INSIDE THE
SAS

WHO DARES WINS

INSIDE THE
SAS

CRAIG PHILIP AND ALEX TAYLOR

BCA
LONDON · NEW YORK · SYDNEY · TORONTO

Page 2: Moving through enemy territory. The SAS
is the world's top unit when it comes to operating behind
the lines and carrying out other clandestine work.

CONTENTS

INSIDE THE SAS

'WE BELIEVE, AS DID THE ANCIENT
GREEKS WHO ORIGINATED THE
WORD "ARISTOCRACY", THAT EVERY
MAN WITH THE RIGHT ATTITUDE
AND TALENTS, REGARDLESS OF
BIRTH AND RICHES, HAS A CAPACITY
IN HIS OWN LIFETIME OF REACHING
THAT STATUS IN ITS TRUE SENSE;
IN FACT, IN OUR SAS CONTEXT, AN
INDIVIDUAL SOLDIER MIGHT
PREFER TO GO ON SERVING AS AN
NCO RATHER THAN LEAVE THE
REGIMENT IN ORDER TO OBTAIN AN
OFFICER'S COMMISSION. ALL RANKS
IN THE SAS ARE OF "ONE COMPANY"
IN WHICH A SENSE OF CLASS IS
BOTH ALIEN AND LUDICROUS.'

DAVID STIRLING

On the night of 16 November 1941, five converted bombers headed westwards through the stormy North African skies. They were carrying 65 parachutists, virtually the total strength of a new, untried formation of the British Army. The parachutists were to drop behind the German and Italian lines and sabotage enemy aircraft on key airfields as part of Operation 'Crusader', General Claude Auchinleck's attempt to throw the *Afrika Korps* out of Cyrenaica.

However, the weather was against them. Severe winds buffeted the aircraft, blowing them off course and dispersing the parachutists as they dropped. Many men were injured on landing and all were far from their planned drop zones. Vital equipment was lost or damaged. The scattered groups of men were in no fit state to carry out the planned operation, so they made their way to the rendezvous with the Long Range Desert Group (LRDG) vehicles which were to provide transport for the journey home. Only 22 men made the rendezvous, the rest had been killed or captured by enemy patrols. The first combat operation by L Detachment, Special Air Service (SAS) Brigade had turned out to be a disastrous failure.

DESERT WARRIORS

One might have expected the higher command to disband the new unit after such a debacle, attributing the losses to another half-baked amateur scheme. The dedicated survivors of the operation, led by their founder, Captain David Stirling, had other ideas, however. Within a few days they were back in action, destroying 61 aircraft in three attacks. The tiny band of SAS pioneers were setting a blazing example for all those who were to follow in their footsteps.

In January 1991, small groups of British soldiers were again roaming the desert, though on this occasion they were in the wide expanses of Iraq and Kuwait. Some were transported by Chinook helicopters, while others rode in specially converted Land Rover vehicles. These men were the forward elements of another major offensive, this time intended to free Kuwait from an occupying Iraqi Army. They scouted enemy positions and attacked the command posts, missile sites, communications centres and other logistics installations. Nearly 50 years after their first raids, SAS men were still fighting their country's enemies.

In the years between these two desert wars, this elite unit has been on numerous operations, many of which are unknown to the public. During World War II, SAS soldiers fought in the Italian mountains, on Aegean and Mediterranean islands, and in northwest

Europe. After the war, they battled in the steamy jungles of Malaya, on the barren, rocky plains of southern Arabia, and on wind-swept islands in the South Atlantic. Closer to home, they have hunted terrorists abroad and in the Irish countryside, and have rescued hostages on the streets of London.

The SAS of the 1990s is a small organisation that is shrouded in secrecy. The regular unit is 22 Regiment, Special Air Service, and comprises four squadrons and a headquarters element. Each squadron is divided into four 16-man troops, each of which is further divided into four four-man patrols. There is also a reserve squadron and various support elements. Training Wing looks after the recruitment and training process for the Regiment, and also supplies instructors to friendly foreign armies. The Counter Revolutionary Warfare (CRW) Wing researches and analyses world terrorism and develops the tactics and technology needed to combat this threat. There is a signals squadron (264 SAS Signals), an Army Air Corps flight, a Demolitions Wing, an Operations Planning and Intelligence Wing ('The Kremlin'), an Operations Research Wing, and services such as transport maintenance, catering, supplies and administration.

22 (pronounced 'two-two') SAS is small for a regiment, with less than 300 combat troopers on strength at any one time. There are also two Territorial Army (TA – the Army's part-time reserve) units, 21 and 23 SAS, which are even smaller, having less support elements. The SAS depot is at Stirling Lines, Hereford, although all British regular and reserve special forces, including the Royal Marines' Special Boat Squadron (SBS), come under the control of the Director, Special Forces, whose Headquarters is at the Duke of York's Barracks in Chelsea, London.

REGIMENTAL PHILOSOPHY

The 'Originals' of 1941 might not recognise some of the equipment used by their successors, but they would certainly be familiar with the basic principles and philosophy of the modern SAS. The use of small numbers of highly trained men to achieve military objectives with the minimum of fuss is a constant thread running through the SAS story, as is the tradition of self-reliant, highly motivated and determined soldiers.

What of the the men that form this secretive and independent unit? The left-wing press has no doubts: SAS stands for Savage and Sadistic. The Regiment is a dumping ground for psychopathic killers who operate with no regard to laws or humanity. The tabloid press is equally sure: every SAS trooper is a steely-eyed, square-jawed superman, able to leap tall

Previous pages: Royal Marines in an observation post (OP). SAS OPs tend to be more covert in nature, being often situated right under the enemy's nose. Such work demands ice-cool nerves and physical stamina, qualities looked for in men who wear the Winged Dagger.
Above right: An SAS trooper photographed in North Africa in World War II. The weapons are Vickers 'K' machine guns which were mounted on SAS jeeps.
Below right: The SAS was involved in mopping-up operations at the end of World War II. Here, a jeep patrol escorts Gestapo agents back for interrogation.

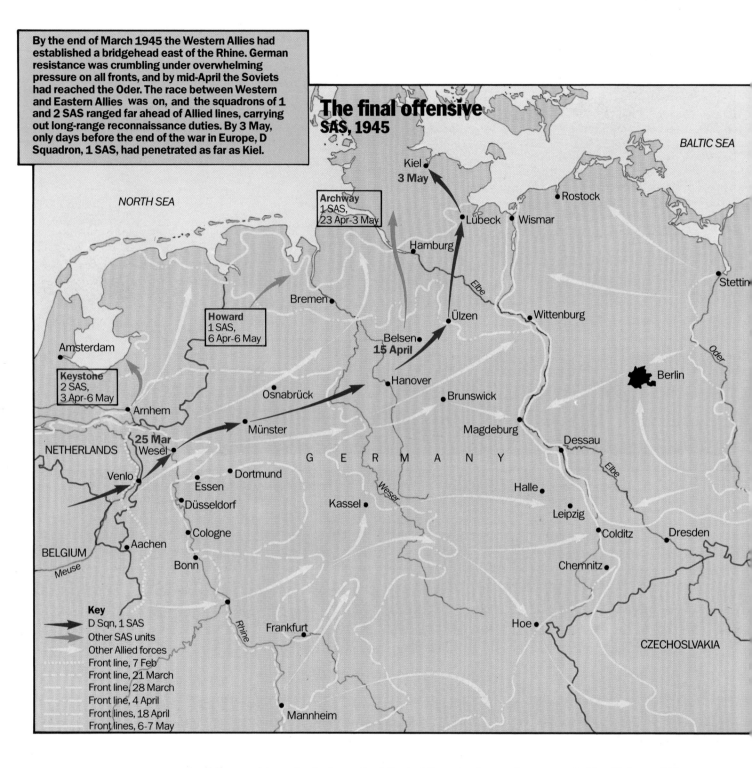

By the end of March 1945 the Western Allies had established a bridgehead east of the Rhine. German resistance was crumbling under overwhelming pressure on all fronts, and by mid-April the Soviets had reached the Oder. The race between Western and Eastern Allies was on, and the squadrons of 1 and 2 SAS ranged far ahead of Allied lines, carrying out long-range reconnaissance duties. By 3 May, only days before the end of the war in Europe, D Squadron, 1 SAS, had penetrated as far as Kiel.

The final offensive
SAS, 1945

BALTIC SEA

NORTH SEA

Kiel
3 May

Rostock

Archway
1 SAS,
23 Apr-3 May

Lübeck Wismar

Hamburg

Stettin

Bremen

Ülzen

Wittenburg

Howard
1 SAS,
6 Apr-6 May

Belsen
15 April

Oder

Amsterdam

Osnabrück

Hanover

Berlin

Keystone
2 SAS,
3 Apr-6 May

Brunswick

Arnhem

Münster

Magdeburg

Dessau

NETHERLANDS
25 Mar
Wesel

Dortmund

G E R M A N Y

Elbe

Venlo

Essen

Weser

Halle

Düsseldorf

Kassel

Leipzig

BELGIUM

Aachen

Cologne

Colditz

Dresden

Meuse

Bonn

Chemnitz

Key
➤ D Sqn, 1 SAS
➤ Other SAS units
→ Other Allied forces
Front line, 7 Feb
Front line, 21 March
Front line, 28 March
Front line, 4 April
Front lines, 18 April
Front lines, 6-7 May

Rhine

Frankfurt

Hoe

CZECHOSLVAKIA

Mannheim

buildings with a single bound while holding his dagger between his teeth. Many thriller writers have SAS or ex-SAS men as their heroes, shooting their enemies between the eyes or breaking their necks with one deadly blow. Both these pictures are obviously false, but how do SAS soldiers see themselves?

When Michael Asher applied to join 23 SAS, one of the TA units, he was told: 'Don't come here expecting to turn into James Bond. There are a lot of myths about the SAS. There are no

piano wires or exploding lighters. What we are looking for first and last are good soldiers who can work alone or in small groups, rather than the big battalions'.

Good soldiers. Two words that sum up the ethos of the SAS. There are no spies, no assassins, no supermen, no psychopaths – the SAS is first and foremost a military unit, manned by superbly trained soldiers. No one can join the regular SAS straight off the street, every applicant must have served at least three years in other units of the Army or in one of the TA SAS units. The volunteer is then put through one of the most challenging and toughest selection processes in the world. To pass this, an individual needs a blend of fitness, self-reliance, initiative and, above all, determination. What the SAS is looking for is soldiers who can think for themselves and who can survive the mental stresses of operating behind enemy lines for long periods. It needs men who can adapt to widely differing types of terrain and climate, and who have the mental flexibility to operate in small, self-contained groups where every man is an essential part of the unit.

THE REGIMENT'S ROLE

Why is such a unit necessary and what does it do? What immediately strikes the observer is how the roles and tasks of the SAS have changed through the years, and how the Regiment has continually adapted to new requirements. Initially formed as a special raiding force, it has been used as a Commando force, a regular infantry unit, vehicle-bound reconnaissance troops, and for long-range reconnaissance patrols. It has trained and lead resistance fighters in occupied territory, befriended and taught native tribesmen, directed friendly aircraft onto hidden or mobile targets, intercepted and ambushed guerrillas, and rescued innocent hostages from terrorist kidnappers. It has also provided medical and educational services to remote peoples, drilled water holes, supplied veterinary skills, and even helped produce electricity in the depths of the Borneo jungle. The SAS is the only fighting unit that claims to have saved more lives through medical care than it has taken in combat.

If World War III breaks out in Europe, the SAS would be at the forefront of the British contribution to the NATO alliance. Patrols would be parachuted or lifted by helicopter into enemy territory to report on military movements and activity, and to locate targets for Allied aircraft. It would also carry out attacks on key headquarters, supply dumps, airfields and communications centres. The TA units would disappear into the friendly countryside, remaining hidden while the enemy forces rolled past. They would then report troop movements along major road and rail routes, providing vital information to NATO intelligence staffs. Thankfully, this nightmare scenario is one which will probably never happen, though no one can be sure.

What of the attitudes of the rest of the Army? At times its relationship with the SAS has been uneasy, with senior officers often misunderstanding the missions best suited to this small unit. Conventionally trained soldiers

OFFICER, 1 SAS, GERMANY, 1945

This officer wears the paratrooper's red beret with the SAS badge and a 'Denison' smock. The 1937-pattern webbing pouches hold a compass and ammunition for his Webley revolver.

SAS badge

red beret

'Denison' smock

1937-pattern webbing

Webley pistol in holster

despatch rider's breeches

motorcycle boots

have also traditionally been suspicious of such independent elites, sometimes accusing it of poaching the best soldiers for frivolous missions which achieve publicity but little else. How much more valuable it would be, they argue, if such men were retained as NCOs and instructors to raise the standards of line units who are, after all, going to be the ones that eventually win a war.

In his study of elite forces, author Roger Beaumont describes the 'selection-destruction

Right: A four-man patrol of the Malayan Scouts poses for the camera before setting off into the rainforest. Note the bergens and machete, essential items for long-range jungle work.

cycle', where the best men are creamed off from other units, trained to a high standard, then used on dangerous missions where casualties are often very high.

The SAS counters by saying that the soldiers it selects are not necessarily the best for a conventional unit. The initiative and self-reliance that is inherent in an SAS trooper does not always suit the more conventional military discipline needed for large, set-piece operations. If the man had been left in his unit he would either not be used to the level of his true capabilities, or he would be unhappy and, if a volunteer, may leave the Army.

The SAS also feels that the 'selection-destruction' argument is not valid in its case. The overall level of SAS casualties through the years has not been excessive, especially considering the circumstances in which it has operated. By training and skilful planning, and by keeping the forces employed to a minimum, the SAS believes that the heavy casualties of a major battle can be avoided. The SAS also points out that many of its soldiers and most of its officers serve with the Regiment for one or two three-year tours before returning to their original units, thus spreading SAS skills and experience throughout the rest of the Army.

The most telling point that SAS supporters make is that in most cases no other unit has had the capability to carry out the tasks given to the SAS. On many occasions the only way of carrying out difficult and dangerous missions without a huge military expedition is to use small bodies of highly trained, skilled and determined men, i.e. the SAS.

The Army seems have come to the same conclusion. The Regiment has survived disbandment and reformation in the late 1940s, occasional threats of dissolution in the 1950s and 1960s, and various attempts to place it under the control of other corps. Today, however, its place seems secure. The men who succeed in achieving the right to wear the Winged Dagger are highly regarded by other soldiers, and even those who try and fail are well thought of. A tour with the SAS is now a benefit, rather than the handicap it once was to the career of an officer. General Sir Peter de la Billière, the British land forces commander in the 1991 Gulf War, is a good example of this. The man chosen to lead the largest British army in the field since the Korean War had a long and distinguished career with the Regiment, and still wears the beige beret.

THE FOREIGN REGIMENTS

Others nations also agree. The Australian SAS Regiment and New Zealand SAS Squadron have similar roles to the British Regiment, and cross-training is carried out between the three units. Most NATO countries have their equivalent units, and exchange training is also carried out with them. The Americans have a huge special forces organisation. The latest and most secretive addition to the US Special Forces is Delta Force, created by Colonel Charles Beckwith after a tour of duty with the British SAS. Delta first came to the public notice after the failed attempt to rescue American hostages held in Tehran in 1980, but since then it has operated successfully in Grenada, Panama and the Gulf.

What of the future? As the recent ending of the Cold War and the changes in the Soviet Union and Eastern Europe show, making confident predictions can be a fruitless business. What seems likely, however, is the increase in the number of small, low-intensity conflicts around the world.

It seems there will still be a place for small groups of dedicated and skilled soldiers. The SAS will adapt to new challenges and roles, using new technology where relevant and developing new tactics. In answer to the question 'What do the SAS do?', the answer has to be 'What do you need doing?'. What seems certain is that the Regiment will continue to display the daring that has enabled it to win through, often against impossible odds, in the past. This is its story so far.

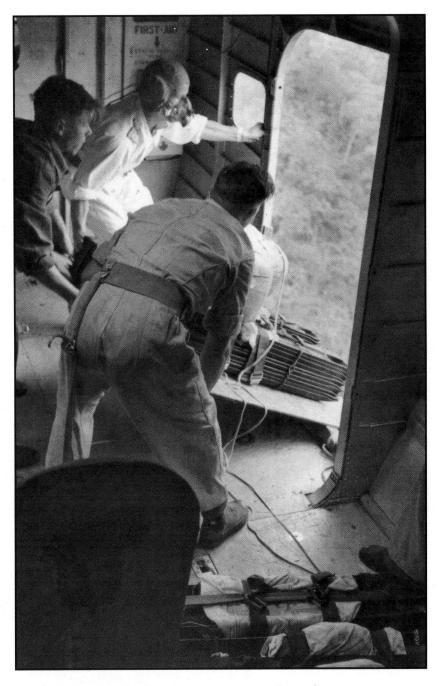

Above: Aerial re-supply in progress during the guerrilla campaign in Malaya. Difficulties of land transport led to the SAS relying on the RAF for logistical support in the field.

CHAPTER 1

THE SAS AT WAR

- WORLD WAR II 1941-45

- MALAYA 1948-60

- OMAN, THE JEBEL AKHDAR, 1958-59

- BORNEO & ADEN 1963-67

- OMAN 1970-76

- ANTI-TERRORISM

- THE FALKLANDS 1982

- THE GULF WAR 1990-91

'I WISH TO SEND MY
CONGRATULATIONS TO ALL RANKS
OF THE SPECIAL AIR SERVICE
BRIGADE ON THE CONTRIBUTION
WHICH THEY HAVE MADE TO THE
SUCCESS OF THE ALLIED
EXPEDITIONARY FORCE.'

GENERAL DWIGHT D. EISENHOWER
OCTOBER 1944

Section I
WORLD WAR II 1941-45

The SAS was conceived in the summer of 1941 by a 24-year-old Scots Guards lieutenant lying in a hospital bed in Alexandria. Tall and gently spoken, David Stirling had led an active childhood, and had been planning to climb Mount Everest after obtaining his Cambridge degree. In preparation for this he had spent the last years before the war climbing in the Canadian Rockies and the Swiss Alps. On the outbreak of war he joined the Scots Guards, but soon became frustrated by the lack of any prospects of action.

By 1940 he had joined No 8 Commando which was sent to the Middle East with two other Commandos to form 'Layforce', a raiding unit named after its CO, Colonel Robert Laycock. Layforce suffered a frustrating existence, used in 'penny packets' to fight in Crete and Syria and throughout the North African theatre. No 8 Commando was to carry out raids along the North African coast, but competing priorities for naval transport permitted only a handful of operations, most of which were foiled by poor weather or discovery by enemy air reconnaissance. The highly trained personnel of Layforce could obviously be put to better use elsewhere, thus the decision was taken to disband the unit.

BORN IN THE DESERT

However, Stirling had decided to take matters into his own hands. Another No 8 Commando officer, Lieutenant 'Jock' Lewes of the Welsh Guards, had 'acquired' in mysterious circumstances 50 parachutes which were en route to India. At the time there were no parachute troops or even parachute instructors in the Middle East, but Lewes and Stirling saw this windfall as a superb opportunity to experiment. Scrounging the use of an old Valentia bomber, the two subalterns and four like-minded Guardsmen, all with no previous training, jumped out over the desert.

With perhaps a certain inevitability, Stirling injured his back and legs on landing, and had to spend two months in the Alexandria Military Hospital. Not one to lie idle, he used the time to analyse the progress of the war in North Africa and how raiding forces such as Layforce could be put to better use. He reasoned that the enemy, because of the geography of North Africa, depended upon one or two vital supply routes and a few key installations stretched along the narrow

inhabitable coastal strip. A well-trained raiding force behind enemy lines could, he argued, cause havoc out of all proportion to the resources expended. These operations would be strategic in nature, therefore the force should report directly to the Commander-in-Chief Middle East, rather than to local senior officers.

STIRLING'S IDEAS

His experiences with Layforce had convinced Stirling that the training, equipment, transport and operational planning for this force should be independent as far as possible. His key assertion was that the best tactical unit to send against any one target was a patrol of only four or five men, rather than the 200 or so deployed by Layforce. Patrols would be inserted by air, land or sea transport depending on the type of terrain and mission. At least 30 targets could be hit simultaneously by 200 men operating on Stirling's principles, rather than one attack using the methods of No 8 Commando. These were well thought out, intelligent and imaginative concepts – the next problem was to persuade the Army bureaucracy that a 24-year-old subaltern was worth listening to.

Rather than send his proposals through normal channels, where they would most likely get lost or stifled in the labyrinthine structure of Middle East Headquarters (MEHQ), Stirling resorted to a typically daring and cheeky ruse to get his ideas directly to the Commander-in-Chief. He turned up (still on crutches) at MEHQ without a pass or appointment, trying to bluff his way past the sentry. The sentry refused him access, but was then distracted by the arrival of a staff car. Seizing the opportunity, Stirling dropped his crutches and limped at high speed past the sentry and into the HQ complex. Realising he only had a few minutes before discovery and ignominious arrest, he entered the first available office to plead his case. Unfortunately for Stirling, the major inside recognised the young lieutenant as the officer who had regularly slept through his lectures at Pirbright in 1939. Beating a hasty retreat, Stirling next headed for the office of the Deputy Chief of Staff, General Neil Ritchie.

Much to Ritchie's credit, he listened to Stirling rather than having him thrown straight out of his office, and promised to mention his proposals to General Claude Auchinleck, his

SAS LIEUTENANT, NORTH AFRICA, 1942

This SAS officer wears his 'wings' over the left breast pocket, signifying he has made three parachute drops behind enemy lines. His traditional Arab headdress, the *shemagh*, offers protection against the sun and can also be drawn over the face in the event of a sandstorm.

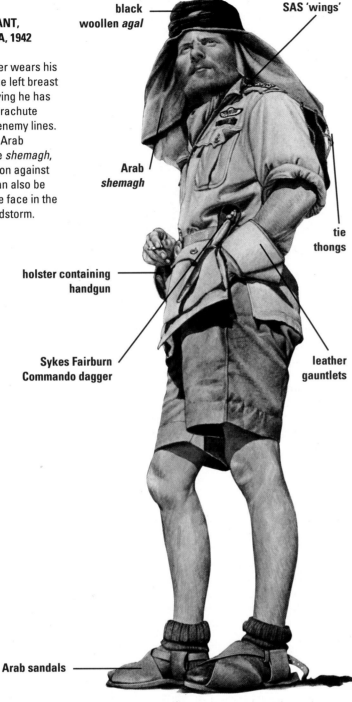

black woollen *agal*

SAS 'wings'

Arab *shemagh*

tie thongs

holster containing handgun

leather gauntlets

Sykes Fairburn Commando dagger

Arab sandals

superior. The result was that Stirling was given permission to recruit four officers and 60 men in a new raiding unit to be known as L Detachment, Special Air Service (SAS) Brigade. There was no actual brigade or detachment – the name was simply a deception to convince the enemy that a new airborne brigade existed in the Middle East.

The first SAS volunteers, known as 'Originals', were largely found from the ranks of No 8 Commando and Layforce. The aforementioned 'Jock' Lewes was an obvious first choice. A quiet, thoughtful man, he was an aggressive fighter who until then had been

successfully leading small raids on enemy frontline outposts. Another officer (this time from 11 Commando) that Stirling recruited was Lieutenant 'Paddy' Blair Mayne. An Irish rugby international, Mayne was a superb fighting soldier revered by his men. However, when off duty a low boredom threshold combined with a quick temper tended to get him into various brawls and scrapes. At the time he was approached by Stirling, he was actually under arrest for punching his commanding officer.

THE FIRST SAS RECRUITS

Many of the first intake of NCOs and privates were Commando-trained ex-Guardsmen, though the SAS took men from any regiment or corps in the Army. The one common denominator was their frustration with petty regimental discipline and the lack of progress in taking the war to the enemy. Many of the names in this group were to become synonymous with acts of daring and courage later in the war. Men such as Johnny Cooper, Reg Seekings, Bob Bennett, Bob Lilley, Pat Riley and others were to set standards that today's SAS men still aspire to.

Selection was not to be automatic, however. Each man was told that he would have to pass a gruelling training programme before taking part in operations. If he failed to meet the standard, he would be returned to his original unit (RTU'd). The infant formation was allocated a training camp at Kabrit in the Suez Canal zone, and the new raiding force that was supposed to set alight the rear areas of the enemy started life equipped with just three tents and one three-ton truck!

While parties were sent out to steal tents and equipment from neighbouring units, a rigorous training programme was devised by Lewes. He placed great importance on the ability of the individual volunteer to survive and navigate in the desert, and even experienced Commandos found the long training marches hard going. SAS soldiers were also expected to be expert weapon handlers and were taught to strip, maintain and fire all forms of friendly and enemy small arms. As there were still no parachute instructors in the Middle East, Lewes devised his own course, the highlight of which involved jumping from the back of a truck travelling at over 50 km/hr to simulate parachute landings. During the first jump from an aircraft, two men were killed when their parachutes failed to open. After a modification to the clip attaching the static line to the aircraft, Stirling, to keep morale up, made the first jump the next day.

The first live operation was planned to coincide with the start of Auchinleck's major offensive into Libya, codenamed 'Crusader'.

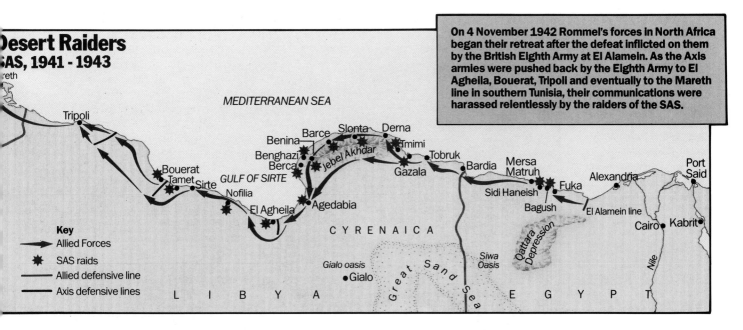

Desert Raiders
SAS, 1941 - 1943

On 4 November 1942 Rommel's forces in North Africa began their retreat after the defeat inflicted on them by the British Eighth Army at El Alamein. As the Axis armies were pushed back by the Eighth Army to El Agheila, Bouerat, Tripoli and eventually to the Mareth line in southern Tunisia, their communications were harassed relentlessly by the raiders of the SAS.

Key
→ Allied Forces
✸ SAS raids
— Allied defensive line
━ Axis defensive lines

The Germans had recently deployed the new 'F' version of the famed Messerschmitt Bf 109 fighter in North Africa, a variant superior to the British fighters then in theatre. L Detachment was given the task of destroying them on the ground as the offensive opened.

DEBACLE IN THE DESERT

On the night of 16/17 November 1941, the SAS went to war. The 65 men of L Detachment were to parachute from five Bristol Bombay aircraft, then individual patrols were to make their way on foot to their targets and place demolition charges on any aircraft they found. Their explosives – Lewes bombs – had been specially designed by Lewes, and provided both incendiary and explosive effects from a light, easily portable package. The raiders were then to withdraw and rendezvous (RV) with a truck-mounted patrol of the Long Range Desert Group (LRDG) which would transport them back to Allied lines.

The mission, however, was a disaster. Strong winds blew the aircraft off course, with many parachutists being injured on landing. Small groups of men were scattered over the German rear areas and many of them were killed or captured. Only 22 men returned and no attacks were made.

Though downhearted, Stirling and the other survivors were determined to persevere and learn from this debacle. An important realisation was that in 1941 parachute insertion was unreliable and that alternatives would have to be found. If the LRDG could extract L Detachment patrols from behind the enemy lines, could it not also take them there in the first place? The LRDG had been formed in July 1940 by a few enthusiasts who had explored the vast uncharted areas of desert

throughout the 1920s and 1930s, solving most of the problems of travelling in the region. They had developed unrivalled experience in desert travel, navigation and survival, and their truck-mounted patrols provided long-range reconnaissance for the British Army in North Africa. Stirling intended to take full advantage of their expertise in such operations until his own force gained the knowledge and the vehicles to operate independently.

Rather than spend time selecting and training more volunteers, Stirling planned two impromptu operations for the night of 14 December 1941. Starting out from the LRDG's forward operating base at Jalo Oasis (also called Gialo), 240km south of Benghazi, Stirling and Mayne were to lead nine men in an attack against the airfield at Sirte, over 560km away, while Lewes would head for El Agheila, and Lieutenant Bill Fraser would mount a third attack on Agedabia airfield on the 21st.

After three days of uneventful travel, an Italian reconnaissance plane spotted and attacked Stirling's party. He decided to split his force and increase the chances of success by attacking in two places. He would take half the group to the original target, while Mayne was to lead the remainder to the airfield at Tamet, another 50km away.

Stirling planned to travel close to the airfield overnight, lay up within observation distance during the day, then plant the charges the following night. During the night march, they actually stumbled onto the airfield itself, but managed to escape and take up their pre-planned position. However, the Italians evacuated the field the next day, leaving the SAS team with no worthwhile targets. Mayne had better luck at Tamet, managing to place

Right: Loaded down with ammunition, the crew of a Vickers heavy machine gun moves forward to engage the enemy in north Italy, April 1945. These men, from 2 SAS, are part of Operation 'Tombola'. Commanded by Major Roy Farran, the mission began on 4 March and ended on 24 April.

Right: Loaded down with ammunition, the crew of a Vickers heavy machine gun moves forward to engage the enemy in north Italy, April 1945. These men, from 2 SAS, are part of Operation 'Tombola'. Commanded by Major Roy Farran, the mission began on 4 March and ended on 24 April.

bombs on 20 aircraft in 15 minutes. He also took his Thompson submachine gun to the officer's mess and sprayed the stunned occupants through the doorway. As the SAS men withdrew under cover of the confusion, he saw an aircraft that had not been attacked. In what has since entered SAS folklore, he climbed into the cockpit and ripped out a section of the instrument panel with his bare hands, thereby disabling the aircraft.

ENTER THE SAS JEEP

Lewes's target was only a staging post, and on the night of his attack held no aircraft. Undaunted, he led his patrol in its vehicles to look for other worthwhile targets. After being intercepted while trying to get close to a suspected army headquarters, they managed to place their charges on over 30 parked trucks before heading back to Jalo. Fraser's attack on Agedabia a few days later was even more successful, with 37 Italian CR42 fighter-bombers being destroyed.

The SAS was finally in action, and proving Stirling's concepts in fine style. By the end of 1941 the unit had accounted for over 100 enemy aircraft, though not without loss. Lewes had been killed in an air attack on his convoy, while Fraser and his whole patrol had not made an RV with the LRDG and were missing. The death of Lewes was a heavy blow, he had been a key figure in the development of the unit. The rigorous training programme that he had devised and overseen was bearing fruit, however. More fortunately, the missing Lieutenant Fraser and his patrol turned up alive and well after an epic two-

week trek through the desert (they had covered over 350km).

At the start of 1942, Rommel's forces were in retreat and the Eighth Army was closing on Benghazi. By this time, Auchinleck had promoted Stirling and Mayne to major and captain respectively, had awarded them both DSOs, and had authorised the recruitment of a further six officers and 40 men. The SAS badge had also become acknowledged by Auchinleck, though some sources say that it was being worn before the first operations. The badge was originally worn on a white beret, but this, following derision from other troops, was soon changed to the beige colour in use today. Specially designed parachute wings were initially worn on the right sleeve, though troopers who had made three parachute drops behind enemy lines were allowed to wear the 'wings' on their chest, a practice which was later discontinued.

Further recruits were gained when a group of 50 Free French paratroopers was given to Stirling. Under their own officer, Commandant George Berge, they were fully integrated into the SAS, though forming a separate squadron. Another independent force that became closely associated with L Detachment was a small group of skilled swimmer/canoeists from the special reconnaissance section of Layforce – the Special Boat Section (SBS). With this influx of new recruits, a series of operations against port facilities was launched.

By July 1942, the pattern of SAS operations had changed dramatically with the addition of a handful of three-ton trucks and around 15 American Willys jeeps. The jeeps were comparatively new to the British Army, but Stirling had seen the potential of these small, versatile vehicles. A number of old Vickers 'K' aircraft machine guns were scrounged from the RAF and these were mounted in pairs at the front and rear of each jeep (some vehicles carried a single Browning 0.5in calibre machine gun in place of the forward pair). The Vickers 'K' was an ideal weapon for the SAS, combining light weight with a ferocious rate of fire. The jeeps were also fitted with radiator condensers and festooned with the extra equipment – fuel cans, food and water containers – necessary to survive in the desert.

The SAS now had the means and training to operate completely independent of any other formation. The procedure was for the whole detachment to set up a forward base inside enemy territory, from where individual raids would be launched – thereby removing the need for long journeys to and from Kabrit before and after each operation. On a raid against Bagush airfield another new tactic was devised which became a standard procedure

for the remainder of the desert war. At Bagush, sentries had been posted around the aircraft which had made placing charges both time-consuming and difficult (several bombs had also failed to detonate). Stirling and Mayne therefore drove their jeeps at speed across the airfield and raked the lines of parked aircraft with machine-gun fire.

These improvised tactics proved so successful that 18 jeeps would be used on the next raid, against Sidi Haneish. The SAS convoy left its forward base on 26 July and arrived at the airfield to find the landing lights on, greatly aiding target identification. The jeeps formed two columns and, like a naval fleet in action, drove in line down the airfield firing broadsides from their massed machine guns. A few minutes later, 40 Ju 52 transports were burning, a significant part of Rommel's logistics backup. The SAS force then split into small parties and travelled independently back to base. Its casualties were light: two men killed, two jeeps destroyed and a number of men suffering from light wounds.

Below: Partisans in north Italy prepare to undertake a reconnaissance of the Alba area in World War II. The man standing in the car is Captain MacDonald, a Canadian officer who was serving with 2 SAS.

M1 THOMPSON SUBMACHINE GUN

The Thompson submachine gun, the legendary 'Tommy gun', was a rugged and reliable weapon that accompanied the SAS on many hit-and-run raids during World War II.

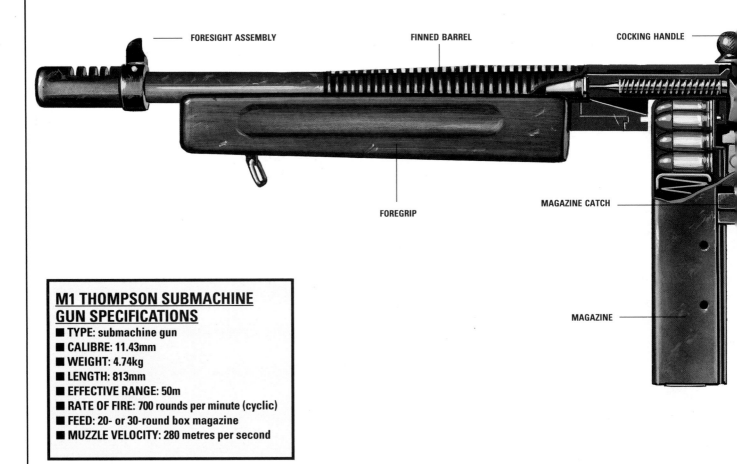

FORESIGHT ASSEMBLY   FINNED BARREL   COCKING HANDLE

FOREGRIP

MAGAZINE CATCH

MAGAZINE

M1 THOMPSON SUBMACHINE GUN SPECIFICATIONS
- **TYPE:** submachine gun
- **CALIBRE:** 11.43mm
- **WEIGHT:** 4.74kg
- **LENGTH:** 813mm
- **EFFECTIVE RANGE:** 50m
- **RATE OF FIRE:** 700 rounds per minute (cyclic)
- **FEED:** 20- or 30-round box magazine
- **MUZZLE VELOCITY:** 280 metres per second

Although the famous 'Tommy Gun' was immortalised in Hollywood gangster movies of the 1930s, the Thompson submachine gun dates back to 1918 when there was a need to develop a weapon that could clear trenches of enemy personnel. By the time the first two models had been produced, the war was over. Nevertheless, development continued and, with the introduction of Prohibition into the United States, the gun became popular with gangsters and, later, the police.

Military sales did not begin in earnest until the late 1920s. The Thompson, or M1928 to give it its official designation, had therefore been around for quite a while by the time the SAS acquired it. However, once they had one, individual troopers were loathe to part with it, and the Thompson accompanied SAS soldiers throughout the Regiment's campaign in North Africa (1941-43), the Sicilian and Italian campaigns (1943-45) and in northwest Europe (1944-45). The SAS ceased to use it after World War II.

Like nearly all submachine guns, the Thompson works by direct blowback action: when the trigger is pulled the breech block is released and moves forward, propelled by a large spring, and picks up a cartridge from the feed. The cartridge is pushed into the barrel chamber and then, once the breech block and round are in position, the firing pin fires the round. The recoil forces produced by firing the round are initially overcome by the forward energy produced by the mass of the

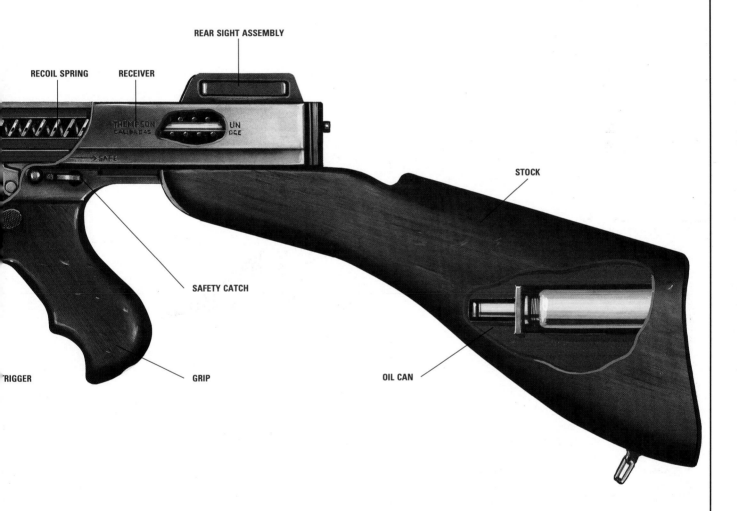

RECOIL SPRING   RECEIVER

REAR SIGHT ASSEMBLY

STOCK

THOMPSON
CALIBRE 45   UN
OCE

SAFE

SAFETY CATCH

TRIGGER   GRIP   OIL CAN

breech block and the spring, with the block remaining in place long enough to 'lock' the system until the recoil forces are able to push back the breech block and its spring to their original position. If the trigger is still pulled then the process begins all over again and continues until the trigger is released.

Despite its widespread popularity among British Commandos, SAS troops and ordinary soldiers – an appeal which may have been due to its 'use' in Hollywood films – the Thompson was

not initially particularly easy to mass-produce because of the large number of complex machining processes involved. However, this problem was resolved somewhat when America entered the war in December 1941. The US Army decided it wanted Thompsons but not until they had been redesigned to fulfil the requirements for mass production. Therefore the manufacturer, faced with the promise of a massive order, simplified the production process and replaced the

drum magazine with a vertical box. This version was known as the M1.

The Thompson was a very accurate weapon, though rather weighty, and was also reliable, a major advantage in SAS-type actions where a jammed weapon could be fatal. In addition, the weapon was very robust and could take a lot of punishment in the field. Later versions tended to have the forward pistol grip replaced by a horizontal foregrip. The 'Tommy Gun' could be fired semi- or full-automatic.

In September 1942, L Detachment was given full regimental status as 1 SAS Regiment. Extra men were obtained from the remnants of 8 Commando or Special Service Regiment, the SBS, and volunteers from a Greek special operations unit (the 'Sacred Squadron'). The new regiment was formed into four squadrons: A, B, C (the Free French) and D (the SBS). The original establishment was 601 men with Stirling, now a lieutenant-colonel, in command. His brother, Lieutenant-Colonel Bill Stirling, was later authorised to raise a second regiment (2 SAS) on similar lines in Algeria.

The SAS continued to operate successfully in early 1943, supporting General Montgomery's final offensive against the *Afrika Korps*. As operations moved into Tunisia, however, problems arose which were a foretaste of what the SAS would face in France. Trying to operate in a much smaller, more heavily populated area than before, B Squadron became vulnerable to detection and attack by security units. Their base was quickly found and occupied, and most of the patrols killed or captured within a few days.

FROM AFRICA TO ITALY

A far worse disaster was to strike, however, one which would have ramifications for the long-term future of the SAS. Unable to keep himself away from the action, David Stirling had tried to lead a small group through Tunisia to meet the British First Army attacking east from Algeria. This time his luck ran out. His patrol was intercepted, and the commander of the most effective raiding formation in the British Army became a prisoner for the duration of the war.

Despite this setback, the SAS in North Africa had destroyed over 400 enemy aircraft, and many supply dumps had been blown up, as had ports, railways, telegraph lines, fuel tankers and numerous support installations. Hundreds of enemy soldiers had been tied up guarding such outposts and combat units had been diverted to spend frustrating days hunting the raiders. Perhaps the last word on the SAS in the desert should be left to its enemy, for Rommel wrote in his diary: 'They caused considerable havoc and seriously disquieted the Italians'. Hitler agreed. In October 1942 he had issued his notorious 'Commando Order' which stated that captured raiders such as SAS men should be turned over to his security police for execution. He wrote: 'These men are dangerous, they should be hunted down at all costs.'

After the North African campaign ended, consideration was given to the future employment of the SAS. Stirling had kept his plans concerning the Regiment to himself, and

no one in higher command had much of an idea what to do with it next. Without his leadership and high-level contacts, the unit was under threat from its detractors, and as a result 1 SAS was disbanded, its components scattered around the Mediterranean. 'Paddy' Mayne's A Squadron was combined with the remnants of B to be renamed the Special Raiding Squadron (SRS). With Lieutenant-Colonel Mayne as its commander, it had an establishment of 250 men and was to prepare for operations in support of the Sicily landings.

D Squadron became the Special Boat Squadron, still using the same SBS initials as before. Now an independent unit, it would carry out a successful series of island raids throughout the Mediterranean and Aegean. The French and Greek SAS personnel were returned to the control of their national armies. Surprisingly, Bill Stirling's 2 SAS was left intact to select and train new recruits in Algeria.

When the Allies went ashore in Sicily in July 1943, the SRS was tasked with attacking the Italian coastal battery at Capo Murro di Porco. A company-strength assault from naval landing craft went totally against all SAS precepts, but Mayne did not have the political clout or military rank to resist the SAS's new role. His men carried out the attack efficiently, destroying a previously undiscovered second battery in the process. The unit was then withdrawn and launched on a second seaborne assault, the capture of the port and harbour at Augusta. 2 SAS sent small groups farther inland to cut telephone wires and railway lines, while the SBS also carried out small raids around the coast.

BLOODBATH AT BAGNARA

The invasion of Italy followed, with the SRS being ordered to capture the port of Bagnara in another assault landing, eventually holding the town for three days before being relieved. The unit's last operation in the Italian campaign was a combined assault on Termoli with the Commandos of the Special Service Brigade. After the Commandos had secured the beach, the SRS moved forward to secure two bridges. The area around the town was quickly taken but, two days later, the Germans launched a determined counterattack. The SRS took its place in the defences and a vicious battle raged until Canadian tanks and some Royal Irish Rangers advancing from Reggio drove the enemy back.

2 SAS then undertook one of the few 'pure' SAS-style operations in the Italian theatre. Operation 'Speedwell' (September 1943) involved small patrols dropped by parachute into northern Italy to disrupt railway lines. While successful, the numbers involved were too few to make a major impact on frontline

Far left: Members of the 'Bulbasket' party photographed in southern France in June 1944. This operation, conducted by B Squadron, 1 SAS, cut several railway lines but was brought to a premature end when the Germans destroyed the team's camp on 3 July. Over 30 SAS soldiers were subsequently executed by the enemy.

Italian Campaign
2 SAS and SRS, 1943 - 1944

ITALY

FRANCE

Turin • • Milan

Maple-Driftwood 7 Jan 1944

Genoa • Venice

Boabab 27 Jan 1944

La Spezia • Ravenna Rimini

Saxifrage 14 Dec 1943

Speedwell 7 Sept 1943

Jonquil 26 Sept 1943

Sleepy Lad 18 Dec 1943

Florence • Ancona

Begonia 2 Oct 1944

YUGOSLAVIA

Pomegranate 12 Jan 1944

CORSICA

Terni •

Candytuft 27 Oct 1943

Pescara

Maple-Thistledown 7 Jan 1944

Rome • Termoli

Combined Operation with Army and RM Commandos 3 Oct 1943

Anzio Cassino

Hawthorn 7 July 1943

Naples • Salerno

Taranto

Jeep Recce, D Sqn 2 SAS with 1 Airborne Div 9 Sept 1943

Marigold 30 May 1943

SARDINIA

Raid on Bagnara 12 Sept 1943

Chestnut 10 July 1943

Reggio

Key
→ Allied forces
✶ 2 SAS raids
✶ SRS raids
▼▼▼ Gustav Line
●●● Gothic Line
++++ Railways

Tunis •

SICILY

Raid on harbour 12 July 1943

Augusta

Snapdragon 28 May 1943

• Pantalleria

Raid at Capo Murro di Porco 10 July 1943

TUNISIA

Narcissus 10 July 1943

Following the Axis surrender in Tunisia in May 1943, the Allies turned their attention to Italy, and the US Seventh and British Eighth Armies landed on the south coast of Sicily on 10 July. The SRS and 2 SAS operated in advance of the main invasion forces, the SRS launching raids against the batteries at Capo Murro di Porco, the town of Augusta and, in September, Bagnara as the Eighth Army crossed the Straits of Messina to mainland Italy. Meanwhile, detachments of 2 SAS were deployed to disrupt enemy rear areas in Sicily in support of the invasion, while other groups operated in the north of Italy, harassing lines of communication to slow down German reinforcement of southern Italy.

On 3 October, as the Allies fought their way up the Italian peninsula, the SRS and a squadron of 2 SAS carried out a major assault landing in conjunction with No 3 Commando and No 40 Commando, Royal Marines, at Termoli in the vanguard of the Eighth Army advance. From October 1943 to January 1944, 2 SAS continued the war against enemy supply lines in central Italy. Deploying by parachute and landing craft, they launched raids against airfields, destroyed railway bridges, ambushed road columns and railway lines. However, overall the SAS suffered from poor logistical support during the Italian campaign.

operations. The bulk of 2 SAS took part in the landings at Taranto and provided jeep-borne reconnaissance patrols ahead of the advancing Allies. A small detachment also arrived during the battle for Termoli (October 1943), fighting alongside the SRS.

As the SAS units were withdrawn to train and prepare for the liberation of France, their commanders reflected upon the frustrations of the campaign in Italy and Sicily (though detachments from 2 SAS would return to northern Italy to conduct a number of operations at the end of 1944). Their men had carried out their assigned tasks superbly, but they were the wrong tasks. David Stirling's concept of small, highly trained groups carrying out independent strategic missions had been largely ignored by senior Army commanders, who saw the SAS as either an elite reconnaissance force or shock troops for

supporting conventional operations. This view was to plague the SAS for the rest of the war, leading to Bill Stirling's resignation in 1944.

THE SAS IN EUROPE 1944-45

The SAS spent the remainder of 1943 and the early part of 1944 in Scotland, regrouping and training for the invasion of France. The SAS star was once more in the ascendant, with the Army authorities deciding to create a full SAS Brigade within Lieutenant-General Sir Frederick Browning's 1st Airborne Corps. The Brigade comprised 1 SAS Regiment (reconstituted from the SRS) under 'Paddy' Mayne, 2 SAS Regiment commanded by Bill Stirling, two French parachute battalions (3 and 4 SAS), and an independent company of Belgian paratroopers (5 SAS). A squadron of the highly secret 'Phantom' signallers from GHQ Liaison Regiment was also attached, as were Army supply and support services.

Most survivors of the original L Detachment were promoted, and Johnny Cooper was commissioned as an officer. He had actually been promoted in the field by Stirling, but had still to attend a recognised officer training course. Brigadier Roderick McLeod was given command of the SAS Brigade and, as it was now part of the airborne forces, the men were ordered to wear their SAS badge on a paratrooper's maroon beret. Many of the 'old sweats' regarded this as an insult and continued to wear their beige berets.

Rapid expansion was now essential, and in some cases selection standards were dropped to get the required numbers of men. The character of the SAS was changing in other ways. No longer the tiny, close-knit, independent unit that had started life in North Africa, it was now under the control of a parent headquarters and was swamped with staff officers, clerks, support services and supply units. The SAS had joined the British Army.

The Army had its views on the correct employment of the SAS in the Normandy invasion. Early plans involved it being used for tactical reconnaissance just ahead of Allied combat divisions. Such a role would have been suicidal for the lightly equipped SAS patrols operating against enemy frontline armoured and infantry formations. These plans drove Bill Stirling to resign his commission in protest, and the plans were changed soon afterwards. The new Commanding Officer of 2 SAS was Lieutenant-Colonel Brian Franks,

the officer in charge of the Commandos who fought alongside the SRS at Termoli.

A few SAS personnel parachuted into France on the night before D-Day – codenamed 'Titanic' – their task being to cause a diversion by simulating a larger parachute attack with explosives, firecrackers, flares and small arms. This was a comparatively minor, and fruitless, operation which resulted in the capture of the party. The main SAS effort, however, was to take place much farther inland.

In the days and weeks following D-Day, squadron-sized forward bases were created behind enemy lines. These were normally in

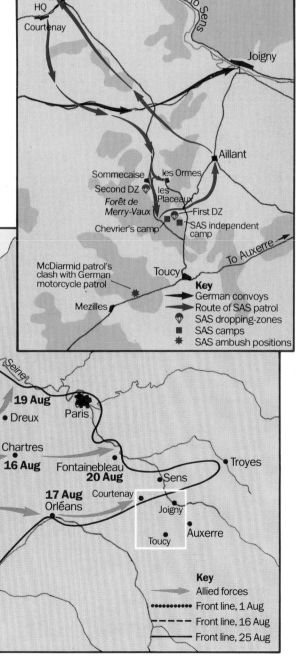

OPERATION 'KIPLING'
C SQUADRON, 1 SAS,
AUGUST 1944

On 14 August 1944, as the US Third Army under General Patton pushed towards the Loire at Orleans, an advance party of C Squadron, 1 SAS, under Captain Derrick Harrison, landed by parachute near Auxerre, 240km behind German lines, and commenced reconnaissance operations. As the Allies drew nearer, the SAS went on the offensive.

On 23 August, Harrison, having heard there were many German troops in the village of Les Ormes, decided to attack. The SAS men, mounted on two jeeps, drove into the village square and started to hit the German vehicles with machine-gun fire. The enemy, crack SS soldiers, overcoming their initial surprise, started to fire back at the SAS soldiers. A fierce battle ensued. Eventually Harrison and his men were forced to retire, minus one jeep, but not before many enemy soldiers had been killed and several of their vehicles set on fire. For his action at Les Ormes, Harrison was awarded the Military Cross.

By 26 September C Squadron had moved to the area around Cosne to rest, effectively bring Operation 'Kipling' to an end. By any measure it had been a great success: the enemy had been continually harassed and many casualties had been inflicted on the Germans.

wooded terrain and were intended to operate for anything up to three months, being supplied by air. From these bases, SAS patrols launched raids and attacks on German transport, communications and supply dumps. They also searched out larger installations, reporting their whereabouts to the RAF.

The SAS was also supposed to supply and support local Resistance (*Maquis*) groups in cooperation with joint detachments from the British SOE (Special Operations Executive) and American OSS (Office of Strategic Services), though inter-service rivalry was a constant source of friction and confusion.

There were many SAS operations during the summer of 1944, and a notably successful one being 'Houndsworth' which commenced on 6 June. Major Bill Fraser's A Squadron, 1 SAS, was given the task of cutting German communications and helping the *Maquis* in an area to the west of Dijon. Dropped into the hilly Morvan area, the SAS strength eventually built up to 144 men, equipped with nine jeeps, numerous machine guns, a few light mortars and even two six-pounder anti-tank guns. The 'Houndsworth' troops carried out over 22 attacks on the main railway line and generally harassed the German supply areas for over three months until early September.

A less successful operation was 'Bulbasket' which was launched at the same time in an area south of Poitiers. After some initial successes, the base's location was betrayed by local collaborators and quickly overrun by German units. Most of the SAS men were captured, then executed. Farther to the north, 'Gain' saw the extensive use of jeep patrols around Fontainebleau, with the SAS driving around in uniform during broad daylight. There was a price to pay for this daring, however, the squadron commander, Major Ian Fenwick, being killed in an ambush.

As the Allied armies advanced, dozens of other SAS actions were carried out across

Right: SAS jeeps in northwest Europe, 1945. By this stage of the war the Regiment's jeeps were more heavily equipped. Note the armoured glass at the front of the vehicles to protect the driver and the front-seat passenger. The trusty Vickers 'K' was still in widespread use, however.

northern France, Belgium and the Netherlands, two of note being 'Kipling' and 'Loyton'. The former involved operations in August and September to the west of Auxerre, near the area covered by 'Gain'. On 22 August, a patrol of two jeeps from 'Kipling' entered the small town of Les Ormes, only to find that a detachment of the SS was preparing to execute 20 civilians in anti-Resistance reprisals. Charging into the town square, the SAS men sprayed the Germans and their vehicles with machine-gun fire. In the confusion, 18 of the 20 Frenchmen marked for execution escaped, although one SAS driver was killed and his jeep destroyed.

'Loyton' covered a series of smaller operations in the Alsace and the foothills of the Vosges and was commanded by Lieutenant-Colonel Brian Franks. Railways, roads and communications were attacked, causing the Germans to employ large numbers of troops in hunting the British. During this

time, the town of Moussey paid the price for giving the SAS food and shelter: virtually the whole male population (210 men) was rounded up and taken to concentration camps. Only 70 survived the war.

By the end of 1944, the Allied armies were moving forward too quickly for the SAS to set up these long-term bases, and it became more of a forward reconnaissance force. At this time 2 SAS detached its 3 Squadron under Major Roy Farran to northern Italy to operate in support of partisans. By the end of December it had a detachment operating in the snow-covered mountainous country north of La Spezia. The party was so successful that at one point the Germans had over 6000 troops hunting the 34 SAS men.

More operations in Italy took place over the next few months, the most important being 'Tombola' in March 1945. Farran set up a large base near Mount Cusna in conjunction with local partisan groups. With the British troops acting as instructors and leaders, the 'Tombola' force carried out a series of ambushes and raids, including an attack on the headquarters of a German corps. The SAS/partisan base became so well established that items dropped to them on re-supply flights included heavy mortars, a howitzer and a Scottish piper complete with bagpipes! On a number of occasions they were even strong enough to fight off the German security battalions hunting them.

The end of the European war saw the SAS Brigade commanded by Brigadier 'Mad Mike' Calvert. He sent out detachments acting as free-ranging jeep-borne reconnaissance patrols for the Allied armies. After hostilities ceased, the SAS was used to search for suspected war criminals and oversee the disarming of 300,000 German soldiers in Norway.

THE SAS IS DISBANDED

Overall, the SAS had contributed greatly to the Allied success. As well as the destruction it caused, it tied down large numbers of enemy soldiers in guard duties and security units. The Brigade paid a heavy price, however, suffering over 300 casualties from the 2000 men deployed. Even though they fought as uniformed soldiers, many SAS men taken prisoner in Europe were executed under Hitler's 'Commando Order'. Immediately after the fighting ended, the victors started to release their servicemen back into civilian life. Army chiefs could see no need for special forces in peacetime, so by the end of 1945 the SAS had been disbanded. Apart from a small team scouring Germany for those who had executed SAS men, there were no British soldiers wearing the Winged Dagger. Stirling's creation appeared to have had its day.

Section II
MALAYA 1948-60

Militarily, the necessity of preserving the wartime experience of the disbanded SAS in some form seemed obvious, but in the climate of cuts in 1946 the formation of a new regiment was impossible. However, the War Office decided to create a Territorial Army (TA) unit which became operational in 1947. The new SAS unit was to be formed by merging with a long-established London-based TA regiment, the Artists Rifles. To be known as 21 SAS Regiment (Artists), the designation (always pronounced 'two-one') was derived by combining the numbers of the wartime 1 and 2 SAS.

Many SAS veterans flocked to join the re-created force which had Lieutenant-Colonel Brian Franks as its commander. At first the Artists Rifles badge (the heads of Mars and Minerva) was worn on a maroon beret, but '21' soon reverted to the traditional SAS badge on the same beret, with Mars and Minerva worn on the sleeve. Any doubts that weekend soldiers could not maintain the standards set by the wartime unit were soon dispelled when, after a few years, soldiers from 21 SAS were again sent to war, albeit of a different type to that envisaged in 1947.

MALAYA IN TURMOIL
To satisfy nationalist sentiments in the area Britain had, in 1948, established the Federation of Malaya consisting of Johore, Kedah, Kelantan, Pahang, Malacca, Negri Sembilan, Trengganu, Penang, Perlis and Selangor. However, the Chinese minority resented Malay dominance and some, mostly communists, turned to violence (the population of the Malay peninsula consisted of some 2,600,000 Malays, 2,100,000 Chinese, 602,000 Indians and several thousand whites). In June 1948, the Malayan Races Liberation Army began attacks on estate owners and rubber planters. The British, in an effort to contain the Communist Terrorists (CTs), declared an emergency and organised a military response.

The country was very vulnerable to rural-based insurgency, being largely covered by thick jungle and scattered with isolated rubber plantations, farms and villages. Skilled jungle fighters, the CTs were able to mount a campaign of terror and intimidation by carrying out selected attacks and assassinations before disappearing back into the bush.

Initially, British troops were largely unable to protect the rural population as demobilisation after World War II had left battalions under-manned, poorly equipped and partly trained.

While the British Army was putting its house in order, an ad hoc anti-terrorist unit known as Ferret Force had been set up in Malaya in July 1948. Made up of former SOE members and native Iban Dyak trackers recruited in Borneo, Ferret Force undertook several successful anti-terrorist jungle patrols, although it was soon disbanded because its members were needed elsewhere.

'MAD MIKE' REPORTS IN
By 1950 the terrorists had killed over 1300 policemen, soldiers and civilians and their strength seemed to be on the increase. The Commander-in-Chief Land Forces, Far East, General Sir John Harding, asked Brigadier Mike Calvert to analyse the situation in Malaya and make recommendations on the strategy to be followed. Calvert was highly experienced in irregular warfare: he had fought with the 'Chindits' in the jungles of Burma and then commanded the SAS Brigade at the end of World War II. His research was not conducted from behind a desk; rather, he determined to see the area for himself. He set out on foot, alone, and travelled through the jungle, meeting the local population and getting an overall 'feel' for the country. His only protection was the rifle he carried. After six months he came up with a two-pronged proposal. First, the CTs would be separated from the native population, both physically and ideologically. Isolated villagers were to be moved and grouped in protected *kampongs*, with strict control over movement in and out of these fortified areas. Food supplies in the *kampongs* would be secured and services such as medical aid would be supplied.

Second, special forces patrols would be sent into the jungle to hunt down CT bases and at the same time win the confidence and support of the indigenous aboriginal tribes. This 'hearts and minds' campaign would eventually cut the CTs off from food and shelter and blunt their ability to intimidate the native population, while simultaneously putting pressure on their previously safe bases. The final operational scheme was known as the 'Briggs Plan' after Lieutenant-General Sir Harold Briggs, the Director of Operations.

Above right: Jungle clearings, such as this one, often indicated a CT camp during the Malayan campaign (the terrorists had to clear the jungle to grow food). When a clearing was spotted from the air, SAS troops were detailed to approach the camp on foot and, with the aid of other units, to destroy it.

Below right: Supplies being dropped to waiting SAS troops from the rear of a Beverley transport aircraft. Such aerial re-supply was essential as each soldier carried a maximum of 14 day's supply of food in his bergen.

Right: Operation 'Termite', July 1954. SAS troopers emplane prior to being parachuted into the jungle east of Ipoh, central Malaya. This four-month operation against the CTs was carried out in conjunction with other British Army and Malay units. Clearings were created for the parachutists by RAF bombers, though this sometimes had the unfortunate result of terrifying the local aborigines.

ENTER THE MALAYAN SCOUTS

Calvert was given permission to recruit his special force, and in 1950 the Malayan Scouts was formed. An initial squadron of around 100 volunteers was hastily put together. It contained men from Ferret Force, the wartime SAS and Commandos, and from other units in the region. This disparate collection also included 10 deserters from the French Foreign Legion. Some of the volunteers were dedicated, skilled soldiers, but others were bored and just wanted to get away from the rigours of military discipline. With virtually no selection procedure and hardly any time or equipment for training, these men formed A Squadron, Malayan Scouts.

B Squadron was created from the reservists of 21 SAS, some of whom had volunteered for service in Korea. These highly trained and disciplined soldiers were diverted to Malaya after the British Government decided, with the entry of the Chinese into the Korean War, that it was politically unacceptable for a British unit to operate behind the lines. C Squadron was recruited by Calvert while on a trip to Rhodesia. With over 1000 applicants, he was able to select around 120 seasoned soldiers of extremely high standard.

Calvert was under pressure to produce results quickly so, following a brief training course at its base at Johore, A Squadron was despatched to operate in the area around Ipoh while B and C Squadrons completed their training. In a remarkably short period of time, a tough, realistic training programme was created. There were no proper ranges at the base camp, so the sports field was used for shooting practice. Drainage ditches were pressed into service as makeshift trenches for grenade training, while other equipment, such as rubber boats, was gradually scrounged.

EARLY JUNGLE PATROLS

By the middle of 1951, the Malayan Scouts had started to take the war to the enemy. A troop of around 12-15 men would create a base deep in the jungle, from where patrols of four men would reconnoitre the surrounding region. Ambushes were set on known tracks and crossroads and the SAS sometimes located CT camps for RAF air strikes. The SAS patrols also made contact with the local tribesmen, providing limited medical assistance and gradually befriending them.

An early patrol led by Lieutenant Michael Sinclair Hill stayed out for a record 103 days, disproving the accepted theory that Europeans could only operate for two weeks in the hazardous jungle environment. At one point, Sinclair Hill was requested by radio not to ask for air support on Sundays, as the aircrew needed to rest. From the depths of the

The failure of the native Malays and Chinese immigrants to agree on the shape of postwar British administration of the colony provoked the Malayan Communist Party to reform its wartime resistance army. The Malayan Races Liberation Army took to the jungle and conducted a terrorist campaign against British colonial administrators and managers of the country's tin mines and rubber plantations. The British government responded with a counter-insurgency campaign based on the coordination of military and police tactics under civil control. Great emphasis was placed on intelligence gathering activities and long-range jungle patrolling.

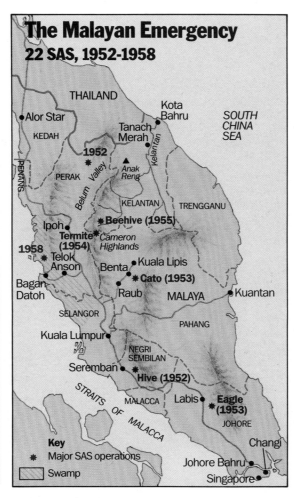

The Malayan Emergency
22 SAS, 1952-1958

Key
* Major SAS operations
▱ Swamp

Malayan jungle came the dry response, 'Tell us when it is Sunday'.

By November 1951 Calvert was invalided home, suffering from exhaustion and illness. His replacement was Lieutenant-Colonel John Sloane, an Argyll and Sutherland Highlander with no previous special forces experience. His first task was to absorb the lessons from the early missions and to solve the discipline problems that had arisen within the unit.

The speed with which A Squadron's volunteers had been recruited had led to some men joining who were unsuited to SAS-style operations. Others were troublemakers who hoped to escape Army discipline, their regiments being only too glad to let them go. Drunkenness, brawling and insubordination were becoming very real problems. The TA volunteers of B Squadron and the Rhodesians of C were more disciplined and professional, and mainly stayed clear of such antics.

Sloane, nicknamed 'Tod', withdrew the Scouts from deep operations while retraining and re-organisation took place. A more conventional military discipline was imposed, general administration improved and a number of men were RTU'd. Major Dare Newell was given the task of raising D

Squadron, this time using proper selection procedures. By February 1952 the Malayan Scouts was ready to return to the jungle.

The first operation in the Belum Valley involved the SAS, Gurkhas, Royal Marine Commandos and the Malay Police Force in an attempt to destroy terrorist food crops growing in jungle clearings. A total of 54 men were to parachute into the jungle canopy; the first use of the technique known as 'tree jumping'.

These trees grow to a height of 20-70m, so each man was equipped with 30m of rope to help him climb down if his parachute caught. A man would crash into the tree tops, not knowing whether his parachute would snag, whether he would be smashed into thick branches, or whether he would plummet through to the dense scrub below. The first time the technique was used there were no serious injuries, although broken bones became a constant hazard in later jumps.

A typical SAS patrol would consist of four men, each one carrying over 30kg of supplies and ammunition in his bergen. They would carry rifles and Bren guns at the ready, although the pump-action shotgun became a popular choice of lead scouts for close-range work. It could take a day to cover five kilometres, with the patrol moving slowly and silently, often stopping to listen every few minutes. The oppressive humidity sapped the strength, and natural hazards included malarial mosquitoes and countless bloodsucking leeches. Rivers could be used for more rapid movement, though the risk of being ambushed increased. Contacts were sudden and vicious, a few seconds of close-range gunfire normally being enough to settle the issue. The CTs would try to avoid contact with the soldiers if possible, and if an ambush was not perfect they would quickly melt into the dense bush.

22 SAS – BACK IN BUSINESS

The 'hearts and minds' concept was an important aspect of these operations. Patrols were despatched to make contact with native villages and to show that the government was determined to protect them from the bandits. The patrol medic became one of the most effective weapons in the SAS armoury, providing basic medical care and attention to isolated villagers. The RAF would also drop medical supplies. Such considerations, combined with martial prowess, created genuine bonds of respect between the aborigines and the British troopers, further reducing the ability of the terrorists to operate undetected.

In 1952, the Malayan Scouts became 22 Regiment Special Air Service. For the first time in the history of the British Army, a TA regiment (21 SAS) had given birth to its regular equivalent. Major John Woodhouse was sent to the UK to start recruiting and put selection and training on a more formal basis. Further re-organisation took place in 1955-56. Woodhouse then returned to Malaya, this time as a squadron commander under the then CO, Lieutenant-Colonel Oliver Brooke. Though the latter had almost no experience of special forces, he was an able leader and a strict disciplinarian. On a more practical basis, he helped devise a two-week ration pack for jungle operations. Brooke was not a desk officer, he was frequently out in the field. Indeed, he suffered a severe leg fracture after 'tree-jumping' into an operational area. A new unit, known as the Para Squadron, was recruited from the Parachute Regiment. C Squadron returned home and was replaced by volunteers from New Zealand. The SAS strength in Malaya was now five squadrons (A, B, D, Para and NZ) – over 560 men.

A new CO also took over in 1955: Lieutenant-Colonel George Lea. Sloane and Brooke had overseen the raising of standards for NCOs and soldiers, Lea was to do the same for the officers. Some were RTU'd and new blood was brought in. Johnny Cooper was again promoted and new additions included Major Harry Thompson and Captain Peter de la Billière; the latter going on to command the British land forces in the 1991 Gulf War. Thompson was responsible for capturing the notorious bandit Ah Hoi, nicknamed 'Baby Killer', in the Telok Anson swamp in February 1958. Thompson and his men spent a gruelling 20 days in the foetid conditions of the swamp before they managed to surround the CTs' camp and force them to surrender.

By 1958 the 'Emergency' had largely been won by the British. Terrorist activity was a fraction of that in 1950 and many CT leaders had been killed or captured. 22 SAS had already suffered in defence cuts, however, being reduced to two squadrons: A and D. A bright spot was the final recognition of the SAS as a separate corps, with the Regiment being removed from the control of the airborne forces. The beige beret was again being worn by SAS soldiers.

THE SAS CONCEPT VINDICATED

In terms of casualties inflicted, the SAS score in the Malayan counter-insurgency campaign was minimal: 108 CTs killed in 12 years of constant operations. Where the Regiment made its greatest contribution, however, was providing intelligence for other formations and winning the confidence of the local population wherever SAS patrols went. The Regiment had also gained invaluable experience in skills such as long-range signalling, jungle navigation and survival, patrol ambush drills

SAS TROOPER, MALAYA, 1960

This trooper wears jungle-green drill fatigues with the badge of Malaya Command worn on the upper sleeve. His weapon is the Australian Owen submachine gun which has the magazine mounted on the top of the receiver.

jungle hat

canvas bergen

machete

Owen submachine gun

jungle-green trousers

canvas and rubber jungle boots

and helicopter operations, all of which would be vital in the years to come. There was no doubt that the long-term future of the SAS as a permanent addition to the British Army was secure, although any thoughts of a restful peacetime existence were soon to be shattered In November 1958, the 70 men of D Squadron were lifted from the steamy Malayan jungle to an environment at the other end of the climate spectrum – the dry and dusty terrain of the Jebel Akhdar, northern Oman. The SAS had another war to fight.

Section III
OMAN, THE JEBEL AKHDAR, 1958-59

The Sultanate of Muscat and Oman lies on the southeast tip of the Arabian Peninsula, bordered in the north by the United Arab Emirates, in the southwest by South Yemen and in the northwest by Saudi Arabia. Most of the population live on the coastal plain, inland of which is a range of rocky mountains leading to empty desert. Oman's location is of strategic significance, as anyone who controls this region can control the supply of oil from the Persian Gulf to the West.

In 1958 Oman was still run as a feudal autocracy, with the Sultan, Said bin Taimur, controlling all forms of government. A major rebellion by disaffected tribes had been suppressed in 1954, but a guerrilla campaign still raged in the country, with some support coming from other Arab nations. Mindful of its strategic interests, Britain had developed close links with the Sultan, and had earlier sent troops to help and train his tiny armed forces. Most of the British soldiers had been withdrawn by 1958, however, leaving only a few training officers and advisers.

STALEMATE ON THE JEBEL

By this time the conflict had reached stalemate. Around 600 rebels were encamped on the top of the Jebel Akhdar, the 'Green Mountain', the highest peak in the north of Oman. The Jebel was really a rocky plain, about 30km long, 15km wide and rising 2-3000m above the surrounding country. Most of this plateau was bounded by steep cliffs, with only a few climbable paths leading to the top. The rebels, led by Talib, the brother of Ghalib bin Ali, the Imam, were skilled fighters, able to camouflage themselves well in the stony terrain, and used a network of caves as supply caches and firing positions. They were armed with rifles, heavy machine guns, mortars, mines and grenades and, unlike the terrorists in Malaya, were prepared to stand and fight if attacked. Operating from this secure base, they were able to dominate the local countryside by mining roads and tracks and fomenting unrest among the rural tribes. Two conventional British/Omani assaults against this natural fortress had already failed and the rebel position seemed impregnable.

The Sultan of Oman still hoped to crush the rebellion, but the British Government, despite its treaty obligations, was reluctant to be seen supporting such a reactionary regime. The British officer acting as the Sultan's chief-of-staff had studied the problem and requested a full brigade to be sent to clear the Jebel once and for all. This request was rejected, so he then asked for at least two battalions of elite troops, either Paras, Royal Marines or SAS. What he in fact received was one SAS squadron and an armoured car detachment from the Life Guards.

FIRST SAS OPERATIONS

D Squadron, 22 SAS, had been lifted straight from the Malayan jungle and had to be hastily acclimatised and trained for its new battleground. The previous eight years had been spent in long, slow-moving patrols punctuated by a few sudden close-range firefights which were over in seconds. The SAS now had to adapt to an open terrain where an enemy could spot men moving at a distance of 500m. Worse, the rebel snipers were also superb shots, easily able to hit a man at half a kilometre while remaining unseen. Soldiers also had to endure incredible variations in temperature. Daytime saw a fierce sun which could cause severe heat exhaustion, but the temperature dropped dramatically when night fell, low enough to freeze the contents of a water bottle. A man could face the risks of heat stroke or hypothermia, both in the space of 24 hours.

The SAS started to reconnoitre the perimeter of the Jebel, examining likely routes to the top. On one of these missions an SAS corporal was killed by a bullet fired from a range of over 400m after he had underestimated the skill of the rebel snipers. This incident led the SAS to change its tactics. All movement was now undertaken at night, with troopers laying up during the day.

In early December 1958, a local sheikh was found who knew a path up the north side of the mountain and was prepared to lead a party from D Squadron to the top. Two troops climbed the 2000m-long track in one night, establishing a toehold on the mountain by the

L4A4 BREN GUN

The Bren gun is a tried and trusted design which has been in British service since the 1930s. Light, reliable and accurate, it was used by SAS troops during and after World War II. Amazingly, it is still in service today.

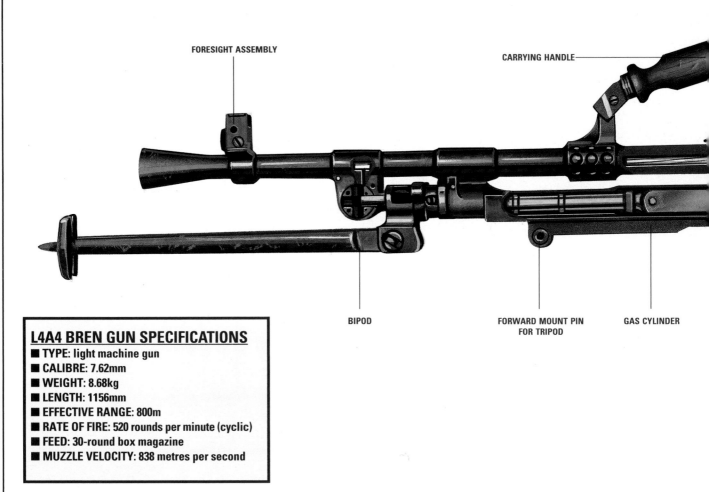

FORESIGHT ASSEMBLY

CARRYING HANDLE

BIPOD

FORWARD MOUNT PIN
FOR TRIPOD

GAS CYLINDER

L4A4 BREN GUN SPECIFICATIONS
- **TYPE:** light machine gun
- **CALIBRE:** 7.62mm
- **WEIGHT:** 8.68kg
- **LENGTH:** 1156mm
- **EFFECTIVE RANGE:** 800m
- **RATE OF FIRE:** 520 rounds per minute (cyclic)
- **FEED:** 30-round box magazine
- **MUZZLE VELOCITY:** 838 metres per second

In the days, weeks and months following the D-Day landings of June 1944, SAS parties were parachuted behind German lines in France and the Low Countries to disrupt enemy movements, undertake sabotage operations, as well as arm the fighters of the *Maquis*, the French Resistance. The latter's main requirement in the summer of 1944 were weapons to arm its men. A major task for SAS teams dropped behind the lines, therefore, was to provide weapons training to *Maquis* recruits. Operation

'Houndsworth', for example, was conducted by a large number of men from 1 SAS – members of 2 SAS were also involved – in the Saone et Loire area of eastern France between June and September 1944. The operation's objectives were to cut a number of railway lines in the area and organise and arm the local *Maquis*.

The SAS on the ground requested air drops in the days after they had landed. The RAF delivered numerous containers filled with ammunition, mortars, explosives, mines and hand grenades.

They also dropped a large number of Bren guns and, in the days following, the SAS trained many Frenchmen in the use of these excellent light machine guns. The method was to train the most intelligent ones to be Number Ones, i.e. firers, while others were given the task of being Number Two and were given hours of instruction in how to change and fill magazines. The results of such labours soon became apparent. The *Maquis*, delighted to have at last a method of hitting back at their occupiers, took to killing Germans with

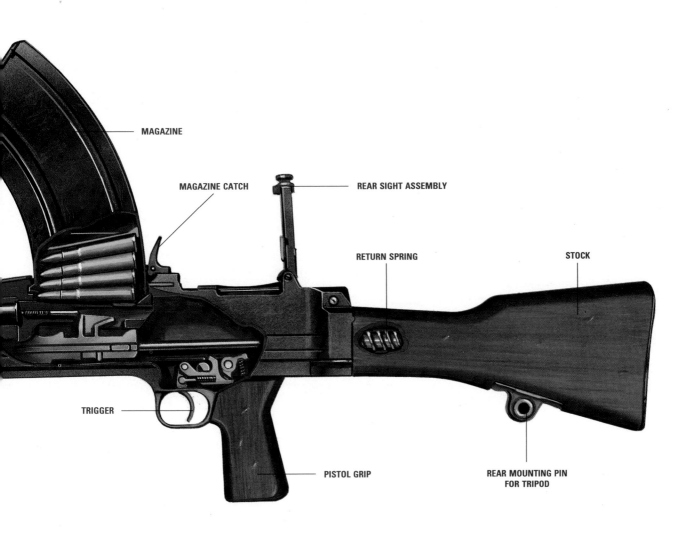

MAGAZINE

MAGAZINE CATCH

REAR SIGHT ASSEMBLY

RETURN SPRING

STOCK

TRIGGER

PISTOL GRIP

REAR MOUNTING PIN
FOR TRIPOD

relish. One example will suffice to show how the *Maquis* put their Brens to good use.

The SAS had heard that a combined force of Gestapo and *Milice* (French paramilitaries who worked with the Gestapo) was planning an attack on a nearby *Maquis* base located in a forest. The SAS informed the Resistance of this and arranged for the RAF to undertake a drop of Brens and ammunition to the base. When they arrived they organised conducted a crash course in their use. The *Milice*

and their German allies approached the forest through a defile. The *Maquis* sited their Brens on both sides of the chokepoint, creating a deadly killing ground below. The enemy advanced in groups of between five and 10 men, unaware they were being watched. When they had moved to within a range of 200m, the Bren guns opened fire. The air was filled with screams as a hail of .303in bullets tore into the ranks of the *Milice*. The latter, caught by surprise, retreated quickly, leaving the ground littered with their dead.

The Bren was one of the finest light machine guns of World War II – some weapons experts would say the finest light machine gun ever. Simple to use, accurate and robust, and able to operate in any terrain, it was a favoured SAS weapon during and after the war. For example, it was used by the Regiment during its operations on the Jebel Akhdar, Oman, in 1958-59, and by jungle lead scouts. The Bren, which is still in service, is now known as the L4, having been modified to fire the NATO 7.62mm round.

Above: Soldiers from A Squadron, 22 SAS, prepare to decamp for another day's patrolling in northern Oman. Soldiering under conditions characterised by very hot days and freezing nights requires high levels of personal stamina and mental fortitude. SAS soldiers in the Jebel Akhdar campaign proved they were capable of Herculean efforts.

morning. The position was precarious, however, and over the next few weeks the soldiers suffered constant sniping and counter-attacks. There were also problems with re-supply drops; on one occasion, for example, the SAS came under attack from its own mortar bombs when a parachute canister split open in midair. Eventually the SAS men were relieved by a detachment of the Life Guards, which continued to hold the position.

SKIRMISHES WITH THE REBELS

Other patrols scouted to the south of the Jebel, and on one occasion the troop commanded by Peter de la Billière fired Carl Gustav and 66mm anti-tank rockets into the mouth of a rebel cave. However, the SAS men came under heavy small-arms fire and were forced to withdraw under cover of rocket and machine-gun fire from RAF Venom fighters. D Squadron became adept at cooperating with the RAF, its men moving into observation positions at night then calling down strikes on suspected enemy locations during the day.

While these patrols were harassing the enemy and obtaining valuable information, it was obvious that more strength was needed before the mountain could be cleared. The British Government had no wish to be drawn into a prolonged conflict. It wanted the

situation resolved with as few casualties as possible, preferably without the British public realising that its soldiers were involved in yet another foreign war. It was also essential to win before the next United Nations debate on the region, to avoid being accused of imperialistic intervention while the conference was in progress. The Army was under pressure to finish the job quickly, using minimal resources with the maximum of discretion. Its solution was to deploy the remainder of 22 SAS (A Squadron) to work alongside D Squadron, the Life Guards squadron and the Sultan's Armed Forces.

DEANE-DRUMMOND'S PLAN

A Squadron arrived from Malaya on 9 January 1959, but only had time for one week of acclimatisation training before the main operation was to commence. The Commanding Officer of the Regiment was now Lieutenant-Colonel Anthony Deane-Drummond, a World War II veteran of Italy and Arnhem. He, together with his squadron commanders, studied aerial photographs to find the best route up the Jebel. A previously unknown path was found to the south. It appeared to be unused and virtually undefended, though for long sections it was totally exposed, with no natural cover. An

attacking force would have to carry all its weapons, ammunition and supplies up this single rocky track, covering a distance of over 3000m in a few hours of darkness.

A SQUADRON'S ATTACK

To increase the chances of ascending undetected, a deception plan involving two diversionary attacks was put into operation. In the early hours of 26 January, A Squadron attacked from the previously captured toehold in the north towards the twin peaks known colloquially to the British as 'Sabrina' (after a well-endowed female TV star of the time). With one troop providing covering fire using all its machine guns, the other three climbed 400m up the steep rocky slope to the top. The enemy position was quickly taken with no losses. While one troop was left behind to hold the peaks, the rest of the squadron then headed south to the village of Tanuf, where the next phase of the deception plan was to take place.

The SAS had been using local donkeys as load carriers in the mountains, but there were doubts concerning the trustworthiness of their handlers. As part of Deane-Drummond's deception, these men were told earlier, 'in strict secrecy', that the actual assault would be from Tanuf. Sure enough, by the day of the

attack, the rebels had re-grouped a large proportion of their forces on the mountain above the village. Not to disappoint them, the second diversionary attack, really a feint, was launched there that evening by a reinforced troop from D Squadron. Making as much noise as possible, it managed to convince the rebels that it was the main force, causing them to waste hundreds of bullets and scores of mortar bombs at the SAS soldiers withdrew.

THE RACE TO THE TOP

Meanwhile, the rest of D and A Squadrons were transported in trucks to the village of Kamah. From here the actual assault was launched, with the SAS leading a column which included another dismounted Life Guards troop and Omani troops, with heavy machine guns and mortars being carried on the aforementioned donkeys. The column struggled to climb the steep, narrow path, at one point coming across a defensive position armed with a 0.5in calibre heavy machine gun. This could have stopped the attack in its tracks, but its crew was asleep, secure in the knowledge that the Jebel was impregnable. An SAS guard was left behind with the snoring prisoners as the rest pressed on.

By 0300 hours the column was nearing the top, but it seemed as if it might not reach it

Above: An Arab donkey loaded with SAS ammunition in northern Oman, early 1959. During the Jebel Akhdar operation, the SAS deliberately gave the handlers false information concerning the direction of the main attack on the rebel positions, knowing it would be passed on to the enemy. The assault, when it went in, therefore, achieved total surprise.

Jebel Akhdar
22 SAS, January 1959

PERSIAN GULF

OMAN

TRUCIAL OMAN (UNITED ARAB EMIRATES)

Awabi
Muscat
Jebel Akhdar
Nizwa

SAUDI ARABIA

OMAN

Masirah

Salalah
Mirbat
ARABIAN SEA

When D Squadron, 22 SAS, was first deployed in Oman in November 1958, the mountain stronghold of the Jebel Akhdar was held by well-armed and entrenched rebel forces. Early in January A Squadron arrived, and 22 SAS started preparations for a decisive assault on the Jebel. At 0300 on 26 January the first phase of the operation began with A Squadron's attack on the Aquabat al Dhafar.

26 Jan 0300 A Sqn reaches 'Sabrina' from the north side of the Jebel and secures the rebel position after a fierce firefight. Leaving 4 Troop to hold the summit, A Sqn pushes on to Tanuf.
1800 A Sqn joins D Sqn in Tanuf. Leaving one troop behind to mount a diversionary attack, the two squadrons travel by lorry to Kamah.

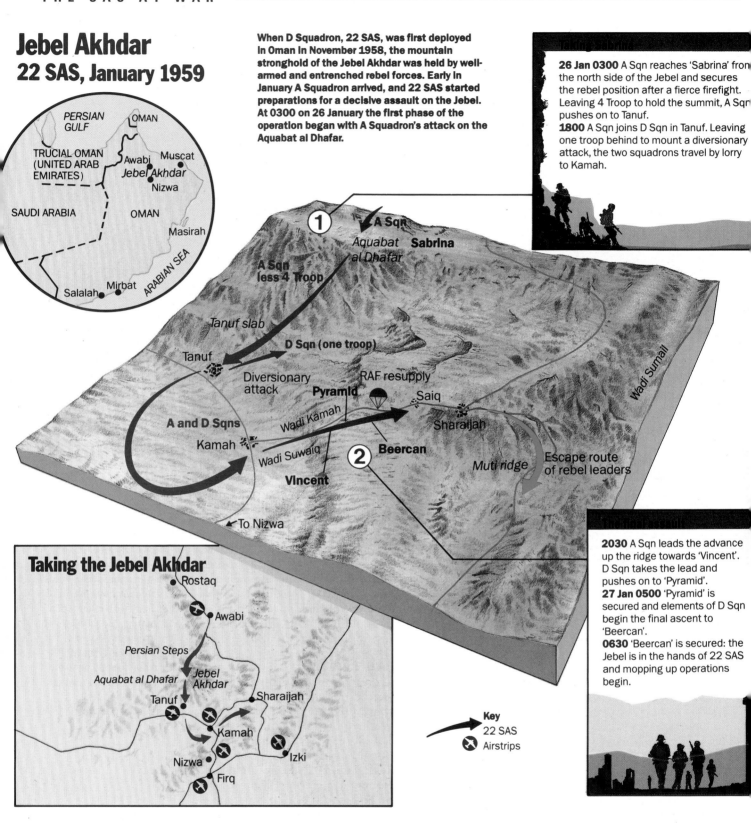

① A Sqn
Aquabat al Dhafar **Sabrina**
A Sqn less 4 Troop
Tanuf slab
Tanuf
D Sqn (one troop)
Diversionary attack
Pyramid RAF resupply
Saiq
Sharaijah
A and D Sqns
Kamah
Wadi Kamah
② **Beercan**
Wadi Suwaiq
Vincent
Muti ridge
Escape route of rebel leaders
Wadi Sumail
← To Nizwa

2030 A Sqn leads the advance up the ridge towards 'Vincent'. D Sqn takes the lead and pushes on to 'Pyramid'.
27 Jan 0500 'Pyramid' is secured and elements of D Sqn begin the final ascent to 'Beercan'.
0630 'Beercan' is secured: the Jebel is in the hands of 22 SAS and mopping up operations begin.

Taking the Jebel Akhdar

Rostaq
Awabi
Persian Steps
Aquabat al Dhafar *Jebel Akhdar*
Tanuf
Sharaijah
Kamah
Nizwa
Izki
Firq

Key
22 SAS
Airstrips

before sunrise. To be caught in daylight, exposed to the rebels above, would have been disastrous, so Deane-Drummond and the CO of D Squadron, Major Johnny Watts, decided that they had to speed things up. D Squadron dumped its bergens on the track and, carrying only small arms, ammunition and water bottles, dashed upwards to the summit. The

dash became a race, with Deane-Drummond, Watts and de la Billière in the front group. They reached the unguarded plateau exhausted, but pressed on to secure the position before sunrise.

As the rest of the force arrived and started to advance across the plateau, daylight brought aerial supply drops and RAF air strikes on the few rebels left guarding the south side of the Jebel, who thought that a full-scale airborne assault was in progress and retreated, their leaders vanishing down the mountain. This defeat signalled the end of the rebellion – the enemy stronghold had been cracked open by a combination of stealth, deception, extreme physical fitness and dogged determination.

The short, sharp Omani campaign had shown that the SAS could adapt yet again to a new role and to different environmental conditions. The Regiment had demonstrated how small numbers of dedicated, skilled soldiers could operate in politically sensitive areas without attracting unwelcome publicity and with the minimum of resources.

In 1960 the SAS returned home to absorb the lessons of the highly successful Jebel Akhdar operation. Its soldiers were sent on a diverse range of training courses: languages, demolitions, sniping, para-medicine, high-altitude parachuting, driving and unarmed combat, while their squadrons were given new equipment, such as specialised long-range radios. Training procedures were refined to reflect the wide range of skills SAS soldiers now needed to possess. In 1960 the Regiment also moved its barracks from Malvern, Derbyshire, to Bradbury – now Stirling – Lines, Hereford, where it remains.

At this time close links were being formed with other special forces units, such as the US Green Berets. The main role of US Special Forces at this time was to train and support indigenous forces in a similar way to the SAS 'hearts and minds' concept, so useful exchanges of knowledge took place. More meetings and sharing of information took place with the SAS units in Rhodesia and New Zealand, and also with the Australian SAS.

TROOPER, 22 SAS, THE JEBEL AKHDAR, 1959

The trooper's L4A4 LMG is in fact a Bren gun modified to accommodate the 7.62mm round. Spare ammunition and water bottles are carried on the 1944-pattern belt.

'Denison' smock

woollen hat

L4A4 Light Machine Gun

gaiters

The lessons learned in Malaya and Oman were also passed on to the TA SAS, with regular officers and NCOs posted as instructors and ex-regulars joining the TA once they left the Army (a second TA Regiment, 23 SAS, had been formed in 1957).

By late 1962, the SAS had a large pool of experienced men and was in good standing with the British Army, and in January 1963 it was called upon to return once more to the hot, steamy jungles of the Far East, but this time to the island of Borneo.

Above left: An aerial picture which illustrates the type of terrain encountered by SAS troops on the Jebel Akhdar.

Section IV
BORNEO & ADEN 1963-67

Malaya, following its independence within the Commonwealth in 1957, created the Malaysian Federation in 1963, along with Singapore, Sarawak and Sabah. This union angered the Indonesia Government, which saw it as a neo-colonialist barrier to its own regional ambitions. The Indonesian state is a large collection of islands with a population of over 150 million, and so it posed a very real threat.

Unrest had already arisen in Brunei, an independent Sultanate in the north of Borneo, with a communist-inspired rebellion breaking out in 1962. This was quickly crushed with the help of hastily deployed British troops, but all the evidence suggested that insurgency in Sarawak and Sabah would continue to escalate with the aid of Indonesia.

'HEARTS AND MINDS' IN ACTION
The border area consisted of thick, often uncharted, jungle, in many places even less habitable than that on the Malayan Peninsula. This time, however, the British had a force of well-trained, experienced jungle scouts in the form of 22 SAS, A Squadron of which was deployed to the area in early 1963. The border extended over some 1500km, and SAS patrols were deployed every 150km. Their task was mainly reconnaissance; they were to detect and locate terrorist teams – at first members of the Clandestine Communist Organisation, later Indonesian troops as well – as they moved through the jungle, providing target information for other units such as the Gurkhas, Paras, infantry and artillery.

A four-man patrol could not hope to cover its assigned area alone, even though the number of usable border crossing points was limited. It became apparent that the SAS 'hearts and minds' tactic needed to be put to full use. There were many small groups of natives living in simple villages throughout the border area, and SAS patrols were to befriend them and enlist them as the 'eyes and ears' of the British. Many SAS men had worked with Iban Dyak trackers from this area during the Malayan campaign, and so already had great respect for their skills. An SAS patrol would arrive at a village and gradually gain the confidence of the inhabitants by supplying medical treatment and practical advice. On one occasion, an SAS sergeant built a water-powered generator to provide the only electric lighting for 600km. He followed this feat by

building an alcohol still from the frame of his bergen, though this skill is not one that is usually taught during SAS training!

Troopers gradually trained a network of irregular forces – Border Scouts – which reported any sightings of strangers. The SAS would also patrol the area themselves, sometimes only in pairs but normally in the standard four-man unit. Many days would be spent moving at the slow, silent pace needed to avoid detection by any enemy nearby. A patrol would sometimes spend 20 minutes out of every 30 totally still, listening for the slightest sound of movement. No one could use luxuries such as soap, toothpaste and tobacco as these unnatural smells could be detected by a skilled tracker (in the jungle smells 'hang' in the air, they do not blow away). Cooking was rare on patrol, the men usually living on cold rations such as tinned sardines. Everyone who went into the *ulu* (a Malay word used by the SAS to describe jungle) lost weight before returning.

Other troops were also involved in the 'hearts and minds' campaign, especially the Gurkhas, and attempts were made to form the native scouts into fighting formations. However, this did not meet with success, and in September 1963 a force of Border Scouts was badly mauled by Indonesian troops at Long Jawi.

INDONESIA RAISES THE STAKES
By mid-1963 the pattern of insurgency was changing. Larger groups, mainly composed of regular Indonesian soldiers, were now coming across the border. These well-trained troops would set professional ambushes and were prepared to engage the heliborne British forces. The 'Confrontation' was escalating into a war, fought in almost complete secrecy, with no public comment from either side.

By the end of 1963, D Squadron had relieved A. It was obvious the SAS was overstretched, so B Squadron was reformed in early 1964 and deployed to the area. The Guards Independent Parachute Company was transferred to SAS control and trained in jungle operations, eventually becoming G Squadron. Other units, such as a company from 2 Para, were also trained for jungle reconnaissance, though they did not operate under SAS control.

In 1964 the Indonesians were building up their strength for a major effort in this

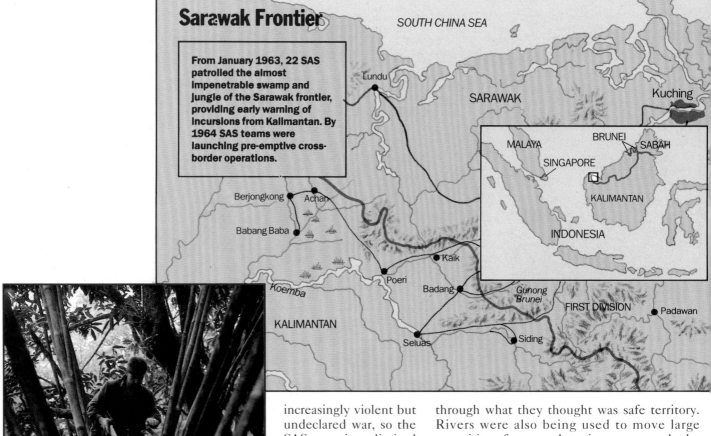

Sarawak Frontier

From January 1963, 22 SAS patrolled the almost impenetrable swamp and jungle of the Sarawak frontier, providing early warning of incursions from Kalimantan. By 1964 SAS teams were launching pre-emptive cross-border operations.

SOUTH CHINA SEA

Lundu

SARAWAK

Kuching

MALAYA

SINGAPORE

BRUNEI

SABAH

KALIMANTAN

INDONESIA

Berjongkong   Achan

Babang Baba

Kaik

Poeri

Badang

Gunong Brunei

FIRST DIVISION

Padawan

Koemba

Seluas

Siding

KALIMANTAN

Above: An SAS trooper, equipped with an Armalite, moves along an aerial walkway in Borneo. Note the olive-green jungle uniform and the bandana to keep sweat out of the eyes. Individual troopers found it almost impossible to keep dry in the jungle. Clothes quickly became soaked in sweat which eventually rotted them.

increasingly violent but undeclared war, so the SAS was given limited permission to cross the border into Indonesian territory. These first reconnaissance patrols – 'Claret' operations – were allowed to penetrate a few kilometres to watch known tracks and rivers and monitor troop movements. They were to avoid contact at all costs and claim map reading error if captured. Later patrols were sent farther into Indonesia, at times to a depth of 20km. The Government insisted that the patrols should remain 'deniable' – thus no identification, dog tags or obvious items of British uniform were worn. Even their boots were non-standard, or the tread pattern was disguised. SAS soldiers were also equipped with American Armalite rifles, ideal for jungle fighting but not readily identifiable as British equipment.

Once the success of these reconnaissance missions had been demonstrated, the politically sensitive step of organising offensive raids was taken. SAS troops started to ambush the Indonesians as they moved through what they thought was safe territory. Rivers were also being used to move large quantities of men and equipment towards the border, so supply boats were ambushed and sunk. The SAS also trained 40 Ibans – Cross-Border Scouts – for long-range operations.

For larger targets, SAS patrols would carry out a reconnaissance then return to lead platoon-strength groups of Gurkhas or other soldiers to the target. Some attacks were supported by artillery and, in emergencies, strike aircraft. 'Claret' raids disrupted the build-up of Indonesian troops by attacking their communications, insertion routes and base camps. A secondary effect was on the morale of enemy troops, who were worn down by the threat of attack in what they thought was safe territory.

By 1965 the SAS squadrons had settled into a pattern of four- or five-month tours, alternating with deployments to Hereford and the troubles in Aden. They had also been reinforced in Borneo by a squadron from each of the Australian and New Zealand detachments. The 'Confrontation' ended when President Sukarno of Indonesia was overthrown in 1966; the new military government having little interest in continuing a lost cause.

As in Oman in 1959, the SAS had won because of its highly trained and disciplined soldiers. SAS casualties were seven dead out of a Commonwealth total of 114; the Indonesians had lost over 2000 men.

Across the other side of the world, however, SAS soldiers had been fighting in yet another trouble spot – but this time the result was to be frustration and failure.

ADEN – THE LOST WAR

Aden sits on the southwest tip of the Arabian Peninsula. In 1963 it was still a British crown colony and protectorate, though the Government had decided to grant it independence. This was seen by Egypt and neighbouring Yemen as a political vacuum waiting to be filled – preferably by them. Backed by Soviet money and weapons, they were fomenting a campaign of rebellion in the Radfan, the bare, rocky area to the north, and urban terrorism in the port of Aden itself.

The British response was sluggish and inadequate. Large, cumbersome, punitive attacks were made into the mountains, further alienating the local population. In April 1964, it was decided to launch another large-scale attack into the Radfan, though the operation was given minimal preparation and had little or no intelligence on the enemy or terrain. The SAS had experience of similar terrain and climatic conditions in Oman, so it was decided to deploy a squadron, even though the Regiment was still heavily committed in Borneo. A Squadron was due in the area for training, so its arrival was brought forward so it could take part in the operation.

THE EDWARDS PATROL

The plan was for an SAS troop under Captain Robin Edwards to infiltrate the mountainous area to mark a drop zone for a parachute landing. The plan went wrong from the start, with the patrol's road transport being hindered by rebel snipers. Edwards' troop then set off on foot, but by daybreak had not reached the cover of the mountain tops. To avoid discovery they decided to spend the day hiding in a rock shelter (sangar). Unfortunately they were discovered by a wandering goatherd and quickly came under attack from around 50 rebels. During the long, hot day, accurate rifle fire pinned down the SAS men in their sangar, preventing any safe exit. They did have a radio, however, and were able to call for artillery and air support. Shells crashed down on the rebel positions and a constant stream of RAF Hunters strafed and rocketed any movement around the sangar. As night fell the SAS troopers escaped, leaving behind the dead bodies of Edwards and his signaller. A tragic postscript was the public display of the dead men's heads in the Yemeni capital, especially as their relatives had been told they were on exercise on Salisbury Plain.

SAS soldiers continued to operate in Aden, though with the British planning to leave in 1967 whatever happened, there was no scope for a 'hearts and minds' policy. The Regiment

CORPORAL, 22 SAS, BORNEO, 1965-66

This soldiers is wearing a 1958-pattern web belt around his waist, upon which is fixed, from left to right, ammunition pouch, 1944-pattern compass pouch, ammunition pouch and 1944-pattern water bottle carrier.

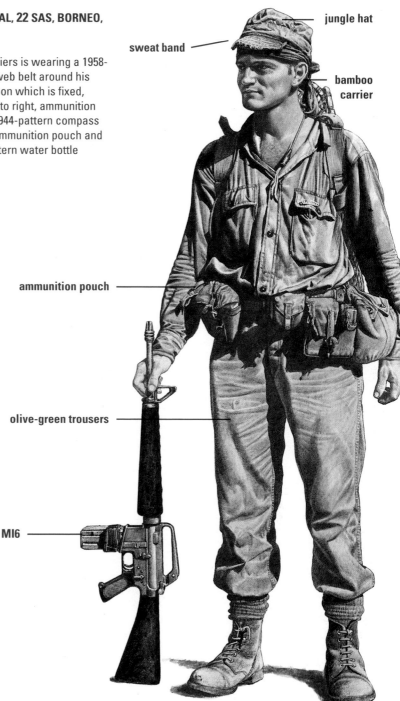

jungle hat

sweat band

bamboo carrier

ammunition pouch

olive-green trousers

MI6

did undertake anti-terrorist operations in Aden town itself, with troopers dressed in Arab clothing patrolling the narrow streets and alleys of the town with concealed pistols. Uniformed policemen and soldiers were sometimes used as 'bait' for terrorists, and a number of would-be assassins were killed in hails of 9mm gunfire. The SAS teams became known as 'Keeni Meeni' squads, the term a Swahili phrase describing the movement of a snake in long grass. For the SAS Aden was a bitter experience.

Section V
OMAN 1970-76

The years 1966-70 were relatively quiet for the SAS, and the four regular squadrons (A, B. D and G) spent most of their time on manoeuvres. Other tasks included VIP protection for friendly foreign leaders and exercises to test the security of British jails. During this period the future shape of anti-terrorist operations was also being examined, while D Squadron was actually deployed to Northern Ireland for a short time, though only as a conventional infantry unit.

In Oman, however, the situation had deteriorated throughout the 1960s, with Sultan Said bin Taimur's repressive regime forcing more and more of the hill tribes into outright rebellion. The Sultan's Armed Forces (SAF) had a number of British ex-officers and NCOs as contract advisers, but it was facing a losing battle in the countryside. Punitive actions such as public hangings of suspected rebels were doing nothing to solve the problem. The strains within the Omani leadership were building and, in July 1970, the old Sultan was overthrown by his son, Qaboos, in an almost bloodless coup.

THE SAS RETURNS TO THE DESERT

The new Sultan had been educated in the West, had trained at Sandhurst, and had relatively modern and liberal ideas for the future of his country. One of his first actions was to invite the SAS back to Oman to help cope with the rebellion. The most intractable problem was in the province of Dhofar. This remote area is in the far southwest of Oman, bordering on South Yemen (which until 1967 had been the Aden Protectorate). The pro-Soviet Yemenis were able to supply the People's Front for the Liberation of the Occupied Arabian Gulf (PFLOAG) – called *adoo* by the SAS – and send reinforcements from their secure bases over the border, while the mountainous terrain made it impossible for the SAF to impose any control over the region.

The initial SAS deployment was only a troop of around 19 men, plus a small personal bodyguard for the young Sultan. The SAS plan (Operation 'Storm') used the tried approach of befriending and gaining the trust of the local population, while simultaneously sending offensive patrols into the enemy's 'safe' havens. The British Government wanted a low profile, so the SAS presence was to be referred to as the British Army Training Team (BATT) so it could be denied any UK combat troops were in Oman.

The 'hearts and minds' strategy comprised a number of elements. It was devised by Lieutenant-Colonel Johnny Watts, Commanding Officer (CO) of 22 SAS, and was called the 'Five Fronts' Campaign. First, SAS parties would deliver basic medical services to the hill tribes by holding clinics in isolated villages. Second, they would provide veterinary support and advice on animal husbandry and help with water preservation. Third, the SAS would establish an intelligence cell to collate and analyse the scraps of information gleaned from friendly locals. Fourth, a psychological warfare operation ('psyops') would be mounted, with leaflets being dropped in remote areas explaining the policies of the new Sultan and offering amnesties to surrendering *adoo*. Finally, troops would be raised to fight for the Sultan.

THE *FIRQATS* ARE BORN

One of the first signs of success was when Mohammed Suhail, one of the main *adoo* leaders (who had been trained by the British when serving in the Trucial Oman Scouts) gave himself up. He had rebelled after becoming disillusioned with Said bin Taimur, but turned himself in when he read of the change of regime in a leaflet. Others did the same and some were persuaded to take up arms against their former comrades. These men and others were trained by the SAS and formed into irregular units called *firqats*, and played a vital part in SAS offensive operations (a major reason why many men defected was their Moslem faith was offended by the atheist ideology of the PFLOAG).

By mid-1971, support from the local tribes was gradually being won and the intelligence picture was improving daily. Around 80 SAS men were now in country and offensive patrols were being stepped up. A number of attacks were launched into the mountainous Jebel Dhofar to remove rebel bases and interdict their supply routes. One such mission was Operation 'Jaguar' in October 1971. A mixed SAS, SAF and *firqat* column – 800 men – made an exhausting night-time climb into the hills then fought a 10-day running battle around the rough airstrips and few water holes on the high plain. British-flown SAF Skyvan tactical transports flew in supplies and ammunition, while SAS teams guided Omani Strikemaster aircraft in strafing attacks on *adoo* positions.

Above right: An SAS team repairing a Land Rover in Oman during the 1970s. The Regiment's campaign in the Gulf state was probably its most successful. When it first arrived in 1970 the majority of the inhabitants of Dhofar were dissatisfied with their Sultan and many were in open rebellion against him. The SAS, by patience, guile and some excellent soldiering, virtually single-handedly reversed the situation.

Below right: An SAS medic administers aid to locals in Dhofar. Medical assistance forms an important part of SAS 'hearts and minds' doctrine, and in Oman troopers were even trained to treat the locals' animals. In addition, the intelligence picked up from these clinics could be invaluable.

M2 HB BROWNING HEAVY MACHINE GUN

Developed in the early 1920s, the Browning was a formidable man-stopper. Mounted on SAS jeeps during World War II, it gave raiding parties devastating firepower.

During World War II, SAS jeeps often mounted a 0.5-inch Browning heavy machine gun in addition to Vickers 'K' machine guns. Bob Bennett, a veteran of D Squadron, 1 SAS, during the war, describes a 1945 SAS jeep: 'Armament consisted of a twin Vickers for the front-gunner, another pair for the rear-gunner and every third or fourth jeep carried one 0.5in Browning heavy machine gun. The driver had a Bren gun. We'd first used the Vickers in the desert, and they fired 500 rounds a minute, which was pretty demoralising to the men on the receiving end. Each gun had a 100-round magazine filled with a mixture of tracer, armour-piercing, incendiary and ball. It was a lethal weapon. Each crew also had a 2in mortar, grenades and plenty of ammunition for their sidearms.'

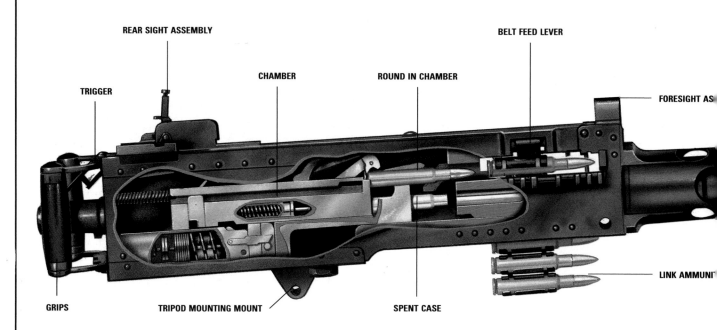

REAR SIGHT ASSEMBLY

TRIGGER

CHAMBER

ROUND IN CHAMBER

BELT FEED LEVER

FORESIGHT AS

LINK AMMUNI

GRIPS

TRIPOD MOUNTING MOUNT

SPENT CASE

The Browning was usually mounted at the front, forward of the passenger seat, the firer protected by a shield of armour plate and bullet-proof glass. The firepower of these vehicles was nothing short of ferocious, the Browning being one of the most formidable heavy machine guns of World War II (confusingly, SAS jeeps also mounted the 0.3-inch Browning M1919 machine gun, and often commentators get the two mixed up).

The Browning is still in service with armies around the world, the reason being simple: it is one of the most deadly anti-personnel weapons likely to be encountered by infantry and, when firing armour-piercing rounds, it is also capable of defeating modern light armour. The most numerous version of the Browning has been the M2 HB, the latter two letters meaning 'heavy barrel'. It can be used to fulfil many roles: as an infantry gun, as an anti-aircraft gun, or as a weapon that can be mounted on aircraft. When used by infantry the machine gun is usually mounted on a tripod, though it can also be fitted to vehicles. Brownings were also produced with water-cooled barrels and were used by the US Navy in World War II as anti-aircraft weapons, being fixed in multiple mountings for use against low-flying attack aircraft. Single water-cooled mountings were often used to provide anti-aircraft defence for shore installations.

The SAS found the weapon to be reliable, accurate and capable of sustained fire, all assets which made it ideally suited to operations behind enemy lines in North Africa and, later, on the European mainland. Though no longer used by the Special Air Service, there is no doubt that the 0.5in calibre Browning will be in service well into the next century, testimony to its claim of being one of the most successful and fearsome heavy machine guns of all time.

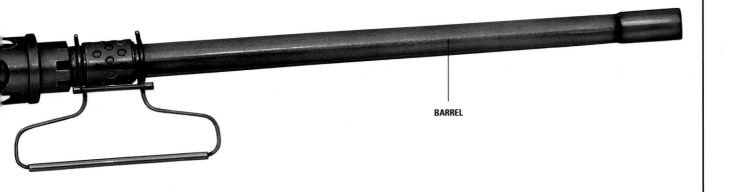

BARREL

M2 HB BROWNING HEAVY MACHINE GUN SPECIFICATIONS
- **TYPE:** heavy machine gun
- **CALIBRE:** 0.5in
- **WEIGHT:** 38.1kg
- **LENGTH:** 1654mm
- **EFFECTIVE RANGE:** 1800m
- **RATE OF FIRE:** 450-575 rounds per minute (cyclic)
- **FEED:** belt
- **MUZZLE VELOCITY:** 884 metres per second

Above: An SAS officer and *firqat* consult with Bedouin camel drivers in Oman, mid-1970s. Individual SAS soldiers established some excellent relationships with their *firqat* comrades, though the latter could be obstinate. During operations, for example, they would often stop fighting until some matter, often trivial, was resolved.
Above right: An SAS 81mm mortar opens up against *adoo* positions in southern Oman. Expert weapons skills were a major reason why small-sized SAS teams were able to hold their own against larger enemy forces.
Below right: Soldiers of the Sultan's Armed Forces (SAF) being transported in a twin-engined Skyvan aircraft. The SAF won a significant victory against the *adoo* at Sarfait in October 1975 which signalled the end of the war in Dhofar.

By 1972 Operation 'Storm' was in full swing, with more and more *firqat* groups being formed, each with two or three SAS advisers. The *adoo* were far from defeated, however, and on the morning of the 19 July they launched their biggest single attack of the rebellion – one which was to give the SAS one of its toughest challenges of any campaign.

THE BATTLE OF MIRBAT
Mirbat lies on the south coast of Dhofar. A cluster of dusty clay buildings, it was protected on the land side by a perimeter of coiled barbed wire some 500m to the north and east. Just inside the northern perimeter were the town's defenders. On the morning of the 19th, these comprised some 30 *askars* (armed Arabs) from northern Oman in an ancient Wali fort to the west. Farther inland was the mud-built BATT House, holding a troop of nine SAS advisers under 23-year-old Captain Mike Kealy. Some 500m farther west, at the corner of the wire, was another small fort holding 25 men of the Dhofar Gendarmerie (DG). The only heavy weapons were a 0.5in calibre heavy machine gun, one 7.62mm GPMG on the BATT House roof, an 81mm mortar emplaced alongside the building, and an elderly 25-pounder in a gun-pit next to the DG fort.

During the night of 18 July, over 250 *adoo* had gathered on the rocky jebel overlooking the town from the north. They were very well armed, being supported by heavy machine guns, 81mm mortars, two 75mm anti-tank recoilless rifles (RCLs) and some RPG and 84mm rocket launchers. Mirbat was to be a massive show of force – if they could take the town and wipe out the defenders, it would be an inspiration to any waverers.

As dawn broke, *adoo* mortar bombs started to rain down on the perimeter wire and the defences. Within a few minutes a hail of mortar bombs and RCL rockets were dropping on the forts and BATT House, and dozens of guerrillas could be seen heading down from the jebel towards the wire. Corporal Labalaba, a giant Fijian, sprinted to the 25-pounder to help the Omani gunner, while other SAS men manned their machine guns on the BATT House roof. Corporal Bob Bradshaw was plotting targets for the SAS mortar, initially against rebel fire-support weapons on the jebel. Urgent radio requests for assistance were sent to the SAS HQ over 65km away, although low cloud and intermittent rain was going to be a problem for any air support (the *adoo* had timed their attack to coincide with the rainy season).

Green tracer ricocheted off the walls of the DG fort, while its occupants and the 25-pounder blasted back at the advancing enemy. The attackers were determined and they soon reached the wire, aiming to surround the DG fort and the gun-pit. They were now close enough to fire anti-tank rockets at the defenders and the fort, and the 25-pounder came under heavy, accurate gunfire.

LABA HOLDS BACK THE HORDES
Labalaba took a grazing hit on the chin, but continued to load and fire the heavy shells as blood poured from his wound. Another Fijian, Trooper Savesaki, made a frantic 500m dash across the bullet-ridden ground between the BATT House and the gun-pit, eventually scrambling into the emplacement unharmed. The Omani gunner was killed by an *adoo* machine gun, so the two SAS troopers continued to load and fire the red-hot 25-pounder at near point-blank range. After a few rounds, Savesaki was hit in the back and Labalaba was left to fire the gun alone.

At 0700 hours, a short lull descended on the battlefield as the rebels regrouped. The cloud was still thick and there was no sign of any air support or reinforcements for the hard-pressed defenders. An attempt to evacuate wounded by helicopter was abandoned when the aircraft came under accurate rifle and machine-gun fire. Kealy was now worried because the men in the gun-pit were not answering the radio. Therefore he and the medic, Trooper Tobin, started out for the gun-pit, though taking a less exposed route than Savesaki. When they were half way across the battle erupted again, with bullets, bombs and grenades crashing into the fort, gun-pit and BATT House.

When the two men arrived at the gun-pit they were faced with a dreadful sight. Labalaba had been killed by a shot to the head, while the wounded Savesaki lay on his

back, firing his rifle with one hand. Tobin tried to tend his wounds but he was also hit by a bullet which fatally wounded him. Kealy was now desperately firing at the rebels who had got through the wire and were surrounding the fort. A grenade rolled into the gun-pit but, miraculously, the fuse was faulty and it did not explode. Kealy shouted

TROOPER, 22 SAS, OMAN, 1970-76

On his belt is a water bottle, ammunition pouch and an escape/evasion survival kit. Instead of the standard British Army SLR, the trooper is armed with a US 5.56mm M16 rifle.

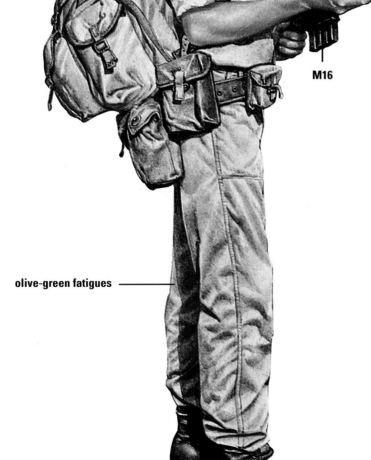

jungle hat

bergen

M16

olive-green fatigues

frantically into his radio for the SAS mortar to drop bombs around the fort and gun-pit.

At the BATT House, Trooper Harris, realising that the range was too short, wrapped his arms around the hot tube and heaved it up against his chest. While he held it there, bracing himself against the recoil, a fellow trooper fired the bombs around Kealy's position.

At this critical juncture, two Strikemaster jets streaked down from the cloud layer and skated over the area at less than 30m. They strafed the *adoo* around the fort and on the jebel, inflicting heavy casualties. However, they soon used up their ammunition and fuel and withdrew, one taking machine gun hits as it went. Another pair were soon overhead though, and they too strafed the rebels. While this was going on, helicopters were dropping SAS reinforcements to the west of the town.

G Squadron had been in the process of taking over from D Squadron in Oman and the men had been about to start a day's weapons practice. When the call came over the SAS HQ radio, they quickly emptied the armoury and bundled into the waiting helicopters. They were landed outside Mirbat and started to work their way towards the flanks of the attacking rebels. The combination of these fresh forces and the air attacks finally broke the will of the attackers and they withdrew, leaving over 30 dead behind them.

THE SAS DEFEATS THE *ADOO*

Mirbat signalled the beginning of the end for the rebellion, for the *adoo* suffered a huge loss of credibility as well as heavy casualties. In 1973, the SAS cleared the area between Salalah and Thamrait, and the next year the whole of central Dhofar was cleared. Though some of the fighting was heavy, the *adoo* were in retreat and disarray. The Dhofar rebellion was finally beaten in October 1975, when a sweep was undertaken in the mountains near the border with South Yemen, resulting in the rebels' supply routes being blocked for good.

For the SAS, the successful campaign had been yet another demonstration of the worth of its low-profile approach. It had been a hard war, and at times the *firqat* had been unreliable and downright infuriating. Nevertheless, the 'hearts and minds' campaign had again proved its worth, being largely responsible for turning the tide. Its next conflict was to be very different, however. The Regiment's new enemies would be drawn largely from within its own society; its battlefields would be on the streets of London, in the farmlands of Armagh, and in the housing estates of Belfast.

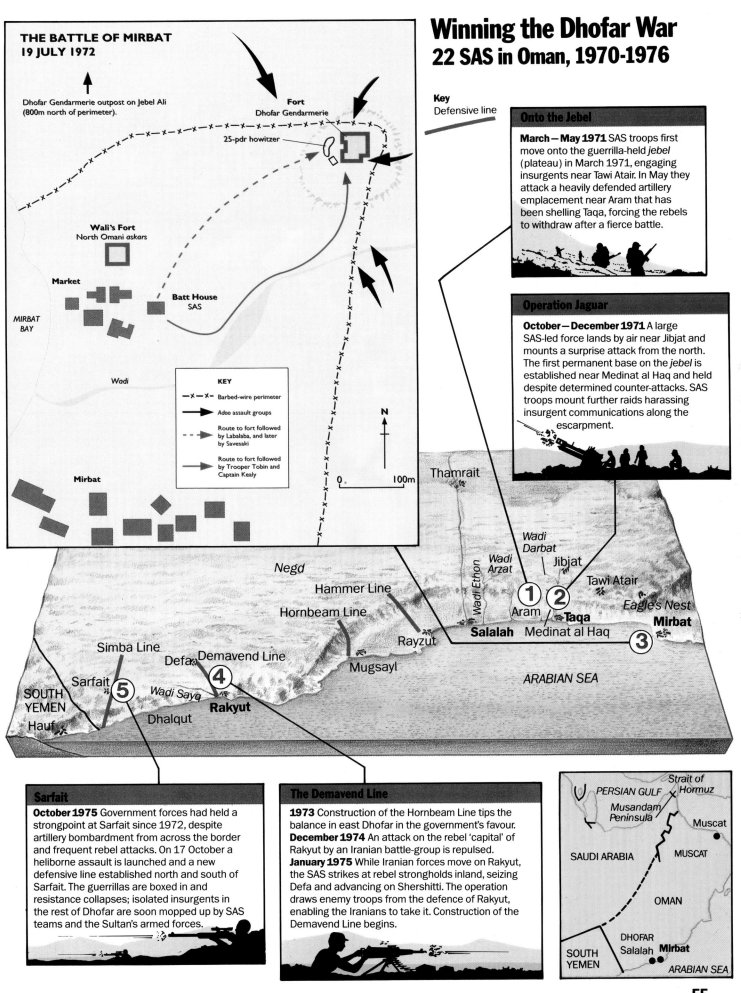

THE BATTLE OF MIRBAT
19 JULY 1972

Dhofar Gendarmerie outpost on Jebel Ali (800m north of perimeter).

Fort
Dhofar Gendarmerie

25-pdr howitzer

Wali's Fort
North Omani *askars*

Market

Batt House
SAS

MIRBAT BAY

Wadi

Mirbat

KEY
- —x—x— Barbed-wire perimeter
- ➔ Adoo assault groups
- ‑ ‑ ‑➤ Route to fort followed by Labalaba, and later by Savesaki
- ➔ Route to fort followed by Trooper Tobin and Captain Kealy

N

0 _____ 100m

Winning the Dhofar War
22 SAS in Oman, 1970-1976

Key
Defensive line

Onto the Jebel

March — May 1971 SAS troops first move onto the guerrilla-held *jebel* (plateau) in March 1971, engaging insurgents near Tawi Atair. In May they attack a heavily defended artillery emplacement near Aram that has been shelling Taqa, forcing the rebels to withdraw after a fierce battle.

Operation Jaguar

October — December 1971 A large SAS-led force lands by air near Jibjat and mounts a surprise attack from the north. The first permanent base on the *jebel* is established near Medinat al Haq and held despite determined counter-attacks. SAS troops mount further raids harassing insurgent communications along the escarpment.

Thamrait

Negd

Wadi Darbat
Wadi Arzat
Jibjat

Wadi Ethon

Hammer Line

Hornbeam Line

Rayzut

Aram
①
②
Tawi Atair

Eagle's Nest

Taqa
Salalah
Medinat al Haq
Mirbat
③

Simba Line
Defa
Demavend Line

Sarfait
⑤
Wadi Saya
④
Rakyut

SOUTH YEMEN
Hauf
Dhalqut

Mugsayl

ARABIAN SEA

Sarfait

October 1975 Government forces had held a strongpoint at Sarfait since 1972, despite artillery bombardment from across the border and frequent rebel attacks. On 17 October a heliborne assault is launched and a new defensive line established north and south of Sarfait. The guerrillas are boxed in and resistance collapses; isolated insurgents in the rest of Dhofar are soon mopped up by SAS teams and the Sultan's armed forces.

The Demavend Line

1973 Construction of the Hornbeam Line tips the balance in east Dhofar in the government's favour.
December 1974 An attack on the rebel 'capital' of Rakyut by an Iranian battle-group is repulsed.
January 1975 While Iranian forces move on Rakyut, the SAS strikes at rebel strongholds inland, seizing Defa and advancing on Shershitti. The operation draws enemy troops from the defence of Rakyut, enabling the Iranians to take it. Construction of the Demavend Line begins.

PERSIAN GULF
Strait of Hormuz
Musandam Peninsula

SAUDI ARABIA

Muscat
MUSCAT

OMAN

DHOFAR
Salalah **Mirbat**
SOUTH YEMEN
ARABIAN SEA

Section VI
ANTI-TERRORISM

At 1726 hours on 5 May 1980, British television viewers watched in awe as black-clad figures stormed the Iranian Embassy in central London. Only when the assault against the terrorist-held Embassy was over did it emerge that the SAS had carried out a dramatic hostage-rescue operation. The television coverage of that operation created, a legend. Henceforth, the SAS were the 'masked avengers of counter-terror' – at least according to the British tabloid press. The sudden rise to 'media stardom' of 22 SAS was regarded with some cynicism by members of the Regiment, who had been quietly carrying out a deadly war against international terrorism for 10 years. After the ignominious British withdrawal from Aden in 1967, the SAS started to look closely at the changing nature of worldwide guerrilla/terrorist activities and how it, as a specialist unit, could respond to them. A young SAS major named Peter de la Billière wrote an article for the Royal United Services Institute Journal, in 1969, entitled 'The Changing Pattern of Guerrilla Warfare'. 'The scope for this type of warfare [urban/-international terrorism] is growing, and successful counter-measures are, as yet, undiscovered,' he wrote. 'Perhaps we should re-think our own clandestine operating procedures to include urban operations, and review how we would deal with another Aden.'

The disastrous German attempt to free Israeli athletes held hostage by Palestinian terrorists during the September 1972 Munich Olympics had convinced the British Government of the need to establish a dedicated hostage-rescue unit. The SAS's counter-terrorist capability was at first limited and sprang from its role of providing bodyguards for key Government ministers and friendly heads of state. To keep track of terrorist threats and train its bodyguards, 22 SAS formed the Counter Revolutionary Warfare (CRW) Wing at Hereford in 1973. This small unit began to develop the concepts and tactics that would eventually come to fruition at Princes Gate in 1980.

Under the command of Lieutenant-Colonel Anthony Pearson, MC, the CRW Team, 'Pagoda' Squadron, was set up in November 1972 to give Britain its first fully fledged counter-terrorist unit. It was tasked with collecting intelligence on terrorist threats,

carrying out direct action against terrorist operations, and pre-empting terrorist activity. 'Direct action' involved a diverse range of skills including hostage-rescue from buildings, aircraft, ships, oil rigs and even nuclear power stations. It also developed hi-tech communications and surveillance techniques to enable these operations to be carried out anywhere in the world at very short notice. In just over a year, the 20-strong 'Pagoda' Squadron was confirmed as a permanent unit of 22 SAS, and since December 1974 it has been on 24-hour stand-by. Initially individual SAS soldiers were posted into the 'Pagoda' Squadron on short-term tours, but by the late 1970s each of the Regiment's squadrons took turns, in rotation, to fulfil the CRW role.

Even at the height of the Falklands and Gulf conflicts, a squadron was always on stand-by at Hereford to respond to terrorist incidents.

FIRST BLOOD AT MOGADISHU

'Pagoda' Squadron's first call to duty came in January 1975 when a deranged Iranian diverted an airliner to Stanstead Airport in Essex. This operation ended peacefully after negotiators talked the hijacker into giving himself up. One SAS soldier, however, was bitten by a police dog! A more serious incident occurred later in the year when the Metropolitan Police cornered a four-man Irish Republican Army (IRA) Active Service Unit in a flat in Balcombe Street, Marylebone, London. The terrorists surrendered after they heard a radio report that the SAS was preparing to assault the flat.

Cooperation and cross-training took place between the SAS and German, French, Dutch and American anti-terrorist units which were also being set up during this period. 'Pagoda' Squadron personnel, for example, were called upon to advise Dutch Special Border Police units dealing with a train hijack in May 1977 by South Moluccan terrorists. When a joint German/Palestinian terrorist cell hijacked a Lufthansa Boeing 737 airliner on October 1977, the SAS was asked to give assistance to the German GSG 9 anti-terrorist unit that was planning to free the 86 passengers and five crew being held hostage. Two members of 'Pagoda' Squadron, Major Alastair Morrison and Sergeant Barry Davis, joined the 26-strong GSG 9 team as they followed the terrorist-held

Above right: The calm before the storm. Two SAS soldiers (left), one carrying a 'frame charge', pictured just prior to the assault on the Iranian Embassy in 1980. Note the police snipers on the right.
Below right: A team is extracted by Wessex helicopter in Northern Ireland. Despite the popular image of the SAS engaging terrorists in firefights, the Regiment's main role in Ulster is intelligence gathering.

L2A3 STERLING SUBMACHINE GUN

The Sterling is one of the more aged submachine guns currently in production. Nevertheless, it is utterly reliable and is used by the SAS for counter-terrorist work in Northern Ireland.

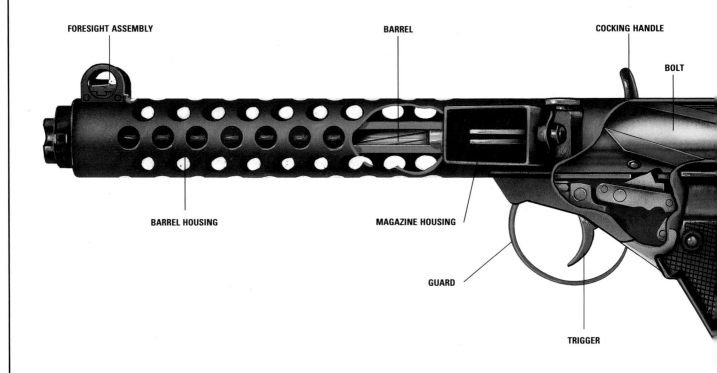

FORESIGHT ASSEMBLY

BARREL

COCKING HANDLE

BOLT

BARREL HOUSING

MAGAZINE HOUSING

GUARD

TRIGGER

The Sterling has been in service with the British Army since 1956. It looks simple, some would say crude, but it is nevertheless a modern submachine gun made entirely from steel and plastic, and has a side-feeding box magazine and a folding stock. Despite its simplistic looks, the Sterling requires more machining than other submachine guns and so its unit cost tends to be higher than its contemporaries.

Nevertheless, it is an extremely reliable weapon that performs well in adverse weather conditions. The gun's bolt, for example, has four special clearance ribs that push any dirt or other foreign objects into special vent holes. In addition, it has an integral firing pin which lines up with the primer only at the moment of firing.

The Sterling was developed at the end of World War II by G.W. Patchett of the Sterling Engineering Company, England. At first, unsurprisingly, it was called the 'Patchett' and could take the same magazine as the Sten gun and the Lanchester submachine gun. However, later versions of the Sterling made it much more effective than its rather simple and crudely engineered predecessors. The standard version, the L2A3, has a curved 34-round magazine, rear flip-type aperture and narrow blade front sights. It is capable of firing semi- or full-automatic.

The SAS mostly use the silenced version of the weapon, the L34A1. It is longer and slightly heavier than the standard version, though many of its parts are interchangeable with those of the L2A3, thus keeping down costs. A silencer casing covers the barrel jacket and the barrel has 72 radial holes drilled through it which permit the propellant gases to escape and so reduce the

muzzle velocity of the bullet. In addition, the barrel has a metal wrap and diffuser tube, the extension tube protruding beyond the silencer casing and barrel. The silenced Sterling is greatly favoured by SAS squadrons operating in Northern Ireland, especially for ambush missions. In such circumstances, it is usually fired semi-automatic, though it is also capable of firing full-automatic for prolonged periods if necessary.

Because of the Sterling's rather awkward shape – especially with regard to the magazine – its size and its relatively low rate of fire, it is not used by the SAS for hostage-rescue operations, the Heckler & Koch MP5 being preferred instead. Nevertheless, the Sterling will continue to be used by the SAS for many years to come, as its accuracy and reliability endear it to troopers on 'sting' operations in Northern Ireland.

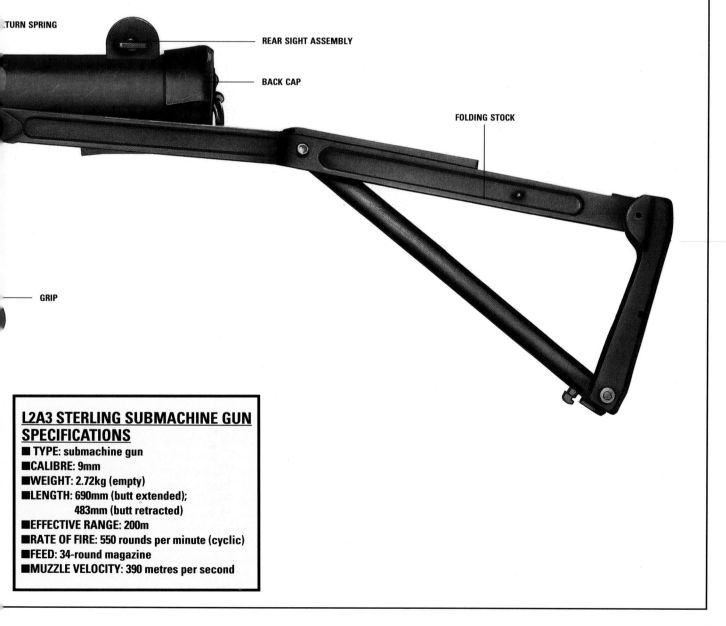

RETURN SPRING

REAR SIGHT ASSEMBLY

BACK CAP

FOLDING STOCK

GRIP

L2A3 STERLING SUBMACHINE GUN SPECIFICATIONS
- **TYPE:** submachine gun
- **CALIBRE:** 9mm
- **WEIGHT:** 2.72kg (empty)
- **LENGTH:** 690mm (butt extended); 483mm (butt retracted)
- **EFFECTIVE RANGE:** 200m
- **RATE OF FIRE:** 550 rounds per minute (cyclic)
- **FEED:** 34-round magazine
- **MUZZLE VELOCITY:** 390 metres per second

airliner around a series of Middle East airports. After the terrorists had killed the aircraft's pilot at Mogadishu airport in Somalia, the two SAS men led the GSG 9 team into action. The SAS threw 'flash bang' stun grenades into the aircraft and then the GSG 9 men stormed the airliner. Three of the four terrorists were killed during the combined British/German assault. All the passengers were freed, only four being wounded.

PRINCES GATE

Three years later, on 30 April 1980, a six-strong Iraqi-sponsored terrorist group burst into the Iranian Embassy in Princes Gate, London, taking more than 20 people hostage, including a BBC sound recordist and police constable. B Squadron, 22 SAS, commanded by Major Jeremy Phipps, was on the scene within hours of the siege commencing. Immediately the SAS began developing plans to break into the Embassy and free the hostages. A high-ranking group of Government ministers and officials at first decided that the best course of action was to negotiate with the terrorists. For five days the SAS prepared and rehearsed meticulously its assault, but was kept on hold as the negotiations dragged on.

By 5 May the terrorists' patience cracked and they shot dead the Embassy press attache, Abbas Lavasani. Listening devices also picked up conversations among the terrorists which included plans to kill further hostages. The time for talking was over. Prime Minister Margaret Thatcher ordered the SAS to storm the Embassy. At 1907 hours the police handed over responsibility for the operation to the SAS. Fourteen minutes later the SAS assault began – Operation 'Nimrod' was underway.

Four SAS men broke into the front of the Embassy after jumping from an adjoining balcony. They blew out the Embassy's armoured windows with a 'frame charge'. An eight-strong rear assault team abseiled down from the roof. This almost ended in disaster when one of the SAS men became entangled in his abseiling rope. He was later to suffer burns after SAS stun and CS gas grenades set the Embassy on fire. As the first team was breaking through windows at the rear of the Embassy, the terrorist leader tried to open fire on them but was brought to the ground by hostage PC Trevor Lock. The SAS men pushed the terrorist away from Lock and then shot him dead as he tried to shoot the policeman. Another terrorist was killed as the SAS swept through the Embassy. He was shot 21 times as he pointed a Browning pistol at an SAS team. BBC man Sim Harris then made his escape through the front window which had earlier been blasted open by the SAS.

In the Embassy's telex room three terrorists started to shoot the male hostages when they heard gunfire and explosions. One hostage was killed and two others were wounded. As one of the terrorist drew a grenade he was shot by the first SAS man to enter the telex room; a second terrorist was also killed. The other terrorist then tried to hide among the hostages. As the latter were being bundled out of the building he was spotted with a grenade in his hands. An SAS soldier clubbed him to the floor with his Heckler & Koch MP5 and he was then shot 39 times. A fifth terrorist was shot in the hallway near the front door.

The hostages were bound and unceremoniously passed along a chain of SAS men into the Embassy's rear garden. Sim Harris then identified the sixth terrorist hiding among the hostages and he was carried off by the police. The lucky terrorist had been guarding the women hostages in a back room and wisely offered no resistance. He escaped with his life.

At 2000 hours Lieutenant-Colonel Mike Rose, Comanding Officer, 22 SAS, handed back control of the Embassy to Deputy Assistant Commissioner of the Metropolitan Police John Dellow, officially ending the SAS involvement. A year later, however, two of the SAS soldiers who participated in the rescue were called as witnesses to the Coroner's inquest into the deaths of the five terrorists during the siege. The inquest jury returned a verdict of justifiable killing.

THE SAS IN GAMBIA

Throughout the remainder of the 1980s, the SAS's hostage-rescue capabilities were called upon twice more, both in very 'unconventional' circumstances. In July 1981, while the Gambian President, Sir Dawda Jawara, was in London attending the wedding of Prince Charles and Lady Diana Spencer, Cuban- and Libyan-backed rebels staged a coup in his capital, taking his wife and family hostage. However, a three-man SAS team infiltrated the capital in civilian clothes from neighbouring Senegal. After a brief stop off in the British Embassy to pick up the latest intelligence, the heavily armed SAS men bluffed their way past the guards holding the president's family. Rescuing the latter, the SAS men then organised an attack by Senegalese troops which broke the coup.

SAS troops were again in action on the British mainland in October 1987, when they rescued a prison officer held hostage for five days by rioting inmates at the maximum security Peterhead Prison, Aberdeen, which housed some of Scotland's most dangerous criminals. The SAS first stunned the rioters with 'flash bang' grenades and then created

confusion by filling the main cell complex with CS gas in preparation for their assault. In a scene reminiscent of Princes Gate, the SAS then abseiled from the roof to the floor of the main prison hall and freed the hostage in a dawn attack. The prison officer suffered only cuts and bruises during his ordeal, and no prisoners were seriously injured in the rescue.

IRELAND – WAR WITHOUT END

In the late 1960s and early 1970s, a 'second Aden' scenario feared by the SAS was actually developing within the United Kingdom itself. After the Roman Catholic civil rights protests were put down by Protestant police and paramilitary units in Northern Ireland during the summer of 1969, British troops were

deployed on the streets of Belfast and Londonderry to keep order. At first they were welcomed by the Catholics as their saviours and protectors. D Squadron, 22 SAS, even deployed openly to the Province for a number of weeks in 1969 to help in the patrolling effort. The 'honeymoon' was not to last, however. By the summer of 1970 the Irish Republican Army (IRA) had launched its terrorist campaign with the aim of driving the British out of Ireland by force of arms.

With its heavy commitment to support the war in Oman, there were few SAS troops available to send to Ireland. During the early 1970s there were never more than a couple of dozen SAS men in the Province at any one time. Despite a very chaotic start, the Army

Above: The dead body of Captain Richard Westmacott lies covered on a Belfast street. Westmacott, an SAS officer, was killed by a burst of machine-gun fire during a gun battle with the IRA in May 1980.

was intent on pressing ahead with its efforts to set up a covert intelligence gathering network inside Republican areas. After a number of embarrassing incidents involving plain clothes Army patrols firing on each other or being arrested by uniformed police, the SAS men with experience of urban guerrilla warfare in Aden were called in to provide professional advice. Only after the ending of the Dhofar War were SAS soldiers available in large numbers for operations against the IRA. The spur for their first official deployment came in January 1976, following a spate of IRA murders in the so-called 'Bandit Country' of South Armagh, an area adjacent to the Irish Republic. These included the killing of three young soldiers when their observation post (OP) was overrun by IRA terrorists, and the murder of 11 Protestants in a bus. Amid much media hype the British Government announced that the SAS was being sent to South Armagh. Ministers admitted that 'presentational' reasons were behind the deployment. It was hoped the Regiment's fearsome reputation would scare off the IRA and reassure Unionist politicians. An advance party of 12 men from D Squadron, 22 SAS, arrived to set up base in Bessbrook Mill in late January 1976. A few weeks later the whole squadron (75 men) arrived. Senior Army officers in South Armagh admitted that their intelligence on the local IRA 'players' (active terrorists) was almost non-existent.

THE SAS IN SOUTH ARMAGH

It was the job of the SAS to fill this void. Unusually, D Squadron was placed under the operational control of the roulement infantry battalion in South Armagh. It specialised in covert reconnaissance of IRA men. SAS teams set up OPs for long periods near the homes of IRA suspects, terrorist arms caches or terrorist rendezvous points (RVs). For weeks at a time SAS teams remained hidden in their OPs, sending back reports on IRA activity. Normally it was left to the police or Army to act on SAS intelligence, but on a number of occasions SAS OPs arrested top IRA men themselves.

The first success for D Squadron came in March 1976, when a team 'lifted' IRA commander Sean McKenna from his home in the Irish Republic and delivered him to a waiting Army patrol just inside the border. The following month, a four-man SAS team was observing the home of an IRA terrorist's fiancée. The suspect, Peter Cleary, was on the run in the Republic, and when he was spotted at the house by a covert SAS OP the team were ordered to make an instant 'snatch'. While they were waiting for a helicopter to airlift them and their 'catch', Cleary tried to break free and was killed in the struggle. On 5

S6 respirator

torch

MP5 submachine gun

body armour

TROOPER, 22 SAS, 1980S

This soldier wears Counter Revolutionary Warfare kit: black overalls, body armour and an S6 respirator with hood. Armament consists of an H&K MPA3 submachine gun and a 9mm Browning handgun, worn low on the right thigh. Three spare MP5 magazines are carried on the left leg.

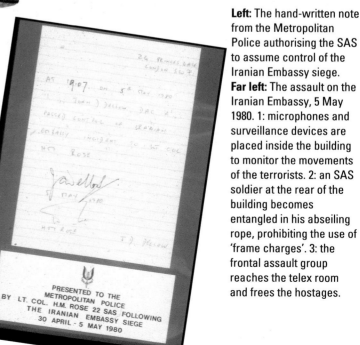

Left: The hand-written note from the Metropolitan Police authorising the SAS to assume control of the Iranian Embassy siege.
Far left: The assault on the Iranian Embassy, 5 May 1980. 1: microphones and surveillance devices are placed inside the building to monitor the movements of the terrorists. 2: an SAS soldier at the rear of the building becomes entangled in his abseiling rope, prohibiting the use of 'frame charges'. 3: the frontal assault group reaches the telex room and frees the hostages.

Right: SAS support troops prepare to give covering fire if required as 'Pagoda' Troop storms the Iranian Embassy. Note the communications equipment worn by the soldier on the right and the silenced MP5 submachine gun carried by the other man.

May 1976, eight SAS men suffered the ignominy of being arrested by the Gardaí after they entered the Republic by mistake.

Further success came the following year, however, in a gun battle with three armed IRA men near Culderry, South Armagh. Seamus Harvey, a local IRA man, was killed by SAS men who had been staking out a terrorist RV, though two of the bullets that hit him were fired by his own men providing covering fire!

AMBUSH AT LOUGHALL

The success of the SAS in South Armagh led to a widening of the Regiment's area of operations, starting in 1978. It would now be available for operations in any part of the Province. Its role would also be very different, and links with Army Intelligence, Royal Ulster Constabulary (RUC) Special Branch and MI5 increased. Prompt collection and dissemination of intelligence was seen as the most effective method of countering terrorist activity. Up until the late 1970s the RUC's Special Branch, Army Intelligence and MI5 all had their own completely separate intelligence gathering operations which included running their own agents and informers inside terrorist organisations. These operations were often poorly coordinated, thus intelligence information was rarely shared between different organisations.

In 1978 the first Tasking and Coordination Group (TCG) was set up in Belfast to coordinate intelligence gathering by all the different agencies in the city. Military and police officers were given the opportunity to pool their resources. When intelligence indicated likely terrorist operations, then SAS teams could be quickly tasked to set up ambushes to catch the opposition 'in the act'. The system was so successful that it was extended to cover the whole of Northern Ireland, with one TCG in each of the RUC's three regions. While the SAS had concentrated on covert reconnaissance during its time in South Armagh, this task now became increasingly the domain of a specialist surveillance unit set up by Army Intelligence.

Operating under a wide variety of cover names, such as 14 Intelligence and Security Company (14 Int Coy) or Intelligence and Security Group (Northern Ireland), its personnel are highly trained in hi-tech surveillance techniques using electronic bugs, covert photography and video surveillance. This unit, together with similar teams from the RUC and MI5, provide much of the raw intelligence to the TCGs on the activities of terrorist suspects. In this new set-up the SAS were tasked for 'executive action' – the ambushing of IRA suspects while committing terrorist crimes.

The Army never comments on the identities of personnel or names their units when undercover soldiers are involved in incidents which result in terrorist fatalities. This leads to a certain degree of confusion on a number of occasions as to whether SAS or 14 Int Coy soldiers have been involved. 14 Int Coy personnel have had their cover blown and have been engaged in firefights with IRA; four of its soldiers have been killed by the IRA; and personnel from 14 Int Coy have also observed terrorist crimes in progress and intervened. In September 1989, a 14 Int Coy patrol in an unmarked car (Q car) saw a Loyalist terrorist murder an innocent civilian in Belfast. The team rammed the terrorist as he was making his get away on a motorcycle and he was killed in the ensuing struggle. A 14 Int Coy patrol even arrested a team of Loyalist

terrorists who had just tried to assassinate the Sinn Fein leader Gerry Adams.

With much of the routine surveillance of IRA members being carried out by other agencies, the SAS has, to some extent, been able to scale down its involvement in Northern Ireland. For most of the 1980s and into the 1990s, only some 20 SAS men have been on duty in the Province at any one time. They have been formed into a detached troop, Ulster Troop, made up of carefully selected personnel. During large-scale operations such as the Loughall ambush in 1987, the extra personnel can be drafted in direct from Hereford. The SAS has been involved in numerous ambush operations against the IRA which have resulted in many arrests and deaths of IRA personnel. Between 1976 and 1987, for example, 25 IRA personnel were

killed by the SAS. As a comparison, in the same period other Army units killed nine IRA personnel, while 14 Int Coy accounted for seven terrorists. Two SAS men have been killed by the IRA and two others have been killed in road accidents while serving in Northern Ireland.

Perhaps the most famous SAS ambush to date took place at the North Armagh village of Loughall on 8 May 1987. Intelligence had revealed that the IRA was going to mount a massive bomb attack on the small village police station. A large-scale SAS operation, codenamed Operation 'Judy', was put into effect to ambush the IRA attack force. Some 40 SAS men were to set up ambush and cut-off positions around the police station, while the RUC highly trained Headquarters Mobile Support Unit and several companies of troops

Above: Following a successful mission, a patrol is extracted by a Lynx helicopter in Northern Ireland. Helicopters were used to evacuate SAS soldiers after their spectacular operation at Loughall in May 1987.

were put on stand-by to seal off the area as soon as the ambush was sprung. The SAS was taking no chances. The killing group made up of Ulster Troop personnel was armed with 7.62mm Heckler & Koch G3-A4K assault rifles and at least two 7.62mm GPMGs. They were positioned inside the police station and in a nearby wood. The remainder of the SAS personnel, 16 men from G Squadron armed with 5.56mm M16 rifles, were assigned as cut-off groups in other parts of the village to stop the IRA men escaping from the ambush. At 1915 hours, a Toyota van followed by a mechanical excavator or digger approached the police station. The van was the IRA's getaway vehicle and the digger's bucket contained a 100kg bomb.

First the van stopped outside the police station and two IRA men got out and, in a scene reminiscent of the gunfight at the OK Corral, sprayed the building with automatic fire from Heckler & Koch G3 and FNC 5.56mm assault rifles. That was the cue for the SAS to open up. More than 1000 rounds were pumped into the van and the digger. In the confusion the terrorists were able to light the fuse of their bomb and it detonated, flattening part of the police station. Fortunately none of the SAS team was seriously injured. The IRA

terrorists were wearing body armour, but they were so close to the SAS that it did not prevent them being riddled with bullets. When the firing stopped eight top terrorists lay dead – the East Tyrone Brigade had ceased to exist. An innocent civilian also died when he accidentally drove through one of the SAS cut-off groups.

Within minutes a large security operation was put into effect to seal off the site of the ambush, so the SAS men could be helicoptered out before the world's media descended on the scene of the Regiment's most successful operation against the IRA.

GIBRALTAR

Under a year later, an SAS mission against an IRA team in Gibraltar was to turn into perhaps the Regiment's most controversial operation. Acting on information supplied by MI5, SAS soldiers were sent out to the British colony to intercept an IRA team that was planning to bomb military bases in Gibraltar. On the afternoon of 4 March 1987, three of the team were followed around Gibraltar by MI5. SAS soldiers in civilian clothes then took over the surveillance with the intention of arresting them. What happened next became the subject of great controversy. According to the

SAS men themselves they were spotted by the IRA team. Thinking that they were about to detonate a bomb by remote control or draw their weapons, the SAS shot dead all three terrorists. Some witnesses said the SAS men had shot the three in cold blood. The situation was made worse by revelations that the three dead were unarmed and had no radio control detonation devices on them.

After a heated inquest the SAS men were cleared. While defending the actions of the SAS, some military sources are scathing about the quality of the intelligence supplies by MI5, which placed the SAS men in the situation of thinking they were dealing with an armed and dangerous IRA team when in fact they were only on unarmed reconnaissance. The Gibraltar incident highlighted the dilemma faced by SAS soldiers when faced with what they believe to be heavily armed terrorists. When operating on British soil, SAS soldiers are governed by the same rules as other soldiers or policeman. Under the 'Yellow Card' rules they can only use firearms as a last resort, and then only to protect their lives. If possible, a warning has to be given, unless by giving that warning the soldier's life is endangered. In so-called 'clean kill' situations, such as Loughall, where terrorists

have already opened, fire the use of firearms presents few problems. The IRA, however, has long maintained that the Special Air Service operates a 'shoot to kill' policy and makes no attempt to arrest IRA suspects. None of these allegations has yet been proved, though in the political quagmire of Northern Ireland this has not stopped the Regiment itself from being branded as a terrorist organisation. It is a no-win situation in a war without end.

Top: Loughall, May 1987. The bullet-ridden Toyota van in which the IRA terrorists made their abortive escape attempt. **Above:** An aerial photograph of Loughall that amply conveys the devastation caused by the IRA bomb. Note the remains of the digger.

THE FALKLANDS 1982

To SAS soldiers living for three weeks at a time in freezing cold and damp covert observation posts (OPs) dug into peat bogs, the Falkland Islands were the 'Costa Hypothermia'. Fighting the Argentinian forces was only half the battle. The unforgiving South Atlantic climate, particularly on the Antarctic island of South Georgia, proved to be just as great a challenge. However, the Regiment contained the expertise within its ranks to enable it to adapt quickly to its new combat environment. Just as well. Like the rest of the British military, the SAS was taken completely by surprise when the Argentinians invaded the Falklands on 2 April 1982.

THE RETAKING OF SOUTH GEORGIA

Within hours of hearing the news on a BBC broadcast, the Commanding Officer (CO) of 22 SAS, Lieutenant-Colonel Mike Rose, had alerted his troops for possible deployment and then contacted the commanders of the Royal Navy Task Force being sent to recapture the Falklands. Two days later, D Squadron, commanded by Major Cedric Delves, flew out from Britain to Ascension Island, a British island almost on the equator in the central Atlantic. It was to become part of the highly secret Task Force 317.9 being formed to recapture South Georgia, which had fallen to the Argentinians on 3 April. Other component units included M Company, 42 Commando, Royal Marines, and 25 men of 2 Special Boat Squadron (SBS), Royal Marines. In total the force mustered some 250 crack troops (the naval component was five ships). This group quickly sailed for South Georgia after its arrival at Ascension, and by 21 April an advance guard had arrived off the island.

The first task for the SAS was to put reconnaissance parties ashore to gather detailed intelligence on the Argentinians before the Royal Marines mounted the main assault. On 22 April, three ageing Wessex helicopters dropped D Squadron's Mountain Troop onto South Georgia's Fortuna Glacier, but the weather was too much even for the SAS – the following day the party's CO, Captain John Hamilton, requested immediate evacuation. When the helicopters returned, the weather conditions caused two of them to crash, though luckily the crews survived. The SAS soldiers on the glacier were rescued only after the surviving Wessex made a daredevil

flight back to pick them up. Undeterred, Boat Troop tried next day in five Gemini assault craft. Only three got ashore, however, the other two being carried away by heavy seas. One crew was rescued by helicopter and the other SAS team temporarily disappeared, though it later got ashore. An attempt by the SBS to get ashore in Geminis was thwarted by floating ice. Nevertheless, by 23 April the SAS had established some OPs around Leith.

Chance now intervened to save Operation 'Paraquet'. At first light on 25 April, the Wessex from HMS *Antrim* spotted the Argentinian submarine *Sante Fe* on the surface approaching the enemy's base at Grytviken. It immediately attacked the submarine and was soon joined by other Royal Navy helicopters. The submarine now made a run for the safety of Grytviken harbour.

Sensing that they had the upper hand, Major Delves and Major Guy Sheridan, M Company, decided to put together a scratch force of Royal Marines and SAS to assault the Argentinian positions. Only two SAS troops, an SBS team and around 24 Royal Marines, in total 75 men, were immediately available because the remainder of M Company was still a day's sailing away in the support ship *Tidespring*. After quick battle orders were issued, the scratch force was shuttled ashore in helicopters. HMS *Antrim* and HMS *Plymouth* started to lay down support fire as the British troops advanced. The 170 Argentinians surrendered without firing a shot.

STRATEGIC RECONNAISSANCE

While the action was unfolding on South Georgia, Lieutenant-Colonel Rose and his headquarters team were sailing south in the assault ship *Fearless*. During their voyage they worked with Brigadier Julian Thompson, the CO of 3 Commando Brigade, to prepare the invasion plan to retake the Falklands. The SAS was required to fill the intelligence void. Two troops of G Squadron sailed south with Admiral Sandy Woodward's Carrier Battle Group and arrived off the Falklands in the final days of April. On 1 May, within minutes of an RAF Vulcan bomber pounding the airport near the Falklands' capital, Stanley, SAS soldiers were put ashore by Sea King helicopters of 846 Naval Air Squadron. Using night vision goggles, the Sea King pilots flew at low level, in pitch darkness and in high

Above right: A Royal Marines 81mm mortar position on Mount Kent during the Falklands War. D Squadron, 22 SAS, was involved in a number of vicious firefights with Argentinian forces on Mount Kent in late May prior to the arrival of the Marines.

Below right: The assault ship *Intrepid* and landing craft photographed in the Falklands. In the air can be seen a Sea King helicopter, the type that was used by the SAS throughout the campaign.

M16A2

One of the most famous assault rifles in the world, the M16 has been used by the SAS in the jungles of the Far East, the deserts of the Middle East and in the Falklands.

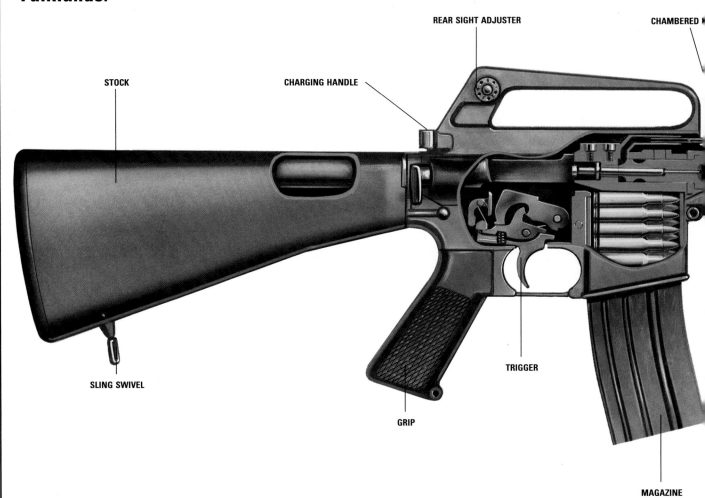

REAR SIGHT ADJUSTER

CHAMBERED

STOCK

CHARGING HANDLE

SLING SWIVEL

GRIP

TRIGGER

MAGAZINE

This weapon, previously known as the AR-15, was developed by Eugene Stoner as a follow-on to the earlier 7.62mm AR-10 assault rifle. First used in anger in the early 1960s, the M16 has since become the standard infantry weapon of the US armed forces. In addition, it is used by at least 12 other countries and is also employed by members of Britain's Special Air Service. The latter has used the M16 since its campaign in Borneo (1963-66), and the weapon has also put in an appearance in the Regiment's

campaigns since then: Aden (1964-67), Oman (1970-76), the Falklands (1982) and the Gulf (1991).

The M16 has several advantages for special forces operations: it is lighter and more compact than its predecessors, the M1 and M14 rifles, thus allowing an individual soldier to carry more ammunition (which is itself lighter than 7.62mm ammunition). It is particularly suited to jungle fighting, being relatively short, light and having a high muzzle velocity which means its ammunition has a high lethality at short

ranges. In desert conditions the rifle performs less well, having poor long-range accuracy and not being able to stand up to sandy conditions. Troops using the first M16s in Vietnam encountered severe problems with jamming and misfires under combat conditions, especially in muddy terrain, until Colt introduced the M16A1 in 1966. This model had a bolt-closure mechanism to ensure rounds were properly seated in the chamber, and it continued in production until 1988, when the improved M16A2 version was

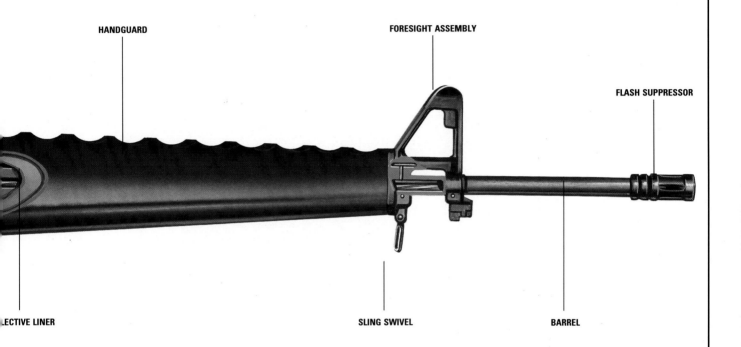

HANDGUARD

FORESIGHT ASSEMBLY

FLASH SUPPRESSOR

LECTIVE LINER

SLING SWIVEL

BARREL

M16A2 SPECIFICATIONS
- **TYPE: assault rifle**
- **CALIBRE: 5.56mm**
- **WEIGHT: 3.18kg**
- **LENGTH: 990mm**
- **EFFECTIVE RANGE: 400m**
- **RATE OF FIRE: 700-950 rounds per minute**
- **FEED: 20- or 30-round box magazine**
- **MUZZLE VELOCITY: 1000 metres per second**

adopted by the US Marines and then the US Army.

The M16A2 has a straight stock, a pistol grip, a round foregrip and an effective flash suppressor – important for SAS teams operating behind enemy lines as one way to spot a soldier firing at you is to watch for the muzzle flash of his weapon. The rifle is made from stamped metal and injection-moulded plastic to simplify the production process and reduce costs. The flash suppressor can accommodate a bayonet and a variety of rifle grenades.

The M16A2 has a three-round burst facility and a single-shot fire mode, the full-automatic mode of the M16A1 has been abandoned in an effort to conserve ammunition in the field.

The M16 is now 30 years old and it faces stiff competition from the newer bullpup designs that are entering service. It will be interesting, for example, to see if it still remains in SAS service now the British Army has the bullpup SA-80. For fighting in a jungle environment the M16 was fine, but US and British special forces are

increasingly being called upon to fight in desert conditions – the 1991 Gulf War against Iraq being a case in point – where the M16's lack of effectiveness beyond a range of 300m becomes all too apparent. In addition, being a precision-designed weapon, the M16 does not stand up well to the hard usage it is often subjected to by elite soldiers. Though it seems set to continue in SAS service until the end of the century, it appears likely that it is reaching the end of its long life, with regard to SAS use at least.

Right: Royal Marines 'yomping' across East Falkland during the conflict. This photograph amply conveys the main features of the war in the South Atlantic: rain, cold and barren terrain. When it is remembered that some SAS four-man patrols spent over three weeks hidden in covert observation posts in this type of environment, then some idea of the standards of SAS training and personnel can be gleaned.

winds, to insert four-man teams at strategic locations throughout the Falklands to gather vital intelligence on Argentinian dispositions. The SAS teams were put down up to 35km from their targets and then slowly covered the distance on foot.

During daylight hours they stayed under cover before making their final approach in darkness. Once in position the SAS teams set up covert OPs overlooking the main Argentinian troop positions around Stanley, Bluff Cove, Darwin, Goose Green, Fox Bay and Port Howard. SBS teams carried out similar missions near Berkeley Sound, Port Salvador and around the eventual British landing site at San Carlos Water. These OPs sent back regular radio reports on Argentinian movements and deployments. An OP near Stanley scored a big success when it called down an air strike on previously undetected Argentinian helicopters.

Some OPs were in position for more than three weeks, with the soldiers having to live on what food they had in their bergens. There was little protection from the severe South Atlantic weather, however, and the OPs were in constant danger of discovery. The Argentinians mounted regular patrols and had radio direction-finding equipment, though the SAS got round this by using 'burst' radio which transmits messages in fractions of a second. On one occasion an Argentinian helicopter hovered low over an SBS OP, blowing away the foliage cover from the 'hide' with its rotor blades. Fortunately the pilot did not bother to look below his machine and so failed to spot the SBS men. Four days before the final ceasefire, an SAS OP was discovered by Argentinian troops near Port Howard and, in a brief firefight, Captain John Hamilton was killed and his signaller captured.

THE PEBBLE ISLAND RAID

As the main British landing force was making its final preparations to put ashore at San Carlos Water, the SAS was tasked with raiding the Argentinian air base on Pebble Island. As it was only a few minutes flight from the proposed beachhead, it posed a potential threat to the landings. The SAS suggested to Admiral Woodward, Carrier Battle Group Commander, that it attack the airstrip and put the Pucara attack aircraft based there out of action. At first the SAS suggested three weeks to prepare for the raid, allowing for detailed reconnaissance, planning and rehearsals. Woodward said five days!

D Squadron, its morale high after South Georgia, was given the mission. After a quick reconnaissance by the squadron's Boat Troop, the raid was scheduled to take place on the night of 14/15 May. Again 846 Squadron delivered the SAS men to their objective, though strong headwinds delayed their take-off from the carrier *Hermes*. Time was at a premium if the raiders were to carry out their attack and get back to ship before daylight made them, and *Hermes*, vulnerable to enemy air attack. At 0700 hours the raiding team opened fire with GPMGs and 66mm LAW rockets, riddling the 11 aircraft on the airstrip with holes. Demolition teams then raced over to the aircraft and planted explosive charges. Fifteen minutes later the task was completed and the SAS started to withdraw. A few Argentinian Air Force personnel tried to intervene but were stopped by gunfire. Within two hours the SAS men were airborne and heading back to *Hermes*. Only two of the raiders suffered minor injuries – the mission had been a stunning success.

ACTION AT DARWIN

D-Day for the British landing at San Carlos Water was set for 21 May. As a diversion the SAS was tasked with mounting a raid against the enemy garrison at Darwin. During the preparations for the raid, a Sea King carrying SAS men crashed into the sea as a result of a birdstrike. Some 18 SAS men from D Squadron died, including many who had taken part in the South Georgia and Pebble Island operations. The raid, however, still went ahead as planned. The heavily armed men from D Squadron opened up on the Argentinians with an assortment of weaponry including 81mm mortars, MILAN anti-tank missiles, GPMGs and M203 grenade launchers. So much firepower was laid down that the Argentinians thought they were being attacked by a full battalion!

D Squadron was in the thick of the action again within days when it was flown forward to Mount Kent, the highest peak in the Falklands. It dominated the approach to Stanley, but was reported by G Squadron's OPs to be unoccupied by the Argentinians. In atrocious weather conditions the SAS held the mountain in the face of constant probing by Argentinian special forces. Night after night the SAS ambushed the Argentinians as they tried to find out what was happening on the mountain. It had originally been intended to reinforce D Squadron almost immediately, but the sinking of the container ship *Atlantic Conveyor* with her precious cargo of Chinook helicopters meant the SAS had to stay on the mountain for five days and nights. On 31 May enough helicopters were scraped together to fly forward an advanced company of 42 Commando, Royal Marines. As the helicopters were touching down the Argentinians chose to attack again. However, the SAS quickly went into action and beat off the attack. On board

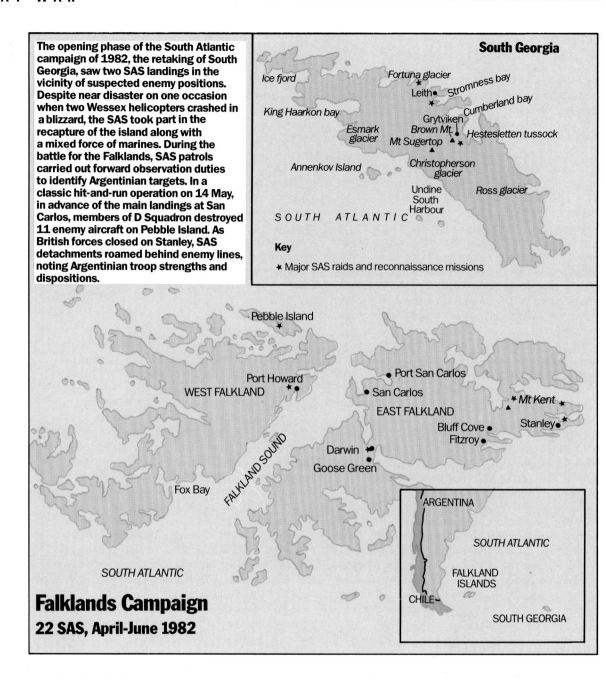

The opening phase of the South Atlantic campaign of 1982, the retaking of South Georgia, saw two SAS landings in the vicinity of suspected enemy positions. Despite near disaster on one occasion when two Wessex helicopters crashed in a blizzard, the SAS took part in the recapture of the island along with a mixed force of marines. During the battle for the Falklands, SAS patrols carried out forward observation duties to identify Argentinian targets. In a classic hit-and-run operation on 14 May, in advance of the main landings at San Carlos, members of D Squadron destroyed 11 enemy aircraft on Pebble Island. As British forces closed on Stanley, SAS detachments roamed behind enemy lines, noting Argentinian troop strengths and dispositions.

South Georgia

Ice fjord
Fortuna glacier
King Haarkon bay
Leith
Stromness bay
Cumberland bay
Esmark glacier
Grytviken
Brown Mt.
Hestesletten tussock
Mt Sugertop
Annenkov Island
Christopherson glacier
Ross glacier
Undine South Harbour
SOUTH ATLANTIC

Key
★ Major SAS raids and reconnaissance missions

Pebble Island
Port Howard
WEST FALKLAND
Port San Carlos
San Carlos
EAST FALKLAND
Mt Kent
Stanley
Bluff Cove
Fitzroy
FALKLAND SOUND
Darwin
Goose Green
Fox Bay
SOUTH ATLANTIC

ARGENTINA
SOUTH ATLANTIC
FALKLAND ISLANDS
CHILE
SOUTH GEORGIA

Falklands Campaign
22 SAS, April-June 1982

the first helicopter was Lieutenant-Colonel Rose and the journalist Max Hastings. In a now famous incident Hastings asked Rose about the operation's chances of success. The SAS officer replied, with characteristic panache, 'who dares, wins'.

FINAL OFFENSIVES
In the final days of the war the SAS continued its low-key reconnaissance operations around the flanks of the British forces to ensure the Argentinians could not spring any last-minute surprises. West Falkland received special attention, along with the Berkeley Sound area to the north of Stanley. In one of these missions an SAS patrol bumped into an SBS unit and an SBS man was shot dead by mistake. On the night of 13/14 June, the SAS

and SBS joined forces for what was called 'a suicide mission'. To divert attention away from 2 Para's attack on Wireless Ridge, a joint SAS/SBS force in four Rigid Raider boats of the Royal Marines' 1st Raiding Squadron was to slip unnoticed into Stanley harbour and lay down a barrage of fire on Argentinian positions. As the raiders approached, however, the crew of an Argentinian hospital ship spotted them with their searchlights. A hail of small-arms fire was directed at the small craft which made a rapid exit from the harbour. Miraculously, only four of the SAS/SBS force suffered minor injuries, though all the Rigid Raiders were so badly damaged they had to be scrapped.

By first light the 11,000-strong Argentinian garrison was in full retreat towards Stanley.

Lieutenant-Colonel Rose, using a civilian CB radio channel, had been conducting a 'psychological warfare' offensive against the Argentinians, though they had ignored his attempts to negotiate. The Argentinian Navy commander in Stanley, Vice-Admiral Otero, now told Rose, via a Spanish-speaking Royal Marines officer, Captain Rod Bell, that General Menéndez, the Commander-in-Chief, wanted a ceasefire. Rose, Bell and an SAS signaller were immediately helicoptered into the heart of Stanley to negotiate. Menéndez at first would only agree to surrender the garrison in Stanley, not his forces scattered throughout the Falklands. Knowing the British force was desperately short of ammunition after its battles around Stanley, Rose bluffed the Argentinians into an unconditional surrender of all their forces. The details of the negotiations were relayed direct to London via the SAS's own SATCOM system.

THE SAS IN ARGENTINA?

While much has been revealed about SAS operations during the Falklands War, one aspect of its participation in that conflict is still cloaked in secrecy. In early May a Sea King was discovered burnt out in southern Chile. The crew surrendered to the Chileans and was repatriated to Britain. What the helicopter was doing has generated a great deal of speculation. Some reports say it landed an SAS force close to the Argentine border. It is alleged the SAS then infiltrated into areas close to Argentinian air bases and sent back early warnings of air strikes to the Task Force. Other theories say it was just a hoax to force the enemy to divert troops from the Falkland Islands themselves. Whatever the truth, it is certain that the SAS made a valuable contribution to the British victory.

NCO, 22 SAS, THE FALKLANDS, 1982

This Fijian NCO wears a civilian Gore-tex jacket to protect him against the cold wind and dampness of the islands. Under the jacket he wears the popular 'woolly-pully' sweater and Royal Marine DPM trousers.

Gore-tex weatherproof jacket

DPM trousers

7.62mm SLR

THE GULF WAR 1990-91

'It was a special operations theme park,' was how one US officer described the role of Special Operations Forces (SOF) during Operation 'Desert Storm'. For the SAS the Gulf War witnessed a return to its World War II desert raiding role, first practised by the Regiment's founder, David Stirling, in North Africa. Operating from remote desert bases, the SAS struck deep inside Iraq and Kuwait to gather intelligence and, later, hunt down Saddam Hussein's Scud missiles. Using hi-tech satellite navigation systems, night vision equipment and laser designators, the SAS was a highly effective force during the war. A heavy price was paid by the SAS for its success, however, with four SAS men being killed and three others being tortured while prisoners of the Iraqi secret police.

THE SAS ARRIVES IN KUWAIT CITY
By a stroke of luck, SAS soldiers were in Kuwait only hours after the Iraqi invasion of the oil-rich state on 2 August 1990. Saddam Hussein had been threatening Kuwait for over a month, and the deployment of Iraqi Republican Guard armoured divisions along the Iraqi-Kuwaiti border in the middle of July had started alarm bells ringing in Western capitals. As a discreet, and rather small, show of support for Kuwait, the British Government ordered a small SAS detachment – under 10 men – to Kuwait at the beginning of August. To avoid attracting attention the soldiers flew out on British Airways Flight 149 from London to Delhi, with a refuelling stop in Kuwait. The Boeing 747 touched down at Kuwait International Airport only hours after the Iraqi invasion. The SAS men found themselves in the middle of a war.

Some reports state they disappeared from the aircraft and made their own way to Saudi Arabia, or simply melted into the desert behind enemy lines. They were then able to collect viable intelligence at key Iraqi military and industrial sites. Whatever the truth, British Airways were very unhappy, and some of its pilots thought that the British Government had given the go-ahead for the aircraft to land simply to allow the SAS men to get into Kuwait, despite knowing that the Iraqi invasion was under way.

After US President George Bush ordered the massive deployment of American forces to Saudi Arabia on 7 August – codenamed

Operation 'Desert Shield' – the British Government soon followed suit. On 11 August, RAF Tornado F3 air-defence aircraft arrived at the massive Dhahran air base. RAF Jaguar strike aircraft took off for the Middle East on the same day. A few days later, British personnel at Dhahran reported seeing a mysterious RAF C-130 Hercules touch down. A large party of SAS and Special Boat Squadron (SBS) soldiers then started to unload laser designators and other SOF equipment off the transport's rear ramp. The men then disappeared into the desert. These were desperate days for the Coalition – there were not yet any heavy tank units in Saudi Arabia. All that stood between Saddam's 5000 tanks and the oil-rich eastern province of Saudi were a few thousand lightly armed US paratroopers and Marines, around 24 US Army AH-64A Apache attack helicopters, a few hundred Coalition aircraft, US Special Forces troops, and the British SAS and SBS.

Had the Iraqis had pushed south, the SAS and its American counterparts would have carried out much the same type of missions they would have conducted in the event of a Soviet invasion of Western Europe. Stay behind parties would have ambushed Iraqi supply columns, headquarters and other key positions, using laser designators to call in air strikes on Iraqi targets.

DEFEATING THE CHEMICAL THREAT
The SAS also had another very unusual mission. Coalition commanders were very worried about the Iraq's chemical warfare capability, but little was known about the types of chemical agents it had in its arsenal. If the Iraqis used chemical weapons, the SAS was to infiltrate the contaminated areas and collect samples of the agents. After bringing the samples back to Dhahran, an RAF Tornado would have then flown them back to Britain's chemical warfare research centre at Porton Down for analysis. An antidote could then, hopefully, have been despatched.

By December 1990, plans for the liberation of Kuwait – Operation 'Desert Storm' – were highly advanced. The SAS was now well established in Saudi Arabia. A, B and D Squadrons, 22 SAS, were in the desert, along with a strong headquarters, signals and support elements. In total, some 400 regular and Territorial Army (TA) SAS men were in the

Above right: When fighting in the desert observe the following rules: wear a head covering, protect the eyes from the glare, and wear some sort of veil to prevent dust and sand getting into the mouth. Operating deep behind enemy lines, SAS troopers in the Gulf War would have been dressed like this soldier, i.e. well protected against the elements.
Below right: The SAS 'Pink Panther' desert Land Rover. Tried and tested, these vehicles performed admirably during the 1991 Gulf War, transporting men and equipment throughout Iraq and Kuwait.

TROOPER, 22 SAS, GULF WAR, 1991

His beige beret, minus the Winged Dagger badge which has been removed, is worn under a camouflage veil. His 7.62mm SLR is also in desert camouflage.

beige beret under veil

desert 'woolly-pully'

SLR

high neck desert boots

Far right: A destroyed Iraqi hardened aircraft shelter. Using designators, SAS teams behind enemy lines ensured laser-guided bombs dropped from Allied aircraft found their targets. Special forces troops operating target markers and transmitting intelligence greatly aided the success of the Coalition in destroying the Iraqi military infrastructure.

Middle East by 16 January 1991. The main SAS base was deep in the desert at the Saudi air base at Al Jubail. Four RAF CH-47 Chinook helicopters of No 7 Squadron's Special Forces Flight were also based there.

The SAS worked closely with the highly secret US Joint Special Operations Task Force (JSOTF) which commanded all American 'black' SOF personnel, such as the Delta Force commandos and SOF helicopters of the 160th Special Operations Aviation Regiment. General 'Stormin' Norman Schwarzkopf, US Commander-in-Chief, was initially unwilling to give these covert forces a large role in the

offensive against Iraq. During his service in Vietnam he had some bad experiences with American 'snake eaters' and complained that their operations inevitably went wrong, forcing conventional units to be sent to rescue them.

Britain's senior commander in Saudi Arabia, Lieutenant-General Sir Peter de la Billière, had commanded 22 SAS in the 1970s and was able to persuade General Schwarzkopf to give the SAS and US Special Forces a chance to show what they could do.

A complex Coalition SOF plan was developed which divided Iraq and Kuwait into distinct Combined Special Operations Areas (CSOAs). This was to prevent 'friendly fire' casualties. One of the missions of 22 SAS was to 'unbalance' the Iraqi High Command with raids in western Iraq. The Regiment was also to interrupt Scud missile operations against Israel, which began on 18 January. The Iraqis would then be forced to divert troops from Kuwait. Southern Iraq and Kuwait – the Kuwait Theatre of Operations (KTO) – was the responsibility of the US Army's Special Forces (Green Berets) and Rangers. Coastal areas were taken care of by the US Navy's SEALs and British SBS. Unlike other British troops, the SAS was never under the full operational control of the Americans. It remained under national command, though SAS officers did coordinate their operations with the JSOTF and the head of the Joint Air Forces, US Central Command, Lieutenant-General Charles Horner.

'PINK PANTHERS' IN IRAQ

As in World War II, the SAS relied on heavily armed vehicles for transport to its targets. These included Longline Light Strike Vehicles (LSVs), but were mostly 'Pink Panther' Land Rovers or Land Rover 90s ('dinkies' in SAS parlance) which were used to great effect. Each vehicle had a Magellan satellite navigation system, two M203 grenade launchers, Stinger anti-aircraft missiles, LAW 80 anti-tank missiles, a front-mounted 7.62mm GPMG, and rear-mounted 0.5in Browning heavy machine gun. For night operations Litton night vision goggles were used by the commander and driver. Trials motorcycles were also reportedly used by the Regiment. The Stingers provided vital defence against marauding Iraqi helicopter gunships, though this threat diminished greatly with the quickly established Allied air supremacy.

The SAS played an important part in the opening of the air campaign. Teams carrying laser designators marked targets for Allied aircraft, the latter's laser-guided bombs homing in accurately on air-defence sites, bunkers, radar sites and command-and-control centres, and military factories.

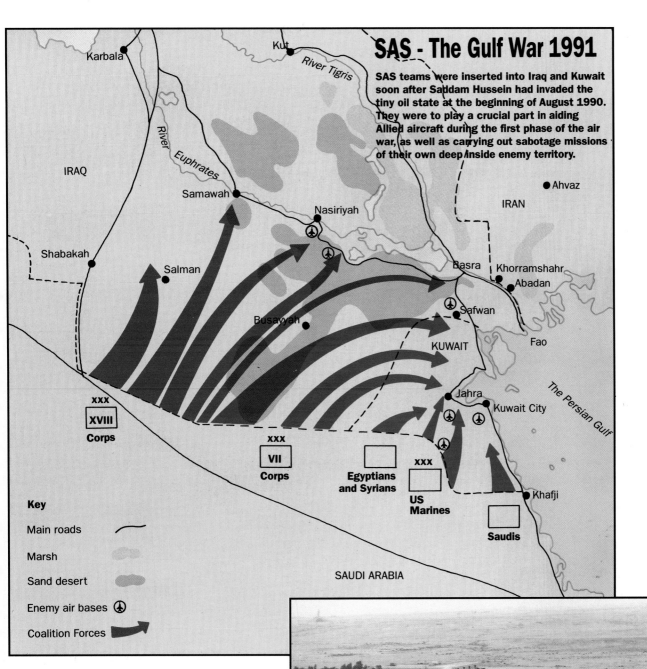

SAS - The Gulf War 1991

SAS teams were inserted into Iraq and Kuwait soon after Saddam Hussein had invaded the tiny oil state at the beginning of August 1990. They were to play a crucial part in aiding Allied aircraft during the first phase of the air war, as well as carrying out sabotage missions of their own deep inside enemy territory.

IRAQ

Karbala

Kut

River Tigris

River Euphrates

Samawah

Nasiriyah

Shabakah

Salman

Busayyah

Ahvaz

IRAN

Basra

Khorramshahr

Abadan

Safwan

Fao

KUWAIT

The Persian Gulf

Jahra

Kuwait City

xxx
XVIII
Corps

xxx
VII
Corps

Egyptians and Syrians

xxx
US Marines

Saudis

Khafji

Key

Main roads

Marsh

Sand desert

Enemy air bases

Coalition Forces

SAUDI ARABIA

As the first air strikes of 'Desert Storm' were being launched (17 January), RAF Chinook helicopters airlifted SAS Land Rovers deep into the empty desert of western Iraq. US HH-53J Pave Low and HH-60G Night Hawk helicopters, with their special electronic and night flying systems, acted as pathfinders for the RAF helicopters. One Chinook was badly damaged when it landed in a minefield, blowing off the helicopter's rear wheels. The pilot, however, managed to get the stricken machine back to base.

Hit-and-run tactics were the order of the day. At first whole troops, 20-30 men, mounted attacks on isolated Iraqi communications sites, supply dumps and convoys. In the early days of the war, when the Iraqi Air Force was still considered a threat, the SAS moved at night

Above: Special forces cooperation in the Gulf. An American Blackhawk helicopter airlifts an SAS Light Strike Vehicle during Operation 'Desert Storm'.

and lay hidden in camouflaged 'hides' during daylight. As the Coalition gained air supremacy, however, SAS operations became more daring. Several prisoners were captured for interrogation, though no senior officers as some reports have suggested. The famous story of SAS troops flying into Kuwait in Egyptian Mi-8 helicopters sporting Iraqi markings to capture a radar site is also described by SAS sources as being 'pure fiction'.

Battles with the Iraqis were often brief, violent, and did not always go as the SAS intended. The raiders had to hit the enemy hard and then quickly break contact. Once away from the target, the SAS team would regroup and take cover in a 'hide', before striking out again the following night. Breaking contact was the most dangerous part of these raids owing to the confusion of battle. One injured SAS soldier, left on the battlefield so his comrades could escape, was taken prisoner by the Iraqis. Three other SAS men died of hypothermia as they tried to escape to Syria when they became separated from their comrades. A fourth SAS man was killed, though his body was later recovered by his colleagues. In addition, four SAS men were wounded and a number were reported captured by the Iraqis in mysterious circumstances. The latter tried hard to hunt down the SAS teams. On one occasion Iraqi special forces troops were airlifted by helicopters in an effort to surround troops of B Squadron. However, the latter beat them off, inflicting heavy casualties (an USAF F-15E Eagle also shot down one of the Iraqi helicopters).

Following Iraq's launch of Scud missiles against Israel on the second day of the war, destroying their mobile launchers became the 'number one' Coalition priority. If the Jewish state had been provoked into striking back at Iraq, the Coalition's Arab members could have dropped out of the war, threatening the entire UN military effort. Conventional aerial reconnaissance methods were too slow to keep track of the highly mobile missiles, so improvised methods had to be adopted to put the Scuds out of business. The USAF and US Navy put heavily armed F-15Es, F-16 Fighting Falcons, A-10A Warthogs and A-6E Intruders on round-the-clock patrols over the Scud firing areas – 'Scud Boxes' – but the pilots needed precise targeting information before they could launch attacks.

SAS: SCUD-BUSTERS

Mobile SAS and US Special Forces patrols were sent into the 'Scud Boxes' to put eyes on the ground. Covert observation posts (OPs) were set up to cover key roads. When Scud convoys were spotted, SAS teams either marked the target with laser designators or passed the grid reference on to an E-3 AWACS command aircraft. Strike aircraft were then sent into action. On one occasion the SAS even fired flares to mark the target for the aircraft. If no aircraft were available then the SAS ambushed the Scud convoy.

On the final day of the war Iraq tried to mount a mass Scud attack on Israel in a last-ditch attempt to try to bring the Jewish state into the conflict. However, Delta Force troops found the 26 missiles and called in air strikes for six hours until they had been obliterated. US pilots had great respect for the daredevil attitude of the SAS. One F-15E squadron commander described them as 'the true unsung heroes of the war'. He said they

located 'maybe one third' of the 20-30 mobile Scud launchers destroyed by his squadron in the war. 'It was effective to have someone able to provide that needle in a haystack information to pinpoint the exact area,' he said. 'Then we could come in with our targeting radars and find those targets.'

The SAS also tried to stop the Iraqi Scud offensive by blowing up fibre optic communications cables linking Baghdad to western Iraq. After infiltrating a number of Iraqi towns, the SAS opened up manhole covers over the cables and dynamited them. The exact number of Scuds destroyed is unclear, with some pundits claiming only 'a couple' of Scuds were accounted for by the SAS. General Schwarzkopf, however, was full of praise for the efforts of the SOF to counter the Scud threat, and he directly credited them with keeping Israel out of the Gulf War. While it proved impossible to put all the Scuds out of action, the SAS made life so difficult for the Scud convoys that they cut down the Iraqi launch rate from eight missiles fired on the second night of the war to only one a night in the final days of the conflict. This limited damage done to Israel to a 'politically acceptable' level.

SAS POWS TORTURED

After the Iraqis agreed to the Gulf War ceasefire they started to hand over their Coalition prisoners of war (POWs). While the captured British, American, Saudi and Kuwaiti airmen were welcomed off a Red Cross plane at Riyadh amid a blaze of media attention, three SAS men were led away from the aircraft by the rear cargo door. Their experiences at the hands of the Iraqis were subsequently revealed to *The Independent* newspaper by US Marine Corps pilot Captain Russell Sanborn, who was held in the same prison: 'The Iraqis hated the British and I would hate to know what damage they did to those men in their hours of torture,' he said. 'The guards would take them out to the interrogation room one at a time and hours later I'd hear them being dragged back in. I could tell from their breathing and moaning that they'd really been worked on.'

'The British prisoners never complained, but sometimes when the guards were out of the cell area I'd hear them giving each other encouragement. I wondered if they were SAS or some kind of special commandos. They were top soldiers of some kind. I looked up to these gentlemen quite a bit. They carried themselves well. After a while the Iraqis obviously began to hold them in high regard and the interrogations slowed. The British prisoners had earned their respect. They were very tough.'

In the KTO the SBS was tasked with spreading confusion and chaos among Iraqi troops in Kuwait City. Working closely with the US Navy's SEALs, the SBS convinced the Iraqis, by leaving false information, that the US Marines were poised to storm ashore on the beaches of Kuwait. It sabotaged Iraqi bases and set up OPs to call in air strikes or gunfire from the two US battleships *Wisconsin* and *Missouri*. The SBS also infiltrated some of the most heavily defended Iraqi positions but suffered no casualties. One SBS team saw an Iraqi ammunition dump explode after a US air strike and flashed a message back to base: 'The blokes have just nuked Kuwait!'.

THE SAS AND SBS ROLE OF HONOUR

The SBS had the honour of recapturing the British Embassy in Kuwait in the final hours of the war, a fitting end to the conflict for the UK's special forces. Britain's secret warriors – SAS, SBS and RAF Special Forces – received numerous awards for gallantry during the Gulf War including four Military Crosses, two Distinguished Service Orders, six Military Medals, one Distinguished Flying Cross, one Distinguished Flying Medal and 24 Mentioned in Despatches. For the SAS it had been a triumphal return to the desert, bringing back memories of the daring raids carried out by David Stirling's recruits in North Africa between 1941 and 1943. The 1991 Gulf War was proof that the SAS is still the world's premier elite unit.

Left: An American CH-47 Chinook helicopter flies over US Marines during the start of the land phase of Operation 'Desert Storm'. Intelligence sent back to Allied headquarters by units such as the SAS enabled the United Nations' forces to build up an accurate picture of Iraqi dispositions and strengths, thus ensuring land and air forces did not stumble into heavily defended zones. **Below:** The result of a chance encounter with the SAS, perhaps? Wrecked Iraqi vehicles in Kuwait.

CHAPTER 2

SELECTION AND TRAINING

- BASIC TRAINING

- CONTINUATION TRAINING

- CROSS-TRAINING

'I WAS A FUGITIVE FROM BULLSHIT. DIDN'T KNOW MUCH ABOUT THE SAS BUT HAD A FRIEND IN IT SO I VOLUNTEERED. THEN I FOUND OUT; BITTER WINTER, SNOW AND FROST, BUT I COULDN'T GO BACK TO MY REGIMENT AFTER ALL THAT AND FACE THE FINGER OF SCORN, SO I PASSED.'

SOLDIER FROM THE BLACK WATCH

Section I
BASIC TRAINING

To become a fully fledged SAS soldier is far from easy. Each year hundreds of volunteers make the attempt to pass SAS Selection Training – few make the grade. While the Regiment has become more specialised and multi-skilled since the 1940s and 1950s, the criteria for acceptance have remained largely unchanged. The SAS is still looking for the same type of soldier as it did back in the early days: one superbly fit, very determined, resourceful, able to think for himself, and able to operate under conditions of extreme stress, isolation and physical hardship.

ANALYSING AN ELITE

A psychologist who once studied SAS Selection Training concluded that the ideal candidate should be intelligent, assertive, happy-go-lucky, self-sufficient, and neither extremely intro- or extroverted. He should not be emotionally unstable but, rather, be a forthright individual who is hard to fool and not dependent on orders. He concluded that this resulted periodically in the SAS having 'too many chiefs and not enough Indians'.

All 22 SAS members are volunteers. Any male member of the Army, Royal Navy, Royal Air Force and Territorial Army SAS is eligible for Selection. Officers must be aged 22-34, while senior non-commissioned officers (SNCOs) and junior ranks can be aged between 19 and 34. All applicants must have just over three years left to serve. This allows the SAS to get value for money from its training. The Selection course is only the first stage of a formal training programme that lasts up to two years. SAS soldiers, however, never stop training until the day they leave the Regiment. After completing a large amount of paper work, candidates are taken on a short visit to the Regimental Headquarters at Hereford – Stirling Lines – where they receive a briefing on what is required of them during Selection Training and some basic information on the Regiment's role and organisation.

Those potential recruits who have not been put off by this are then called to attend one of the twice-yearly courses, one in the summer and the other in winter, run by 22 SAS Training Wing at Hereford. This organisation is manned by some of the Regiment's most experienced SNCOs, who ensure the highest standards are maintained. Candidates aspire to join the SAS for many reasons. Those who are attracted by its 'gung-ho' media image will soon be weeded out by the Selection process. Those trying to join the SAS because their existing military careers are in trouble will also find SAS Selection daunting, as will soldiers who cannot work as an individual within a small team. Those wishing to excel at soldiering will find that Selection is the toughest test they have yet faced.

Determination and the will to win earn candidates top marks on SAS Selection. During a lake-crossing exercise, for example, one candidate who could not swim still passed the test because he dived into the lake anyway. The SAS directing staff (DS) running the exercise admired his 'bottle', and overlooked the fact that they had to rescue him from the lake.

THE COURSE WITH NO MERCY

What is Selection Training? It consists of a three-week build-up period (two weeks for officers) followed by Test Week. After starting with a standard Army Battle Fitness Test, the regime is a daily diet of road marches to start with, followed by timed route marches across the Brecon Beacon mountains in southern Wales. These start out as team efforts, but gradually the size of groups is reduced as men fail until the candidates are marching solo.

At the start of Selection, bergens weighing 11kg are carried by individuals, though by the end of Test Week the weight has been increased to 25kg. In the 1960s the bergens were filled with bricks, but now food, clothing and other survival gear can be carried. Map reading and cross-country navigation are vital skills for SAS soldiers so they have a key part to play in Selection Training. A surprisingly large number of candidates, particularly those from non-line units such as the Royal Corps of Transport and Royal Signals, have little experience in these skills as they are usually carried out by officers and NCOs in more regular units. However, aspiring SAS men must learn these skills fast or fail the course.

These route marches are the core of Selection. They are not only designed to test candidates' physical fitness and map reading ability, but also all the other qualities needed to become an SAS soldier. They are set in all weathers and at night, so candidates have to fight not only the clock but also the elements. High degrees of stress are introduced into

Previous pages: Two SAS soldiers take a break during a training exercise. The Regiment does not compromise when it comes to entry requirements: only the best and most able recruits get in. Even when 'badged', SAS soldiers are constantly undergoing training. There's no such thing as a fully trained SAS soldier.

Above right: A sunny day for prospective Paras on Pen-y-Fan, the highest peak in the Brecon Beacons. The area is subject to rapid weather variations – just right for SAS Selection Training.

Below right: On Selection, each man is given a bergen, a map, a compass, and then the grid reference for the first rendezvous. When he reaches it, he will be told the next one, and so on. All the while, he is being timed and watched for any signs of weakness – the strain can become intolerable. Worse, he starts off with company but, as the course progresses, he is left on his own.

Far right: Out on his own, a prospective member of 22 SAS undertakes the 'Fan Dance', the solo, timed 60km march that is the culmination of Test Week of Selection Training. Failure means he will be RTU'd without a second thought.

Below: The SAS is looking for men who will keep on going when their limbs are screaming for them to stop. Mental and physical endurance are the order of the day.

these marches by a system of rendezvous (RV) points manned by Training Wing DS. Only when soldiers reach an RV are they told the location of the next one, and so on. Not surprisingly, the failure rate is high as physical injuries and sheer exhaustion take their toll of the candidates. If soldiers drop out because of injury or just give up, they are immediately returned to their parent unit (RTU'd). The candidates' stamina and judgement are also eroded by the pace of the course. They are turfed out of their beds at 0400 hours every day and return well past 2200 hours.

TEST WEEK – THE TOUGHEST HURDLE

In Test Week the pressure intensifies with the distances and times required to complete the marches being increased and decreased respectively. It culminates in a 60km endurance march, known as the 'Long Drag' or 'Fan Dance' because it involves the candidates having to run up Pen-y-Fan, the highest peak in the Brecons, in 20 hours. This is likened to running up the side of a house because of the mountain's almost sheer slopes. Again candidates have to pass through RVs

manned by DS to receive the information necessary to complete the next phase of the march. Even in good conditions the 'Long Drag' is hard, but candidates are given no dispensation because of the weather. In mid-winter, driving rain, snow and gale-force winds make venturing out on to the mountain a matter of survival. A number of prospective SAS soldiers, and even fully fledged members of the Regiment, have perished on Pen-y-Fan. The most famous victim was Major Mike Kealy, who joined a 30-strong contingent of Selection candidates on a night march across the mountain during a blizzard in February 1979. In the time-honoured SAS fashion, his bergen had been filled with bricks rather than survival gear. Soaked to the skin from driving snow and his own sweat, Kealy was found on the route suffering from advanced exposure and all efforts to revive him failed. Exposure has claimed other victims, and another died when he was swept away while crossing a swollen river.

Through the 1960s the DS adopted a policy of 'negative motivation', or 'beasting', designed to test candidates' willpower. A ritual

REMINGTON 870 SHOTGUN

This pump-action shotgun is used by the SAS for counter-terrorist and hostage-rescue work, when a weapon with good stopping power at short ranges is called for.

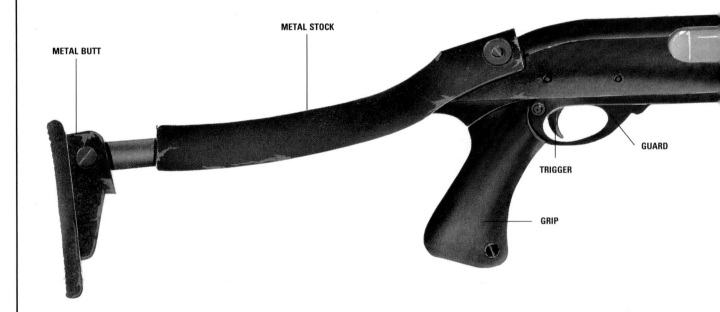

METAL BUTT

METAL STOCK

EJE◀

GUARD

TRIGGER

GRIP

Surprising as it may seem, the SAS has employed shotguns long before the Regiment assumed a Counter Revolutionary Warfare (CRW) responsibility. While fighting in Malaya in the 1950s, for example, individual SAS troopers often carried Browning autoloader shotguns when on patrol in the jungle. During a chance encounter with the enemy, shotguns could send a wide spread of shot in the general direction of hostiles. With the introduction into service of semi- and

full-automatic assault rifles, specifically the M16 and the SLR, the shotgun fell from favour (a major disadvantage of shotguns is that they require constant attention and cleaning to keep them in working order because they are hunting weapons – thus they are really unsuited to general campaign work).

However, in the early 1970s the Regiment assumed a CRW responsibility. This meant that SAS squadrons received training in counter-terrorist and hostage-rescue skills. The

latter invariably meant storming buildings, trains, aircraft and the like to free innocent hostages from the clutches of armed terrorists. As well as requiring expert weapons skills to identify and neutralise armed opponents in a matter of seconds, methods had to be devised to effect rapid entry into rooms. The shotgun was back in business.

There are two main reasons why the shotgun is popular for hostage-rescue work. First, the stopping power of a

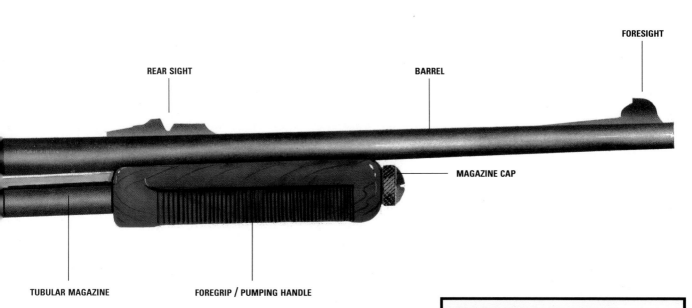

FORESIGHT

REAR SIGHT

BARREL

MAGAZINE CAP

TUBULAR MAGAZINE

FOREGRIP / PUMPING HANDLE

REMINGTON 870 SHOTGUN SPECIFICATIONS
- **TYPE:** pump-action shotgun
- **CALIBRE:** 12-gauge
- **WEIGHT:** 3.60kg
- **LENGTH:** 1060mm
- **EFFECTIVE RANGE:** 40m
- **RATE OF FIRE:** manual
- **FEED:** 7-shot tubular magazine
- **MUZZLE VELOCITY:** varies according to cartridge used

single cartridge can be prodigious. An SG round, for example, containing nine soft lead balls travelling at around 400 metres a second is equivalent to a nine-round burst from a submachine gun. Second, and more important, shotguns can fire a wide variety of ammunition, from armour-piercing and buckshot to high-explosive and gas. It is this variety that is attractive to hostage-rescue units such as the SAS.

The Remington is used mainly to blow door hinges prior to an assault team's entry into a room, and for such purposes it has been widely used in Northern Ireland. For example, the Royal Ulster Constabulary or British Army will receive a tip-off that a certain flat contains suspected IRA terrorists, prompting the despatch of an SAS squad to investigate. The team, protected by body armour, will blow open the door with a Remington and then burst inside. Sometimes they will be successful, other times not, but a Remington is always present.

Like most shotguns operated by counter-terrorist units, the Remington is rugged and operates with a simple mechanical pump-action system which does not jam at crucial moments. Once inside the room the shotgun can be used as a devastating anti-personnel weapon, though only if a terrorist is on his or her own, as a spread of shot can also kill a hostage. The Remington, which is also used by the US Marine Corps, will remain in SAS service for the foreseeable future.

BUD COOK.

BUD WAS A
CHRONIC
FIRE-ARM WAVER
HE DIED QUITE
YOUNG
STILL A SHAVER.

TODD..

UNDER THIS SOD
LIES MORTIMER
TODD,
HE PUT HIS TRUST
IN A RUSTY ROD.

RIP
FRANK HOE
FOOLS MAY
COME
FOOLS MAY
GO
THIS ONE
WENT
HE WAS TO
SLOW

BILLY MISE
HE DIDNT
PRACTISE
HERE HE
LIES

R I P
BILL DAY
FORGOT TO
LOAD
HERES HIS
PLOT

Above: Black humour at Stirling Lines, Hereford, but proof that the rigours of Selection and Continuation Training have a very real purpose – to stop soldiers getting sloppy and then being killed needlessly.

was made of loading useless bricks into bergens during marches. At RVs DS would deliberately try to get candidates to rest or cheat. If they fell for the bait then they were promptly RTU'd. A so-called 'sickener' factor was employed to try to weed out those poorly motivated and weak candidates. For example, on marches candidates would be told to RV with the truck back to camp at a certain time, but when they arrived at the RV the truck would drive off. The DS then told the candidates that the truck had moved to an RV 16km away. Those who gave up were RTU'd. From the 1970s onwards, 'positive motivation' became the norm and the term 'sickener' was dropped. Now candidates are encouraged to press on to the next RV and their motivation and stamina are tested by being asked to perform unexpected tasks, such as re-assembling a foreign-made firearm.

This new attitude came about because of a need to reduce unnecessary wastage rates during Selection, and recognition that willpower can be tested in other ways. For aspiring SAS officers, however, the 'sickener' factor still applies. Before progressing on to the main course undertaken by all ranks, officers are put through an ordeal called

Officer Week. Training Wing SNCOs delight in 'beasting' the 'Ruperts', as the officers are known, through a series of route marches and other physical jerks. In the evenings they are required to complete staff exercises, or appreciations, of special forces-type tasks such as planning a Commando raid or deep-reconnaissance patrol. The prospective SAS troop commander then has to defend his plan from cross-examination by SAS SNCOs and troopers, who have many years of experience of doing these types of operations for real. This usually results in the officer's plan being totally 'rubbished'. It is not uncommon for officers to make 'real fools' of themselves during these sessions. Therefore, candidates are warned beforehand that it is no shame to fail Selection, so as not to totally undermine an individual's confidence.

One SAS officer has said this process, combined with Selection Training, results in around six per cent of applicants passing. Officers only serve in the SAS as troop commanders for three years before being posted back to their parent regiments, though they can come back to a more senior post later in their careers. As a result, 22 SAS has become very short of junior officers. The

Regiment's increased workload in recent years has meant new officers are expected to undertake complex missions almost immediately on joining. This further increases the pressure during Selection to pick only the best candidates which results in a vicious circle of even fewer officers passing. This problem, know as 'creeping excellence', started to affect the SAS as a whole in the mid to late 1980s, resulting in the strength of the Regiment dropping below establishment, often with troops having 10 to 12 men instead of their full complement of 16. Some SAS personnel put the problem down to the influx of Parachute Regiment soldiers and SNCOs after the Falklands War. By the mid-1980s the latter made up 52 per cent of the Regiment's strength. In turn this led to ex-Para NCOs failing a disproportionate number of candidates from non-Para units during Selection. Needless to say, this is a subject of some controversy within 22 SAS. Selection for the two Territorial Army SAS regiments is equally stringent, but it is organised to allow the part-time soldiers to complete selection over 10 consecutive weekends. As with 22 SAS Selection Training, the pressure is gradually increased as candidates progress through the weekends. Unlike the regular SAS unit, however, prospective TA SAS soldiers can join up without having any prior military experience. The wastage rates are very high with only one or two candidates passing some Selection courses. The DS are looking for exactly the same qualities in TA soldiers as their Regular Army counterparts. If candidates do not come up to scratch on a weekend, they are simply told not to bother turning up for the next one. Veteran SAS NCOs serving as DS with the TA express great surprise at the diverse backgrounds of candidates trying to join the TA units. They often have wider experience and mental flexibility than their Regular Army counterparts, who have been brought up to think in a regimented military fashion. One 22 SAS officer, however, expressed a certain exasperation at the 'military naivety' of some TA SAS soldiers.

The prospective SAS soldiers who complete the endurance march and pass the other parts of Selection are then gathered together and told the good news. This is rapidly followed by the bad news concerning Continuation Training. They are sent home on a relaxing weekend break and told to report to Hereford for first parade on Monday morning.

Above: Early SAS training in the North African desert in late 1941. These men are jumping off the back of lorries in an effort to simulate parachute landings. The whole idea was rather harebrained, the only tangible result being a spate of broken limbs. As a result, it was quickly abandoned.

Section II
CONTINUATION TRAINING

After being judged as the 'right material' to become an SAS soldier by passing Selection, aspiring members of the Regiment have to acquire the necessary skills to take their place in the ranks. If they pass the next 14 weeks of Continuation Training, plus jungle and parachute training, they earn the right to wear the SAS beige beret and Winged Dagger badge. They are, in SAS parlance, 'badged'.

Continuation Training schools them in SAS patrol tactics, elementary signalling, first aid, demolitions and combat survival. This is followed by jungle training and a static-line parachute course – the whole takes around six months. Training Wing now takes a more benign view of its charges. However, students can still be RTU'd at any time if they fail to meet the SAS's exacting standards (indeed, fully fledged SAS troopers can also be RTU'd if they commit any serious misdemeanours).

LEARNING TO FIGHT THE SAS WAY
Training Wing's facilities are second to none in the Army. It employs tried and tested methods of instruction which combine theoretical lessons with practical demonstrations, and then the students have to put what they have learnt into practice. Tactical training concentrates on the basic SAS operational unit: the four-man patrol. Four patrols combine to form a troop, and each 'Sabre' (fighting) Squadron has four troops. Students are taught how to move tactically across country, by day or night, and how to set up and operate observation posts (OPs). While other Army units deploy short-term patrols, the SAS teaches its soldiers how to operate deep behind enemy lines for long periods. The patrolling skills necessary to do this type of work are very different to those employed by the infantry. They are enshrined in SAS standard operating procedures (SOPs). Each member of the patrol, for example, has his own specific skill, though other members of the patrol will also have his skill as a safeguard against any casualties the unit may suffer.

An intensive course in weapons skills is also included in Continuation Training. This involves learning to fire all the weapons in the SAS arsenal, such as the Heckler & Koch MP5 submachine gun, M16 assault rifle, mortars, the MILAN anti-tank weapon, and 'enemy'/foreign weapons such as the AK-47 assault rifle (fully trained SAS soldiers spend hours on ranges honing their weapons skills).

Equally important is the ability to operate radios. Units which operate behind enemy lines must have the means to transmit intelligence back to headquarters. While much is made of the SAS's satellite communications systems by the media, troopers are also taught the basics of signalling. Of particular importance is the theory and practice of setting up antennas to communicate over long distances. SAS soldiers have to be able to pick OP sites that are not in radio 'black spots'. The SAS still uses Morse code, the only British Army regiment to do so. Morse is more easily understood than voice communications over long distances, but recruits require special instruction to get up to the SAS standard transmitting and receiving standard: eight words a minute. Special codes and call sign systems peculiar to the SAS also have to be learnt by students. Some 30 different radio sets are used by the SAS which requires a high level of technical knowledge. The procedures for calling in air strikes and artillery fire also feature in Continuation Training. First aid skills are next on the agenda for aspiring SAS soldiers. The Regiment takes battlefield first aid very seriously. On patrols deep behind enemy lines the normal military medical back-up of casualty evacuation helicopters, ambulances and regimental aid posts is not available. SAS first aid training is much more advanced than that taught to regular soldiers.

HANDLING EXPLOSIVES
Basic demolition skills and techniques are also taught during Continuation Training. This enables students to handle explosives safely, learn the attributes of different types of explosives, and understand how to place them to cause the maximum amount of damage. Sabotage operations behind enemy lines are almost impossible without this type of knowledge.

A number of tests also take place during Continuation to assess the likely speciality the student will undertake when he is finally 'badged', such as languages. A number of

Above right: Effecting a river crossing. Continuation Training involves teaching students how to move unseen through hostile territory, an essential skill for units such as the SAS which operate behind the lines.
Below right: A casualty care simulation. For deep-penetration units, learning advanced first aid is essential as there are often no opportunities to call in evacuation helicopters or vehicles to take a wounded man to hospital.

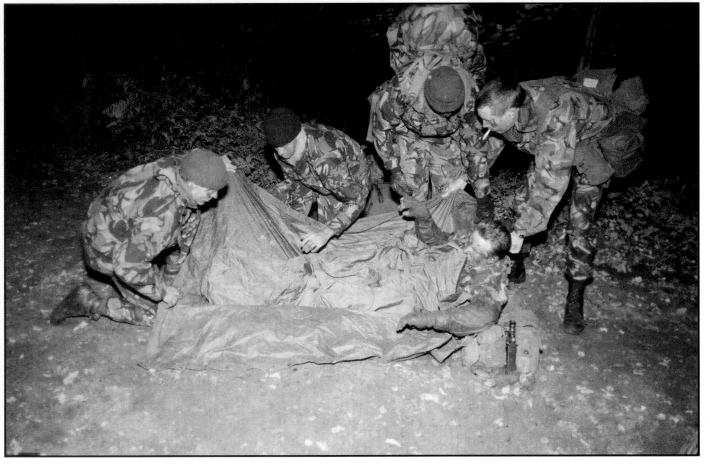

initiative tests are also included to start getting students to think in 'special forces' mode. At one time these included developing plans for bank raids or escaping from prisons, but after some adverse publicity they were confined to purely military subjects. The students then progress on to combat and survival training which culminates in Escape and Evasion (E&E) and Resistance-To-Interrogation (RTI) exercises. This phase of Continuation Training starts gently enough, with students being taught how to build makeshift shelters, 'bashas', from trees and leaves, how to trap wild animals with snares, and how to cook their catches. Lurid stories have emerged about students having to eat hedgehogs and rats. Rats are not recommended because they are usually very skinny and have little meat on them. The purpose is to enable SAS soldiers to live off the land behind enemy lines if they get separated from their troop or patrol.

After a week of learning the theory the students put their knowledge into practice during an E&E exercise. They exchange their SAS smocks and combat trousers for 1940s-vintage battle dress and greatcoats, and are dropped off in one of Britain's more remote regions. Sometimes they are given a few matches, a watch and a knife, on other occasions they are told to get on with it. To make the exercise more realistic, an infantry or Parachute Regiment battalion is sent out to hunt them down. The Paras in particular think this is fun and take great delight in giving their SAS rivals a hard time, particularly those who are recognised as being ex-Paras.

RESISTING INTERROGATION

Captured student are hooded, bound and then manhandled into Land Rovers and trucks. They are shown little mercy by their captors. All through the exercise the Training Wing staff are tipping off the 'hunter force' on their student's likely hiding places, sometimes even setting up fake rendezvous (RVs) to get them caught. Those who manage to avoid capture, however, are soon sharing the fate of the others. Those who make it to the final RV are unceremoniously turned over to the 'hunter force' for delivery to the interrogation centre, run by the Joint Services Interrogation Unit and members of 22 SAS Training Wing. There is no escape from this phase of the exercise.

Although the Army is loath to admit it, the treatment the captured students receive verges on what some would call torture. In theory, the abuse they receive falls within the limits set by the Geneva Convention because the students are not physically tortured, but this is only really a question of semantics. The first hours of the interrogation centre on sensory deprivation. After being hooded, the students have little idea where they are being taken or what is happening to them. To prevent them sleeping, they are forced to stand spread-eagled against a wall or, alternatively, squat in stress-inducing positions. With the student suffering from fatigue and having no idea where he is or what is going to happen next, the interrogation starts. The intention is make him reveal information which would be valuable to the enemy. He is only supposed to give his name, rank, service number and date of birth. Any other questions must be answered: 'I cannot answer that question'. If he gives any information away, he automatically fails the course. Various interrogation techniques are employed to try to break the students. The famous 'Mr Nice/Mr Nasty' technique is an old favourite, but interrogation sessions are also mixed with more sensory deprivation to increase the pressure on students.

PUSHING MEN TO THEIR LIMITS

As the interrogation progresses, it is closely monitored by psychological and medical experts to assess how the students are handling their ordeal. It is standard for the interrogation to last about 24 hours, but the students do not have any idea how long they are expected to hold out which further tests their willpower and physical strength. Over the years a number of techniques have been developed to try to break students' willpower. Hooded men have been deceived into thinking they are about to be savaged by dogs, or that real torture is taking place in the room next door. In reality, the staff are only hitting an old mattress while simulating groaning sounds. On other occasions interrogations are carried out by female personnel while the students are stripped naked. Internal medical examinations in front of female personnel are also used to undermine the machismo of self-proclaimed 'hard' men.

The psychological aspects of the interrogation are considered the most important part of the RTI phase. Students are totally at the mercy of their interrogators, and it is under these circumstances that their will to win, to resist to the bitter end, is tested to the limit. SAS soldiers captured by the Iraqis during the Gulf War received special attention in Saddam Hussein's secret police torture cells. From all accounts they took brutal punishment but did not break, suggesting that the SAS RTI exercise sifts out those who would crack easily under interrogation.

Those who pass the RTI exercise are then flown out to Brunei to undertake jungle warfare training. Ever since its reformation in Malaya, the SAS has put a high premium on jungle warfare skills. Jungle survival skills are

Far left: SAS troopers are taught to arrive at their targets by land, sea or air. Here, two soldiers are engaged in a seaborne approach to an enemy position.

Below: Like this Royal Marine, SAS soldiers are taught how to construct jungle 'bashas' during Continuation Training.

taught first. Of particular importance are jungle navigation and ambush skills. During a final exercise, students are sent out on a four-man patrol through the jungle under realistic tactical conditions. Throughout the exercise they have to carry out a number of operational tasks. Failure means men are RTU'd which is a cruel blow for those who have made it this

first is made from a static balloon. The remaining jumps are made from RAF C-130 Hercules aircraft at 300m using static-lines – the parachute is automatically opened by a line attached to the aircraft. One jump must be made at night and another must be what is called an operational descent. This takes place from a C-130 which flies at only 130m for an

Above right: An SAS trooper in Borneo during the campaign against cross-border infiltrators. Jungle training ensures individual troopers are well equipped to fight in this physically demanding environment.

Below right: One of the more comfortable ways to travel through the jungle – an SAS riverboat in Borneo in the early 1960s.

far. The final phase of Continuation Training is the four-week basic parachute course at the RAF's No 1 Parachute Training School at RAF Brize Norton, Oxfordshire. After the ordeals involved in early phases of SAS training, this is positively laid-back. The course is run by RAF Parachute Jump Instructors and SAS participants are treated no differently to those from other regiments (former Paras who already have their wings are exempt from the course).

Students first have to learn about the characteristics of PX1 Mk 4 and PX1 Mk 5 main parachutes and PR7 reserve. In total, they have to make eight parachute jumps. The

hour to simulate a low-level tactical flight into enemy air space. In the final approach to the drop zone (DZ), the pilot puts the aircraft through a series of tactical manoeuvres to avoid colliding with the ground. This also serves to shake up the parachutists in the fuselage before the aircraft climbs to 250m for the actual jump. For the students the relief of safely reaching earth is combined with the knowledge that they have successfully passed Continuation Training and are now members of 22 SAS. Unlike other soldiers on the course, the SAS men do not receive standard parachute wings; rather, they are awarded the unique SAS 'Sabre' wings.

Section III
CROSS-TRAINING

Cross-training is one of the reasons why the SAS, despite it relatively small size, is so potent as a military unit. Having troops and patrols filled with multi-skilled soldiers enables these units to function effectively even after they have suffered 25-50 per cent casualties.

Within every SAS 'Sabre' Squadron there are four 16-man troops, each one having a specialist role. Boat Troops concentrate on amphibious warfare; Mobility Troops specialise in operating Land Rovers, fast attack vehicles and motorcycles; Air Troops are the experts on freefall parachuting; and the Mountain Troops concentrate on mountain and arctic warfare. During their SAS careers, soldiers serve with different troops to enable them to learn as wide a range of skills as possible. This means, for example, that freefall parachute jumps can be made by SAS teams into arctic regions if necessary. As in Continuation Training, the four-man patrol, commanded by a corporal, is the basic SAS unit, and new arrivals are assigned to a patrol for the duration of their initial three-year tour with the SAS. Within his patrol the new recruit is expected to specialise in one of the four patrol skills, regardless of the speciality of his troop.

HALO INSERTION TECHNIQUES
The patrol skills are medicine, demolitions, communications and languages. Soldiers are selected for specialising in a patrol skill on the basis of their performance during earlier phases of training, with those who show aptitude for a particular skill being steered towards it. Needless to say, the new SAS recruits have a busy time during their 12-month probationary period with the Regiment. It would be wrong to say, however, that there is such a thing as a fully trained SAS soldier, they are always learning new skills.

Perhaps the most dangerous skill taught to SAS soldiers is High Altitude, Low Opening (HALO) parachuting. It was developed to allow the silent insertion of troops behind enemy lines by parachuting from an aircraft at high altitudes and so unseen from the ground (also, the aircraft cannot be heard from the ground). SAS soldiers assigned to an Air Troop are sent on a six-week course to learn this hazardous technique. At the end of the course an SAS soldier is able to freefall from 10,000m,

day or night, carrying a rifle and a bergen strapped below his parachute (the 'chute is deployed at 760m). The high altitude also means oxygen has to be used. HALO is loosely based on civilian freefall parachuting, in that the parachutist remains stable by adopting the starfish position as he hurtles towards earth at a terminal velocity of 190km/hr. Civilian sports jumpers use a special manoeuvre to allow them to open their 'chute manually and still preserve their stability. SAS soldiers carrying bergens cannot do this, so their parachutes are fitted with an automatic opening device. One SAS man is known to have died during an operational HALO decent because his bergen shifted, causing him to spin out of control. Icing-up of face masks is another major problem (as well as frostbite), and so HALO training includes learning the drill to wipe away the ice with both hands, while retaining stability.

BOAT TROOP SKILLS
An important skill learnt during HALO training is manoeuvring to allow the patrol to land as close together as possible. Jumpers will endeavour to land together in an area away from known enemy positions. This can involve manoeuvring behind mountains or into valleys before opening their 'chutes (care must also be taken to avoid opening it within earshot of enemy forces). Jump suits are made from radar-absorbent material to reduce the radar cross-section of individual jumpers. As a result, only the most highly trained radar operators or advanced computer systems are able to tell when transport aircraft have dropped HALO teams.

In theory HALO jumping sounds a very attractive method of covertly inserting teams behind enemy lines, but even the SAS recognises that it is only to be used as a last resort. This is because of the risks to the jumpers in flight and the possibility of them being blown off course, scattered, or landing among the enemy.

SAS Boat Troops specialise in amphibious warfare, their preferred craft being Gemini inflatable assault boats or Klepper canoes. In addition, their members must also learn combat swimming/diving and parachuting into water. As well as launching their boats from ships, Boat Troops practise operating from submerged Royal Navy submarines.

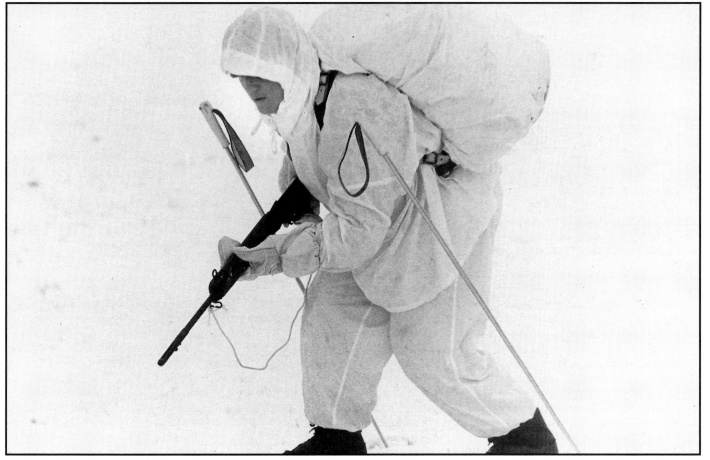

STEYR AUG

Revolutionary in design and appearance, the AUG has been seen in the hands of SAS troopers since its introduction into service in the 1980s. Despite its rather fragile look, the AUG is one of the most robust rifles currently in existence.

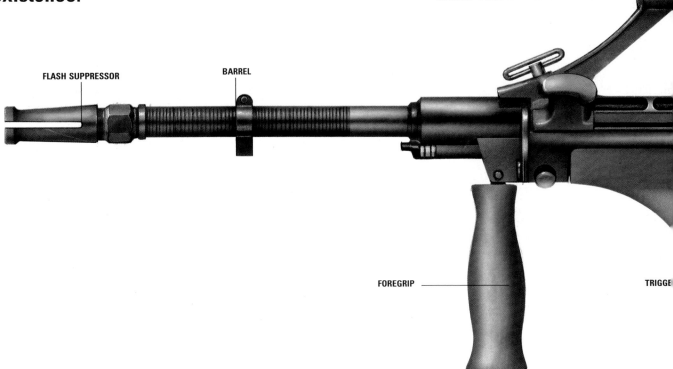

TELESCOPIC SIGHT AND CARRYING HANDLE

FLASH SUPPRESSOR

BARREL

FOREGRIP

TRIGGE

STEYR AUG SPECIFICATIONS
- **TYPE:** assault rifle
- **CALIBRE:** 5.56mm
- **WEIGHT:** 3.60kg (empty)
- **LENGTH:** 790mm
- **EFFECTIVE RANGE:** 400m
- **RATE OF FIRE:** 650 rounds per minute (cyclic)
- **FEED:** 30- or 42-round magazine
- **MUZZLE VELOCITY:** 970 metres per second

The Steyr AUG is one of the new 'bullpup' assault rifles. This means the mechanism is set back in the stock so that the bolt is alongside the firer's cheek and the magazine is behind the trigger. This allows the use of maximum barrel length in a weapon of short overall length. The stock of the AUG is made of high-quality plastic and the receiver is an aluminium casting with steel inserts for the barrel lugs and bolt guides. An integral part of this casting is the optical sight, which also acts as a carrying handle. Interestingly, the magazine is transparent, allowing the firer an instant check on the number of rounds left. The AUG has no fire selector switch because the firer uses the trigger to select the firing mode. The first pressure on the trigger allows single shots, while pulling past this allows automatic fire. One additional advantage of the AUG is that it can accommodate right- or left-handed firers simply by exchanging the bolt.

One of the great virtues of the AUG is its interchangeability – it can be converted to different modes quite easily. Thus it can be used as a parachutist's rifle, a submachine gun, or as a standard assault rifle, in addition to becoming a light machine gun by merely fitting a heavy barrel.

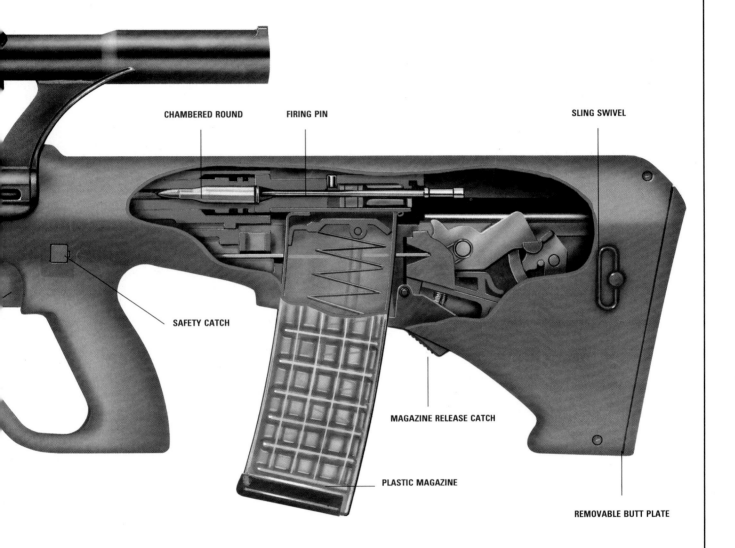

CHAMBERED ROUND

FIRING PIN

SLING SWIVEL

SAFETY CATCH

MAGAZINE RELEASE CATCH

PLASTIC MAGAZINE

REMOVABLE BUTT PLATE

The AUG fulfils all of the criteria for modern assault rifles. It is effective up to a range of 400m (early studies this century revealed that most infantry combats took place at ranges well below 400m), it fires 5.56mm ammunition which is smaller and lighter than conventional rifle cartridges – 7.62mm and larger – but allows automatic fire to provide an increase in firepower compared to single-shot weapons. In addition, the recoil forces are relatively low, enabling the rifle to be reasonably lightweight and of a simple construction.

Tactically, assault rifles such as the AUG have had a considerable impact upon the conduct of warfare, not only on standard infantry tactics but also on the way special forces fight. Assault rifles allow fire saturation tactics which can lay down an awesome amount of firepower. Obviously SAS teams operating behind enemy lines need to watch their expenditure of ammunition. Nevertheless, a four-man team firing controlled bursts can, using weapons such as the AUG, still hit an enemy with a devastating amount of firepower delivered in a matter of seconds. This gives a four-man patrol a greater chance of survival in a firefight with a larger force.

Parachuting into water is not without its dangers, however, especially if the jumpers become entangled in their 'chutes after hitting the water. These skills have two main aims: to facilitate the covert insertion of reconnaissance patrols via a shoreline; and underwater sabotage. SAS soldiers who serve in Mountain Troops are often to be found in remote parts of the world honing their skills at rock climbing, ice and snow work on some very dangerous mountains.

Desert operations are the preserve of the Mobility Troops, which have specially equipped Land Rovers known as 'Pink Panthers' because of their distinctive camouflage. The modern-day equivalent of the Long Range Desert Group jeeps, the 'Pink Panthers' are optimised for desert travel. They are heavily armed with GPMGs and other weaponry, but also carry large quantities of water and fuel to give them long range. Corrugated iron channels are also carried to get bogged down vehicles out of soft sand.

Desert navigation is a skill still taught to SAS soldiers despite the development of satellite navigation systems. Technology has a habit of not functioning at the moment it is needed, so troopers learn how to use sun compasses, theodolites and astro-navigation techniques. Because of its campaigns in the region, the SAS has good contacts with many armies in the Middle East and regularly conducts training in Oman, the United Arab Emirates, Saudi Arabia and Jordan.

THE SAS 'KILLING HOUSE'

SAS squadrons deployed as the Regiment's CRW unit are put through an intense training routine to prepare them for the role. Great emphasis is placed on Close Quarter Battle (CQB) skills, which are vital during siege-busting operations. SAS soldiers practise these skills in the 'Killing House', in which they have to gain entry and kill a group of 'terrorists' without injuring the hostages. Those soldiers selected to serve in the SAS Ulster Troop also receive extra training before being assigned to this elite unit.

The SAS's CQB training owes its existence to the Regiment's 'Keeni Meeni' operations in Aden against Arab terrorists. By the early 1970s, these skills had been translated into close protection or bodyguard courses run by the then newly formed CRW Wing. At first, the SAS used standard British Army CQB ranges, where wooden silhouette targets randomly sprung up as a patrol moved down a mock-up of a typical city street. However, this lacked the necessary realism for SAS soldiers preparing to rescue hostages from the inside of an airliner, for example, so the CRW Wing developed the CQB concept further. The

'Killing House' was built. Originally a single room, its interior could be modified to allow a variety of scenarios to be simulated. Dolls were used to 'play' terrorists, with 'live' hostages also being used. SAS men would then burst inside and instantly differentiate between the 'good guys' and the 'bad guys'.

Closed-circuit television cameras monitored the progress of students as they cleared the room. However, in 1986 one of the 'live' hostages made a wrong move and had his brains blown out. The system was modified. Now a video projection system is used which projects images between two rooms onto life-size wraparound screens. One room has 'live' terrorists and hostages in it, while the other is stormed by the rescuers. Both groups can interact and shoot at each other in perfect safety (each exercise is recorded on video for subsequent appraisal). Special low-charge rounds are used and the walls of the rooms are coated with a material that prevents ricochets.

SAS men receive heavy coaching on how to enter rooms and select targets in under four seconds. In a typical week each man will use in excess of 5000 rounds in the 'Killing House'. By the end of the course the reaction times and firearms skills of the soldiers are superb. As a 'party piece' for visiting politicians, generals and other VIPs, the SAS lays on an impressive demonstration of its shooting skills. One SAS man will stand against a plywood board while another shoots bullets around him. The first SAS man will then stand to one side to reveal a neat line of holes that trace the outline of his body.

'BUSH DOCTORS' AND MIDWIVES

Medical skills, as mentioned earlier, are highly regarded in the SAS and patrol medics undertake an intensive course of medical training. In addition to SAS training, they also spend time in hospital casualty departments to gain experience of dealing with real trauma victims. SAS medics also learn how to become so-called 'bush doctors', able to dispense medicine to locals in SAS operational areas. Midwifery is of particular importance in this situation. The provision of basic health care is an important part of the SAS's 'hearts and minds' counter-insurgency tactics which proved their worth in Malaya, Borneo and Oman. Indeed, the SAS claim it has saved more lives in these campaigns through its medical prowess than it has taken in combat.

Signallers are coached up to a high standard by the SAS on a three-month course. Signalling is a skill acquired by most members of 22 SAS at some point in their careers. It is not uncommon for even the most junior SAS soldier to be up to Regimental Signaller standard, a level of skill not usually found

Above: The subskimmer, shown here, allows teams to infiltrate hostile shorelines covertly. They can travel underwater or on the surface, and can be left on the seabed while the crew goes ashore.
Right: The preserve of Mobility Troop or Mountain Troop? This snow bike facilitates speedy movement through arctic terrain and is ideal for special forces soldiers.
Far right: When a helicopter cannot land, a useful skill is to be able to abseil to the ground while the aircraft hovers in mid-air. Such drills require a high level of training.

among soldiers outside regimental or squadron/company headquarters. As a Regimental Signaller, an SAS soldier is able to control a whole radio net as well as operate his own set. He is also able to instruct other soldiers in the use of radios.

LANGUAGES AND DEMOLITIONS

Language skills are highly prized by the SAS but they take time to develop. Those SAS soldiers who have shown some aptitude for languages are sent on special courses at the Royal Army Education Corps School of Languages at Beaconsfield. Linguists at first are only expected to have a basic command of their language to enable their patrol to conduct behind-the-lines operations in foreign countries. Eventually, however, they will become fluent. While Arabic and Malay were important during the 1960s and 1970s, they were supplanted by East European and Scandinavian languages in accordance with the perceived threat from the Warsaw Pact.

The Regiment's unpreparedness for operations in the Falklands was indicated by the fact that Lieutenant-Colonel Rose, 22 SAS's commander at the time, had to rely on a Spanish speaking Royal Marines officer to interpret for him during the surrender negotiations. This deficiency has now been

rectified in case of a future war with Argentina. The 1991 Gulf War is likely to see the SAS again putting an emphasis on Arabic.

SAS men who showed promise with demolitions during Continuation Training are allowed to develop this skill to an advanced level. They learn about making simple and advanced booby traps, sophisticated trigger mechanisms and the like.

Right: Wessex helicopters with SAS soldiers in Borneo during the 'Confrontation' with Indonesia. The introduction of the helicopter into military use has greatly aided units such as the SAS, but it has also forced troopers to learn new skills regarding the flying characteristics of these aircarft, how to emplane and deplane from them, and drills for establishing landing zones.

Soldiers and NCOs who survive their three-year tour with 22 SAS have the option of further stints. It is not uncommon for them to serve with the Regiment for the rest of their military careers. They progress on to a variety of positions in the Regiment, many of which are very exotic. Staff sergeants can become troop commanders in the place of junior officers or squadron quartermaster sergeant majors. The high point for most SAS SNCOs is to be a 'Sabre' Squadron sergeant major.

Outside the 'Sabre' Squadrons, SNCOs fill key positions in Training Wing, CRW Wing, TA SAS units or the 'Head Shed' (senior officers). They run the Selection and Continuation Training courses, as well as developing more advanced training routines.

For officers their careers in the SAS are at first limited to a three-year tour and then they have to return to their parent unit. This is because the Regiment's size prevents them acquiring the necessary experience to progress through the officer promotion maze. On being 'badged' SAS, officers are posted as troop commanders with the rank of captain, even if they started Selection as a lieutenant. However, the only way for them to progress up the promotion ladder afterwards is to leave 22 SAS and pass the necessary exams and courses to get to major (in 1979 the promotion problem was eased somewhat when SAS officers were exempt from having to pass the Camberley Staff College entrance examination). Having reached the rank of major, officers with SAS experience can go back to Hereford to command squadrons or fulfil other specialist positions. If successful, an officer may go on to lead the Regiment.

'TRAIN HARD, FIGHT EASY'

SAS soldiers never consider themselves fully trained and are constantly learning new skills or enhancing existing ones. The Regiment is also constantly monitoring the performance of its soldiers to ensure they keep up to scratch. At any point during their SAS careers soldiers can be RTU'd if they stray from the Regiment's exacting, some would say harsh, standards. An SAS patrol, for example, playing the 'enemy' on Exercise 'Brave Defender' in 1985 was deployed against a TA infantry battalion. When the latter turned the tables on the regulars and discovered their 'hide', all four SAS men were RTU'd. 'Train hard, Fight Easy' is the motto of Training Wing. It is not uncommon for SAS soldiers to return from active duty and comment that such and such an exercise was more difficult. Bravado, perhaps, but for men who daily push themselves to their limits and regularly risk their lives in routine activities, it is not such an outrageous thing to say.

TACTICS

- FOUR-MAN PATROLS

- WEAPONS SKILLS

- EXPLOSIVES AND SABOTAGE

- BEHIND ENEMY LINES

- COUNTER-TERRORIST TACTICS

- HOSTILE ENVIRONMENTS

'THE REST OF THE LADS, HAVING STORMED OVER THE BALCONY AT THE FRONT AND BLASTED THEIR WAY INTO THE FIRST FLOOR OF THE BUILDING WITH A WELL-PLACED EXPLOSIVE CHARGE, WERE NOW SYSTEMATICALLY CLEARING THE UPPER ROOMS, ASSISTED BY A WINNING COMBINATION OF THE STUNNING EFFECT OF THE INITIAL EXPLOSION, THE CHOKING FUMES OF THE CS GAS, THE CHILLING EXECUTION OF WELL-PRACTISED MANOEUVRES AND THE SHEER TERROR INDUCED BY THEIR SINISTER, BLACK-HOODED APPEARANCE.'

SOLDIER 'I' ON THE IRANIAN EMBASSY

Section I
FOUR-MAN PATROLS

'I want a body bag waiting on the LS [landing site] for us when we arrive', was how an SAS patrol commander announced his return from a mission in South Armagh on a spring night in 1976. Within minutes the four-man SAS patrol was carrying the dead body of a wanted terrorist from their helicopter at Bessbrook Army base. The target of the operation had been 25-year-old Peter Cleary, who was believed to have taken part in a string of terrorists crimes. He was on the run in the Irish Republic, but intelligence revealed he would slip across the border to attend a party at his girlfirend's house near Forkhill.

VICTORY BY STEALTH

The house was only 50m from the border. The SAS patrol was tasked with watching the house to see if Cleary made an appearance. A number of days beforehand, the four-man patrol had been inserted by helicopter at night some distance from the objective. They then approached the house on foot and established two observation posts (OPs). The men had to eat, wash and defecate inside their 'hides'. With the patrol split, sleep was impossible. Each pair had to remain constantly alert in case Irish Republican Army (IRA) terrorists or local people, who almost universally supported the former, detected the SAS men. If found, the latter could expect little mercy.

The combined effect of sleep deprivation and the risk of imminent detection put the SAS men under great stress. However, just after 2100 hours on the night of 15 April, the SAS men sighted a man who they thought to be Cleary. They made a positive identification and moved into the house to arrest him. After leading him away to a nearby field, the SAS soldiers called for a helicopter to lift them and their prize out. Because they were so close to the border, the request had to be approved by brigade headquarters (senior Army officers were worried about political flak if the aircraft crossed the border by mistake). For 50 minutes the SAS men had to wait in a field guarding Cleary. They were in a very exposed position as Cleary's relatives would have instantly told the IRA of his capture.

At 2325 hours the helicopter finally got clearance to pick up the SAS team and their 'catch'. It was a further 10 minutes before it reached the SAS men. When it dropped out of the sky towards the LS, three of the SAS men went forward to guide it down. Amid the noise of the approaching helicopter, Cleary jumped the remaining SAS man who was guarding him. Cleary grabbed the end of the soldier's rifle. The SAS man pulled the trigger three times and the IRA 'staff officer' fell dead.

While every SAS operation is unique, the snatch operation against Cleary contains all the ingredients of a typical SAS four-man patrol mission. The factors SAS patrol commanders have to consider include the insertion of the patrol, its approach to the objective, actions while in the OP, and how to safely get back to base. The insertion of an SAS patrol has to be meticulously planned to ensure the enemy has no indication of what is happening. Secrecy is the best defence for lightly armed SAS patrols.

WHY THE FOUR-MAN PATROL?

The four-man patrol is the smallest SAS operational unit and the cornerstone of the Regiment's art of war. The idea of a small-sized unit was originally conceived by David Stirling during World War II, and was later refined by Brigadier 'Mad Mike' Calvert and Lieutenant-Colonel John Woodhouse in Malaya. Four men was established as being the ideal number as it would enable a patrol to have mobility, secrecy and sufficient firepower if required. The lack of numbers is more than compensated for by each patrol member being a multi-skilled individual with more than one patrol and troop skill. How does a four-man patrol operate?

After being inserted by helicopter, for example, the patrol goes into all-round defence until the aircraft is safely out of the area. After making sure it is not being observed by the enemy, the patrol will move off towards its objective. Each man in the patrol has a pre-rehearsed task. On the move one will be the 'point' man or lead scout, and will guard the front 180-degree arc of the patrol. The next two men will cover the patrol's two flanks, and the 'Tailend Charlie' will watch the rear to make sure the patrol is not being followed. Along the route the patrol will move through a series of pre-designated rendezvous points (RVs), which are usually easily recognisable features such as bends in rivers or corners of woods. While helping navigation, they are also a key part of SAS anti-ambush drills. If the patrol gets 'bumped' by the enemy, the commander will have little

opportunity to give orders, so patrol members automatically follow a pre-arranged drill: they simply run like hell out of the ambush's 'kill zone' and make it back to the last RV. If that is compromised they will then attempt to make their way back to the next RV. The same procedure is also followed if some of the team become separated from their fellow patrol members.

Movement is usually conducted at night to decrease the likelihood of ambushes. If a patrol cannot reach its objective under the cloak of darkness, then it will take cover in a 'hide' or laying-up point during daylight and continue the march when darkness returns. The patrol needs to carry all the weapons,

When the patrol commander is happy with the choice of his OP, he will lead his troops into it and establish a working routine. First, it has to be camouflaged. It is normal for SAS men to dig themselves shell scrapes around one metre deep, then cover the hole in the ground with chicken wire. Vegetation is then used to cover the structure concealing the SAS men inside. This camouflage has to be regularly changed to ensure it keeps its colour and does not look different from the surrounding vegetation.

Inside the 'hide' the SAS men cover the earth floor with plastic ground sheets to keep them dry. Enemy locations are kept under observation with high-powered telescopes and

Right: Highly practised movement drills, such as this all-round defence tactic, ensure four-man patrols can hold off larger enemy forces, at least temporarily, with some ease. Another procedure is the head-on contact drill, whereby each member of the patrol, once the enemy has been encountered, moves into a position that allows fire to be directed at the opposition forces without hitting a comrade. If the patrol is marching in file and, for example, enemy soldiers are encountered by the lead scout, then the other patrol members will flank left and right and bring their weapons to bear instantly.

ammunition, equipment, water and rations it needs to survive. This can result in SAS men having to carry bergens weighing up to 50kg which makes silent movement at night very difficult. As the patrol approaches its objective, the commander will bring his men together in a final RV (FRV). Once he is happy this is secure, he will move off to make a reconnaissance of his OP position. This is a key part of the mission. Here the commander's experience begins to tell. It is unusual for Intelligence to provide patrol leaders with much information about the ground and enemy forces in the vicinity of the OP – this is, after all, one of the jobs of the SAS. It is up to the patrol commander to move in close and find the best site for his OP. He must consider four factors: can he see the objective; can he establish communications with higher headquarters from the OP site; how secure from detection by the enemy is it; and is it suitable to live in for up to a month?

night vision devices. This equipment places great strain on the users' eyes, so the occupants will take turns to operate it. Sighting and situation reports have to be sent back to higher headquarters at pre-arranged times to enable senior commanders to get an overall picture of what is happening on the battlefield or behind enemy lines. The mission of the OP is to observe the enemy, under no circumstances is it to compromise its position by engaging the enemy, no matter how enticing the target.

Inside the OP, the men have to eat, sleep, urinate and defecate without revealing their location to the enemy. Cooking hot food is not possible, at least during the day, so patrols have to live on a diet of cold biscuits, cheese and sweets. The men urinate and defecate into different plastic bags. If the substances are combined they have a tendency to explode, covering the inside of the OP in very unpleasant matter! It is usual for the patrol to carry only two sleeping bags with it. Two men 'hot-bed' with each other, i.e. while one is on duty the other sleeps. Most patrols stay in position for up to two weeks at a time, but if they need re-supplying then helicopters will be tasked to link up with the patrol.

The most critical items for patrols are radio batteries. If their rations run low the men can

It is possible to transmit away from the OP position, but then the signaller runs the risk of being discovered while moving outside the 'hide'. The next greatest danger to covert OPs are dogs. Properly trained, they can sniff them out quickly and lead enemy troops straight to the SAS position. By limiting movement outside the OP to an absolute minimum, SAS

put their survival training into practice, but without functioning communications equipment the OP is useless – it cannot perform its primary task: the transmission of intelligence. Re-supply drills are as laborious as moving across country. Secrecy must be maintained at all cost.

EVADING THE ENEMY

OPs are very vulnerable to detection by the enemy. The most dangerous threat are enemy direction-finding (DF) systems that can pinpoint radio signals. Only through good signalling skills and hi-tech burst transmission equipment is it possible to avoid being DF'd.

patrols lessen the chances of being discovered by enemy infantry or helicopters.

However, if the OP is compromised the patrol commander has a number of options. Fighting it out is not a very good proposition given the likelihood of the enemy having greater numbers and firepower. At night a rapid retreat, or 'bug-out', with the intention of meeting up at a pre-arranged RV is a good option. In Northern Ireland, for example, SAS OPs are usually supported by a Quick Reaction Force (QRF) – consisting of either British Army soldiers or members of the Royal Ulster Constabulary – at a nearby base which can be mobilised to get the OP out of trouble

Above: One great advantage of the four-man patrol is that its small size allows it to move through hostile territory undetected. Secrecy is increased by moving at night and laying low during the day.

Right: The early days. David Stirling, the Regiment's founder, with an SAS jeep patrol in the North African desert in 1942. During the war Britain had, at first, used its special forces troops in large-scale operations which often resulted in failure. Stirling's idea was to use small-sized teams to infiltrate behind enemy lines and hit many targets simultaneously. His concepts have endured into the modern era.

if it is compromised. Helicopter QRFs were used in Oman, but during the 1982 Falklands War this luxury did not exist. SAS patrols watching the Argentinians were on their own if they were discovered.

Extracting patrols from OPs is also fraught with difficulties. For example, the tactical situation may have changed since it was inserted and the OP could now be in the middle of a major enemy concentration area. Extraction drills are basically insertion procedures carried out in reserve. The most dangerous extractions are those which involve the patrol moving on foot through a friendly frontline. Not only does this take the patrol into no-man's-land, where the enemy is on a

high level of alert, but there is also the very real danger of being mistaken for the enemy by friendly forces.

Some of the most dangerous and difficult OPs ever mounted by the SAS took place during the Falklands War. Watching over Stanley, East Falkland, for 26 days, for example, was Captain Aldwin Wight and his four-man patrol from G Squadron, 22 SAS. From his position on Beaver Ridge, he was able to observe all the Argentinian positions around Stanley, the capital of the Falklands. Unfortunately, his OP was so close to the enemy's positions that there was little chance Wight and his men could have escaped if the position was uncovered. They were also in the

longest of any established during the Falklands War. To gain intelligence on the enemy, and also avoid detection, Sergeant Mather constantly changed the position of his OP. At Goose Green, Corporal Trevor Brookes discovered his OP was directly under the main Argentinian helicopter route between Stanley and Goose Green. For 16 days his OP stayed in position, despite frequent enemy air searches and foot patrols. Royal Navy Sea Harriers carried out a successful air strike against a fuel dump at the Goose Green airstrip thanks to information supplied by Brookes. When 2 Para later mounted its successful attack on the settlement, his information proved of great value.

THE SBS IN THE FALKLANDS

Sergeant Mather and Corporal Brookes both received the Military Medal for their efforts, while Captain Wight received the Military Cross. The Royal Marines' Special Boat Squadron (SBS) also sent patrols ashore in the Falklands to establish OPs at the same time as the SAS. They shared many of the experiences of their Army counterparts. They too had some close calls, such as dodging Argentinian patrols near San Carlos. One SBS team, as it was approaching its OP position, spotted a group of Argentinians moving forward to occupy exactly the same piece of ground. Rather than compromise the patrol, the Marines went to ground. In the confusion two men became separated from their colleagues. The patrol commander made for the agreed RV, but the missing Marines were nowhere to be seen. He then had to withdraw to a pre-arranged RV and link up with a helicopter. Some 12 days later, a search party found the missing men at the patrol's final RV. An SBS team overlooking San Carlos Water from Ajax Bay thought they had been compromised when seven enemy helicopters landed near their position and 100 troops began a sweep of the area. The Marines, convinced that they were about to be captured, sent an uncoded radio message back to the Task Force stating they were about to be discovered. Luckily their camouflage concealed their position and the Argentinians did not find them. The team was extracted by helicopter later that night.

middle of an assembly area for Argentinian helicopters, an excellent target if the patrol could have relayed this intelligence back to headquarters.

Communications difficulties at first prevented them from reporting the presence of the helicopters. Eventually, however, they were able to pass on the vital intelligence and RAF Harriers staged an air strike which destroyed four of the enemy aircraft. There was little cover from the elements in their high OP position, where weather conditions alternated between freezing rain and gale force winds, intermingled with a few freak clear days. At Bluff Cove, Sergeant Joseph Mather's OP was in position for 28 days, the

THE ULTIMATE FIGHTING UNIT

The covert OP is the principal tactic used by the SAS to gather intelligence on enemy forces. SAS soldiers must be able to set up OPs in all terrains and climates, and then survive in them for long periods. They are a major test of stamina, endurance, willpower and nerves. The risks are enormous but, if successful, the rewards are worthwhile.

Above: A British Para OP. SAS OPs tend to be more covert in nature, and are often situated right under the noses of the enemy.
Right: A Lynx helicopter comes in to pick up a waiting patrol in Northern Ireland. SAS four-man patrols have been used to conduct some very successful operations in Ulster, such as the arrest of IRA terrorist Peter Cleary in April 1976.
Far right: A Sea King helicopter of 846 Squadron (the unit which transported the SAS on the Pebble Island raid) prepares to extract troops in Norway. SAS patrols frequently train in the area as part of their arctic warfare brief.

Information from SAS and SBS patrols, for example, was the key to the British victory during the Falklands War. The four-man patrol, as envisaged by David Stirling over 50 years ago, is the ideal tactical unit which enables the Regiment to fulfil a diverse number of roles, such as intelligence gathering, sabotage and the like. Its small size means each member of the patrol can be under constant strain during a mission which can test a man's nerves and stamina to the limit; in a four-man patrol there is nowhere to hide. However, one would expect nothing less from the Special Air Service.

Section II
WEAPONS SKILLS

One of the most basic skills for any soldier is the ability to shoot his personal weapon accurately and speedily, but for SAS soldiers handling weapons must be second nature. Training starts immediately after Selection and initially follows the standard British infantry pattern. As a number of SAS recruits come from non-infantry units, tuition begins at a fairly basic level. The trainee is reminded of the basic principles of marksmanship and weapons handling, then moves on to simple range exercises.

He is given coaching on how to hold the weapon correctly, how to aim, and how to squeeze the trigger smoothly. At this stage all targets are fixed and firing is conducted from static positions. The standard positions are lying, kneeling on one knee, and standing upright. Only when these basic principles are firmly grasped will the recruit move on to more advanced drills.

As the SAS art of war is based around the small-sized unit, such as the four-man patrol, in action it is absolutely essential that each man's weapon works every time. A great deal of time is therefore spent on learning Immediate Action Drills (what to do if a weapon jams) until they are carried out automatically, even if the firer is in complete darkness.

LEARNING TO AVOID STOPPAGES

Prevention is better than cure, however, so great emphasis is put on correct maintenance and cleaning techniques. Troopers spend hours stripping, maintaining and reassembling firearms, and are taught how to look after weapons in all environments. For example, if the standard amount of oil is put on a cleaned weapon when in sandy, dusty conditions, grit will stick to the oil and soon clog up the mechanism. In such conditions, therefore, the weapon must be kept dry. The soldier also needs to know the best way of keeping small arms working in the jungle or in arctic conditions. If a patrol is hundreds of kilometres behind enemy lines, a visit to the armourer is not an option!

Training starts with standard British Army infantry weapons. SAS recruits are shown how to get the best from the L1A1 Self-Loading Rifle (SLR) and its replacement, the SA-80 rifle. Unlike most infantry units, troopers also spend a lot of time with the Browning 9mm pistol because it is an important element of

SAS Close Quarters Battle (CQB) drills. They also learn to use the L2A3 Sterling sub-machine gun. Once the characteristics of these weapons are fully understood, the soldier progresses on to slightly more specialised tools. The American M16 assault rifle has been a favourite SAS weapon since the Borneo campaign in the 1960s, as has the pump-action shotgun, though the latter is now used mainly for counter-terrorist work as opposed to jungle patrolling, so extensive training is carried out on these weapons. Troopers are also taught the capabilities and limitations of silenced weapons such as the L34A1 Sterling.

SAS troopers are trained to fight anywhere in the world, so it is essential they are familiar with as many foreign weapons as possible. This not only helps them understand the good and bad points of any small arm that is likely to be used against them, but also enables them to use any captured hardware when they are operating behind enemy lines, as well as allowing them to train insurgents if necessary. This being the case, the Russian AK series plays a large part in this training and, to a lesser degree, Chinese weapons.

ADVANCED WEAPONS TRAINING

Training then moves on to learning more advanced skills, with soldiers taking part in much more difficult and challenging firing exercises. Night firing, for example, is practised extensively, both by the light of flares and with image intensifying night sights. The soldier will also carry out battle runs, where he has to dash forward then engage targets quickly at various ranges. Targets can be made to pop up without warning and disappear after a few seconds if not hit. To provide distractions, thunderflashes and other pyrotechnics are also used. Shooting accurately under these conditions is completely different to firing at static targets set up at fixed ranges. Time limits are constantly applied, and should a weapon jam, the trainee is expected to clear the stoppage and carry on with no extra time being allocated. Eventually, after hours on the ranges, bringing a weapon to bear speedily and accurately onto a target becomes instinctive.

SAS patrols augment their firepower by carrying machine guns and support weapons. Of the former, the general purpose machine gun (GPMG) is by far the most popular. Capable of firing up to 1000 rounds per

Above right: A party of men from 2 SAS service their weapons during Operation 'Canuck', northern Italy, in early 1945. Note the Browning 0.5in heavy machine gun and ammunition boxes. The Browning, often mounted on World War II SAS jeeps, was a formidable man-stopper.

Below right: SAS soldiers in Malaya in the 1950s. The man in the foreground is carrying an M1 Carbine, a semi-automatic rifle, which, because of its compactness, was ideal for jungle fighting. Due to poor visibility encountered in jungle terrain, contacts with the enemy are often short and confused. Therefore, troopers must be able to fire their weapons accurately and speedily from the hip.

L42A1 SNIPER RIFLE

Based on the venerable Lee-Enfield .303in rifle, the L42A1 was used by the SAS until the early 1980s. Despite its rather basic design, the Regiment found it performed well in adverse weather conditions.

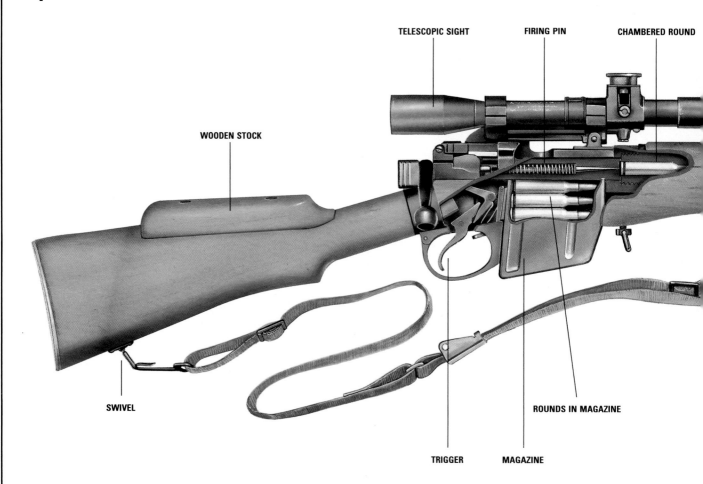

TELESCOPIC SIGHT   FIRING PIN   CHAMBERED ROUND

WOODEN STOCK

SWIVEL

ROUNDS IN MAGAZINE

TRIGGER   MAGAZINE

At the centre of the debate concerning which sniper rifles are best suited for military use lies a contradiction. The best rifle is the one with the most powerful sights, image intensifying or infra-red for example, which can ensure a first-round hit at 1000m range or beyond. However, experiences of snipers in the field soon revealed that the best sights were totally unsuited to campaign work because they were too delicate. Therefore military sniper rifles

are a trade-off between reliability and robustness on the one hand, and performance on the other.

The military sniper has two main tasks: to 'take out' key enemy personnel, and to hit other snipers. Both these tasks can involve hitting targets at ranges of up to 1000m, though usually it is below this figure. This contrasts with police and counter-terrorist sniping, where the targets are at much closer ranges. The L42 possessed most

of the attributes needed to be an effective military sniping weapon. It was robust and reliable, having all the virtues of the .303 Lee-Enfield design as well as a heavy barrel. It fired the 7.62mm NATO cartridge, a round which has good stopping power at long ranges.

Its one drawback was that its accuracy was not as great as more modern systems. However, this in itself was not a great hindrance to its performance as the military sniper's

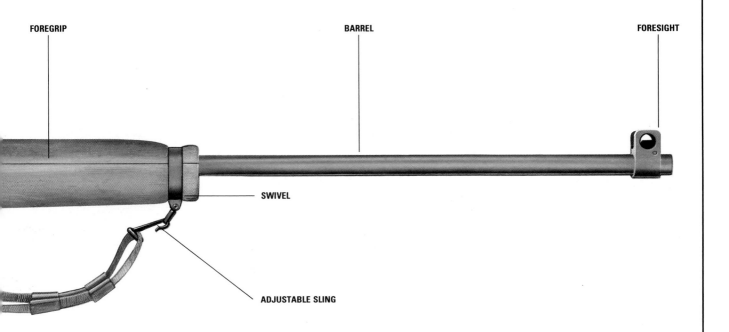

FOREGRIP

BARREL

FORESIGHT

SWIVEL

ADJUSTABLE SLING

L42A1 SNIPER RIFLE SPECIFICATIONS

- **TYPE:** bolt-action sniper rifle
- **CALIBRE:** 7.62mm
- **WEIGHT:** 4.43kg
- **LENGTH:** 1181mm
- **EFFECTIVE RANGE:** 800m
- **FEED:** 10-round box magazine
- **MUZZLE VELOCITY:** 838 metres per second

task is, first and foremost, to hit his target. Though he will be looking for an immediate kill, the fact that he has incapacitated his foe is enough. After all, the enemy's resources will be taken up transporting the wounded man to rear area medical facilities. In addition, a man severely wounded by a sniper can lower enemy morale just as much as if he had been killed.

For the SAS, the L42's ability to stand up to punishment and still perform was

an important factor. In Oman, for example, SAS patrols were operating in the scorching heat of the desert with their L42s, but the latter still worked well when used. In the Falklands some years later, the rifle was working in sub-zero temperatures and damp conditions – testimony to its ability to stand up to the rigours of almost any battlefield.

The design of the rifle is straightforward and differs little from that of the No 4 Mk 1 rifle on which it is

based. Notable differences include the telescopic brackets fitted to the left side of the body to take the Telescope, Straight, Sighting, L1A1, which is modified from the Telescope Sighting No 32 Mk III of the No 4 rifle. These brackets also allow use of an image intensifier. All in all, the L42 was an excellent weapon that provided the SAS with a reliable rifle that could perform exceptionally well in most weather conditions.

Far left: A member of the Malayan Scouts learning jungle warfare skills with the aid of a fencing mask and an air rifle. The rifles fired darts which, though unlikely to kill, caused painful minor wounds – an incentive to always be on guard. Through constant training the Scouts became effective jungle troops. Weapons used by the Scouts and, later, by the SAS in Malaya included the Owen submachine gun and the M1 Carbine.
Left: SAS troops wait for a helicopter to land in Borneo in the 1960s. The men are armed with M16 assault rifles. The M16 and its smaller variant, the Colt Commando, are still used by the Regiment today. Their high-velocity 5.56mm rounds are lethal at short ranges.

minute, the GPMG can give a four-man patrol devastating firepower, though carrying its ammunition can be back-breaking work.

Support weapons used by the SAS include the 66mm LAW (Light Anti-tank Weapon) single-shot rocket launcher which packs a reasonable punch in a small package. It is also useful for destroying trenches or bunkers. Other weapons that SAS troopers receive intensive training on are mortars, especially the 81mm version.

The next stage is to apply the individual's weapons skills to both patrol and troop battle drills. Through the years the SAS has developed standard operating procedures (SOPs) for moving and fighting in small groups in all kinds of terrain. Many of these SOPs have now passed into Army use, and it is no coincidence that the standard infantry tactical group is the four-man fireteam. Anti-ambush drills are also practised until reaction is automatic and instinctive.

Right: The Colt Commando is an excellent weapon for short-range firefights. Its 5.56mm round tends to shred everything that gets in its way and also 'tumbles' (careers off in all directions inside the body as opposed to following a straight track). In addition, its smaller calibre means more ammunition can be carried by individuals – a useful attribute for units such as the SAS which operate behind the lines.

Even when a trooper becomes 'badged' SAS, he continues to learn new weapons skills. A major role for Regiment is teaching foreign armies or supporting indigenous fighters and resistance groups, such as in France – the *Maquis* – in World War II or Borneo – the Border Scouts and Cross-Border Scouts – in the 1960s. To fulfil such tasks the SAS needs qualified instructors, so the trooper may find himself sent on an instructor's course. He may also be sent on courses to learn how to use more sophisticated systems such as the MILAN anti-tank weapon and the Stinger surface-to-air missile.

Another specialist skill is that of the sniper. The SAS has always believed in the value of snipers, especially for killing high-value targets behind enemy lines. Selected trainees

Left: The Browning High Power, the handgun currently used by the SAS. Contrary to popular belief, SAS soldiers in engagements do not use 'double taps', preferring instead accurate and sustained firepower to put down an opponent.
Below: One of the reasons why SAS soldiers are so proficient with their weapons is that they spend hours on the range honing their skills. In combat this means they can wield their weapons instinctively and with deadly accuracy.

undergo a gruelling course in which they are expected to learn how to move covertly across any terrain and to lie in wait for hours for a suitable target. Personal camouflage is vital, and snipers are taught how to use strips of painted hessian to enable them to blend into the background. He needs to be a superb shot, able to hit a man-sized target with his first round at over 500m. For such work the SAS currently employs the Accuracy International PM bolt-action rifle

Other SAS weapons skills include Close Quarter Battle (CQB) drills. Originally developed from the training methods used by the undercover 'Keeni Meeni' squads in Aden in the 1960s, SAS CQB techniques have become renowned as being the best in the world. CQB skills are essential for the bodyguard and anti-terrorist roles and form a major element of advanced weapons training. Every time a squadron takes its turn in the CRW role, its soldiers have to go through a CQB refresher course, which is reinforced by constant practice during the tour.

LEARNING SKILLS IN THE 'KILLING HOUSE'

Troopers first practise their individual skills – snap shooting at pop-up targets – with pistols, submachine guns or pump-action shotguns. They have to get these basic techniques almost perfect before progressing on to team tactics and hostage-rescue training.

At Hereford there is the famous 'Killing House', a live-firing complex which is a warren of corridors and rooms with specially protected walls to absorb stray rounds. The whole building is covered by TV cameras and exercises are recorded for later debriefings. 'Terrorist' targets are in some of the rooms, together with 'hostages'. The rescue team has to be able to enter a room, identify the targets and shoot them within a few seconds, without hitting any of the hostages. The SAS soldiers move continuously from room to room (which may be filled with smoke), firing with deadly accuracy as they go. They have to be able to change magazines instantly and clear any jams or stoppages without holding up the attack.

Originally the targets were standard Army paper ones, with the hostages marked in a different colour. The Regiment then used to practise with live SAS personnel playing the hostages and the assault team firing live rounds at the targets all around them. This practice was discontinued after a sergeant 'hostage' was accidentally shot dead. A much more sophisticated and high-tech system is now employed. The terrorists and hostages are played by real people who are in a different, but identical, room. A TV camera system projects a view of this room onto a paper screen covering one of the walls of the assault

room. As the team enters, they are confronted with the confused picture of moving, yelling people, some of whom are hostages and others terrorists. They have to identify their targets and engage them within seconds. After the first shots roar out, the picture is frozen to enable a clear analysis of the results.

The exercises then get more complex, with distractions such as stun grenades and smoke thrown in for good measure. The troopers learn to cope with the reduced vision caused by wearing gas masks and the weight of heavy body armour. Multi-team exercises are also practised which require a high degree of coordination between the patrols. When describing SAS training, sources often refer to the 'double tap' with a handgun, two rounds fired in quick succession to the centre of the body or, if circumstances allow, to the head. In his published memoirs, Soldier 'I', an SAS sergeant, describes such a CQB exercise: 'In I went and headed straight for the cluster of figure-eleven targets propped up on their rickety stands in the far corner. Usual thing, I thought quickly, my eyes doing a radar scan of the room. Four terrorists and three hostages.

'Ba...Bang, Ba...Bang, Ba..Bang. Three double taps in less than three seconds, six neat holes in three terrorist heads.'

SAS ENGAGEMENT DRILLS

As journalist Mark Urban has pointed out in his book *Big Boy's Rules*, the 'double tap' is rarely used when the SAS soldiers have to shoot for real. During the Princes Gate rescue mission, and when ambushing IRA terrorists, SAS troopers have poured bursts of fire into their targets until there was no doubt that they were dead. In the intensity of close-range combat, there is no room for finesse.

Other commentators have sometimes asked whether such expert shots could shoot to wound rather than to kill. The SAS response is that 'shooting to wound' is only found in the pages of fiction. If it is asked to break a terrorist siege, it will be because hostages are being killed and all hope of a peaceful resolution has gone. In this case, the main priority for the SAS troopers is to rescue the hostages alive, as well as stay alive themselves. They have to make sure that every terrorist is instantly 'neutralised'; that he or she cannot fire a weapon, throw a grenade or detonate a bomb. Shooting at arms or legs may leave a determined terrorist alive to flick a switch or shoot a hostage. Heavy and sustained firepower to the body, on the other hand, ensures an opponent is totally neutralised.

CQB skills have also been used in Ulster in a number of ambushes. These typically occur at very close range and often in poor light, where quick, accurate shooting is essential.

Left: One of the weapons SAS troopers get very familiar with is the Heckler & Koch MP5 submachine gun, shown here being carried by members of 'Pagoda' Troop during the storming of the Iranian Embassy in 1980. Troopers will train with it intensively while part of the CRW squadron. This means endless hours in the 'Killing House' shooting at targets, as well as learning rapid magazine change and malfunction clearing drills.

However, even such highly trained soldiers as SAS troopers face problems of target identification in CQB scenarios. When there is time to plan an attack in detail, such as at Princes Gate, it is easier to differentiate between terrorists and hostages. In the less controllable ambushes in Northern Ireland, though, a total of six innocent people have been mistaken for gunmen and accidentally killed by the SAS. In the intensity of close-range combat it is easy to make mistakes.

What is clear, however, is that SAS soldiers are trained to an exceptionally high level with all infantry firearms, whether rifle, sub-machine gun, handgun or machine gun. Even if he has never seen an individual weapon before, the SAS man is expected to quickly learn and adapt to its characteristics and use it accurately and effectively. Because SAS soldiers fight mostly in small teams, great emphasis is placed on weapons skills. Here, the SAS has developed CQB techniques to such a pitch that rescue teams can storm a building defended by determined, well-armed terrorists and kill them without loss to themselves. What gives SAS soldiers the edge is their high levels of skill with small arms, an expertise which is the result of receiving expert tuition, and the hundreds of hours spent on ranges and in the 'Killing House'.

Section III
EXPLOSIVES AND SABOTAGE

The first SAS missions in World War II were to blow up Axis aircraft on the ground, and the sabotage of enemy installations and materiel has remained a role of the Regiment ever since. There are many types of explosive devices and sabotage techniques that the SAS employs; the actual method chosen will depend upon the target and the environment.

Most military demolition charges are made from various types of plastic explosive; common types are C-4, C-3 and Semtex. Plastic explosive (or *plastique*) is remarkably safe to handle, it is almost immune to shocks, is resistant to water and chemicals, and if set alight by matches burns slowly rather than exploding. Another benefit of *plastique* is that the charge can be moulded to the shape required, giving the best possible contact between the charge and the target. Some *plastiques* are mixed with aluminium powder to increase the incendiary effect of the detonation. Others have special compositions to improve water resistance, and these often form the filling of anti-ship limpet mines.

HOW TO DETONATE EXPLOSIVES
To turn this stable material into a bomb, a detonator (also known as a blasting cap) is needed. This is usually a tube containing a small amount of impact-sensitive explosive (or initiator). The blasting cap is pressed into the charge or taped to the outer edge, and when it is set off the shock wave is enough to trigger the main charge. Detonators can be activated by a number of methods: by a clockwork or electronic timing device, by a manually operated electrical generator, a radio command system, or by a simple burning fuse.

An old-fashioned, though reliable, delayed action mechanism is the time pencil, used by the SAS on Lewes bombs during World War II. This type of detonator had a spring-loaded firing pin pointing at the impact-sensitive initiator. A thin wire held the firing pin in place and alongside this wire was a glass ampoule containing acid. If the detonator was squeezed, the ampoule shattered and the acid ate into the thin wire. Eventually the wire broke and the spring slammed the firing pin into the initiator, causing it to explode. They could be set for minutes or hours as required.

If two or more charges are required to detonate simultaneously, they are linked by detonating cord. This has a core made from PETN explosive which causes the cord to explode instantaneously along its entire length. If a blasting cap is pressed against one end, detonating cord will provide enough energy to explode *plastique* at the other. If two charges are linked with cord, the explosion of one will cause almost simultaneous detonation of the other.

More sophisticated systems include the use of shaped charges. Here, the explosive has a 'V'- or cone-shaped cut-out from the face nearest the target. When detonated, the explosive power is focussed towards the cut-out, creating a much more powerful shock wave in that direction. Shaped charges are useful if the target demands a specific cut, like a steel girder or concrete bridge support. If shaped charges are correctly positioned the quantity of explosive needed is usually small.

SAS patrols are taught to use the minimum of explosive for any target. If a patrol is on foot behind enemy lines, all explosive and detonating materials must be carried by the troopers, along with their ammunition, food, radios, radio batteries, clothing and weapons. If they are operating from vehicles or have easy access to aerial re-supply, the weight factor is not so critical.

PRIME SAS TARGETS
The SAS prefers to use the simpler, more reliable detonation methods such as manual pressure triggers. If a charge misfires, it is usually impossible for an SAS team to return to the target and try again. SAS demolition experts are also taught to use two independent detonation systems where possible, to further reduce the chances of a misfire.

Targets include installations such as airfields and their aircraft. The machines themselves are relatively easy to destroy, the normal method being to place very small charges in the cockpit, on the undercarriage and nose cone (an example being the Pebble Island raid during the Falklands War). Other 'soft' targets on an airfield include fuel dumps and tanker vehicles. Many air forces now park their combat aircraft in concrete shelters which

Above right: An exercise involving explosives and soft-skinned vehicles. Units such as the SAS can wreak great havoc behind enemy lines with very small quantities of explosives.

Below right: Bridges are a favourite target for deep-penetration units. Destroying a strategically placed bridge can cause the enemy great inconvenience by interrupting the movement of men and materiel to the front.

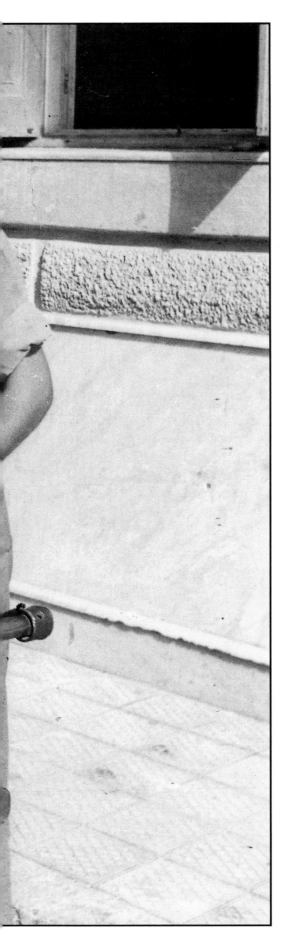

makes a sabotage attack on a major base much more difficult. In this case it may be easier to kill the highly trained pilots than destroy their machines.

Bridges are also a common target, though modern concrete structures are surprisingly difficult to destroy. The best way to attack a bridge is to place charges at each end of a span, between the supports, causing a complete length to fall in. Other methods include blowing the supports along one side only, so the bridge's own weight causes it to twist and break. The sabotage team must create a gap longer than the enemy's readily available military bridging systems. Given sufficient engineering resources most demolitions can be repaired, so the timing of the attack is vital if maximum disruption is to be caused. For example, a good time to blow an important bridge would be as a friendly offensive starts, when the enemy supply system is most likely to be over-stretched.

Railways are much easier targets, although they are also simpler to repair. Sabotage teams will concentrate on key junctions, points or signals or even the bridges over which the lines cross (during World War II, for example, SAS teams operating in northwest Europe in 1944-45 cut enemy railway lines on 164 separate occasions). Tunnels are virtually impossible to collapse with the limited quantities of explosive available to an SAS patrol, though a small charge on the line inside, triggered by the weight of a passing train, can be effective.

SAS patrols may also be ordered to disrupt enemy command, control and communications networks. Radio masts and telephone wires are vulnerable but can be easily repaired. The saboteurs will instead attack the transmitters, switching gear or telephone exchanges. A similar proviso applies to industrial targets such as dams and canals. A dam is too strong a target for an SAS patrol, though the pumping mechanism is not. A few kilos of explosive will shatter canal locks and create flooding, and destruction of the lock mechanism will block a canal until repairs can be made.

UNDERWATER DEMOLITIONS

Specialist techniques are needed for underwater targets. Ships or metal objects can be attacked using magnetic limpet mines. These small devices can be easily carried by a diver and clamped onto the underside of the vessel. Limpet mines only contain a few kilos of explosive, so more than one must be placed to guarantee penetration of sufficient water-tight compartments to sink the target. Water pressure dramatically increases the effect of even small quantities of explosives, and the swimmer must be well clear before

Left: Members of 2 SAS fusing mines in the Mediterranean, 1943. Ever since its creation, the Regiment has trained its soldiers in the employment of explosive devices. During World War II the SAS specialised in cutting railway lines and disabling enemy aircraft on the ground.

Right: A white phosphorus grenade explodes during a training exercise. As well as laying demolition charges, SAS soldiers are expert at setting booby traps. Rigging trip-wires to grenades to create an ambush can slow an enemy pursuing force, as well as contributing to the lowering of an opponent's morale.

detonation. Anti-ship operations are mainly the preserve of the modern Special Boat Squadron (SBS), but the SAS likes to retain its own speciality in this field.

Technology has also given new capabilities to sabotage teams. If it is carrying a radio and laser designator, the SAS patrol can 'illuminate' structures and installations for friendly aircraft to attack with laser-guided munitions. This requires a great deal of coordination and virtually perfect communications, but does allow a small team to inflict massive amounts of damage. This technique was used extensively during the 1991 Gulf War, with SAS teams locating and designating Scud mobile missile launchers for Allied aircraft to attack.

BOOBY TRAPS

Sophisticated detonators and charges may not be available behind enemy lines, so SAS demolitions training includes extensive tuition on booby traps and improvised explosives. Makeshift explosives and incendiaries can be manufactured from materials such as weed-killer, petrol, powdered soap and other readily available substances. Conventional military ordnance such as grenades, shells or aircraft bombs can also form the basis of a booby trap or improvised mine.

A lethal booby trap can be created by putting explosive into innocuous items and equipment. For example, a standard-issue torch can be packed with explosive and fitted with a trembler switch, ready to detonate if it is moved. When left outside a barracks, for example, the torch will soon be picked up. A supposedly empty drinks tin can be similarly treated and is almost bound to be kicked by passer-by. At its simplest a booby trap can be a nail sunk vertically into the ground, with a round of ammunition resting on it, pointing vertically upwards. If someone stands on the bullet the pressure pushes the nail into the cartridge, firing the round upwards.

Such booby traps rarely cause significant damage to an army. Their main effect is on the morale of enemy soldiers. If a few devices are scattered around the enemy's rear echelons, the effects are considerable. Normal activity becomes much more difficult, with men becoming reluctant to move or enter buildings without slow, careful checking. This author well remembers being on a major NATO exercise and waking up to find '22 SAS' chalked on the side of his supposedly guarded vehicle. After a few nights during which shadowy figures occasionally appeared, throwing thunderflashes, firing blank ammunition and 'roughing up' sentries, the whole area was a mass of rumour and counter-rumour, with nervous rear echelon troops shooting at anything that moved.

Many such techniques were developed during World War II and now form the basis for today's skills. Security agencies and special forces around the world frequently exchange information on new techniques, especially those developed by terrorist and guerrilla forces. When the Australian SAS deployed to Vietnam, for example, it faced some of the most ingenious booby-trap experts of modern times. This information was passed on to the Regiment during exchange postings and joint training exercises.

A closely related style of operation is the sabotage of known terrorist arms caches. Explosives and detonators are tampered with, rendering them ineffective. This has occasionally been carried out in Northern Ireland, and when one of its bombs fails to explode, the IRA can never be sure whether it was just an ineffective fuse or deliberate sabotage. Another technique could be to sabotage the detonators so that they trigger an explosion immediately they are set, killing the bomber. There is no evidence that this method has been used in Ireland (the risk to innocent civilians probably prohibits its use).

ANTICIPATING THE ENEMY'S MOVES

The SAS man is also trained to recognise situations where booby traps and terrorist bombs may be used against him. The first principle is to analyse the threat. SAS troopers have to be able to 'think terrorist'. If acting as a bodyguard, the soldier has to think ahead all the time, planning the future movements of his client in such a way as to minimise the risk of attack. Simple drills such as taking circumspect routes, changing cars regularly, arriving at, and departing from, public functions at unpredictable times all serve to make a terrorist's life more difficult. The bodyguard also has to be able to examine a car quickly and effectively, with a good knowledge of the possible places a bomb could be hidden. He must also be aware of any danger spots on his client's route, such as sharp bends, culverts, drainage ditches and small bridges, where a bomb could be conveniently placed. Similar skills are needed for troops operating against terrorists, such as in Northern Ireland.

Whatever the roles and missions of the SAS in future years, it seems likely that demolitions and sabotage will play a large part in the operational repertoire of the Regiment. Improved technology will make explosives more powerful or lighter, and fuses more sophisticated and reliable. What remain unchanged, however, are the tactical skills needed to identify the best target, get the explosives into position and place them at the points where most damage is caused.

Section IV
BEHIND ENEMY LINES

The SAS is a deep-penetration unit that specialises in operating behind enemy lines. Small-sized teams can achieve results in the enemy's rear areas far out of proportion to their size, but only if they can keep the upper hand. This mean avoiding larger forces in a straight fight. Contact is, if possible, avoided at all costs because it will only get in the way of the main tasks of SAS teams in enemy territory: intelligence gathering, sabotage, and fomenting unrest among the population if possible. However, when targets of opportunity become available, SAS teams will seize the initiative and engage in what can sometimes be spectacular actions.

THE PEBBLE ISLAND RAID

The Pebble Island raid during the Falklands War has entered SAS folklore. It began after the commander of the British Task Force, Admiral Sandy Woodward, was thinking aloud at his morning conference on 10 May 1982 about how to neutralise the threat to the British landing at San Carlos Water from the Pucara ground-attack aircraft based on the island, which was only 45km from the proposed beachhead. The Admiral's SAS advisor promptly suggested that his troops could deal with them. The following night a Sea King from 846 Naval Air Squadron inserted two four-man patrols from D Squadron's Boat Troop onto West Falkland. After landing, the Boat Troop men quickly set up an observation post (OP) to watch the island. They had four Klepper canoes with them to cross the 16km stretch of sea to Pebble Island to make a close reconnaissance of the objective that evening, but terrible sea conditions put paid to that idea.

On the night of 12/13 May, the weather having abated, the SAS team got ashore. Leaving four men to guard the canoes, the Boat Troop commander led a reconnaissance team forward to look at the airstrip. What they saw were 11 aircraft including six Pucaras. The terrain was flat with no cover and so the party went to ground until the following night to avoid detection. Only on the morning of 14 May did D Squadron's commander, Major Cedric Delves, get the vital information needed to plan his attack. That night two Sea Kings lifted off HMS *Hermes* with 45 men from D Squadron and an artillery spotter on board. High winds delayed the launch of the

Sea Kings so the SAS men had to move fast when they were put down on Pebble Island. The Boat Troop captain met the assault force commander at the landing site (LS) and quickly briefed him on the Argentinian dispositions. The SAS force was split into several groups: an assault force of 20 men, a reserve troop, parties to secure the flanks of the assault force, and a fire support team with 81mm mortars. The Boat Troop men would protect the mortar team. Scouts from Boat Troop led the different groups to their positions. The 6km march was covered quickly despite each man being burdened with extra ammunition and two mortar bombs. All the groups were in position by 0700 hours, though the attack was well behind schedule. The original plan to destroy the airstrip and kill its defenders was scrapped. The SAS had to be content with the 'brassing up' of the aircraft.

HITTING THE ENEMY HARD

HMS *Glamorgan* was called up and ordered to put down fire on the Argentinian troop positions. Under cover of this heavy fire the assault force moved forward and placed demolition charges on the aircraft. Soon the airfield was ablaze as the aircraft were blown apart and *Glamorgan* scored a number of hits on a fuel dump. One SAS soldier earned the nickname 'Pucara Paddy' for his skill at blowing up enemy aircraft. Their job done, the SAS soldiers began to withdraw. Casualties had been very light: one soldier injured by shrapnel and another by a land mine explosion. The Argentinians tried to follow but were met with M203 grenade and small-arms fire. After 30 minutes of action the raiders broke off contact and made their way to the helicopter LS. The Pebble Island raid was hailed as a great success, though hardly anything went according to plan. It worked because of the basic soundness of SAS tactical concepts, plans and sheer daring which were flexible enough to stand up to quickly changing circumstances.

Careful planning, based on accurate information from the reconnaissance party, allowed the attack force to select a helicopter LS out of the enemy's view, thereby facilitating an undetected march to the objective. With the element of surprise on its side, the SAS was always one step ahead of the

Above right: On patrol in Malaya. The SAS and, before it, the Malayan Scouts were tasked with hunting down Communist Terrorists deep in the jungle. It was a nerve-racking business. Visibility in the jungle was inevitably poor, and the threat of ambush was never far away.

Below right: An SAS jeep behind enemy lines in northwest Europe, late 1944. This vehicle, from 1 SAS, is hunting for German snipers. In addition to the Vickers 'K' machine gun at the front, there is a covered Lewis gun on the rear of the jeep.

Argentinians. The division of the SAS force into several groups was based on the Regiment's standing operating procedures (SOPs). In addition to the assault force, which actually moves forward to close with the objective, protection parties are needed to stop other enemy forces interfering with the main attack. Fire support is needed to eliminate any enemy defenders who try to resist the attack. A reserve is essential to deal with the unexpected. When behind enemy lines stealth is imperative to avoid detection and maintain the element of surprise, especially for small-sized forces. Slick battle tactics were the key to success at Pebble Island. All the SAS men knew their drills and procedures, and they only required quick confirmatory orders for the operation to get under way. The raid commander kept a tight grip on what was happening and ensured good coordination between the various groups. Good fire support kept the enemy on the defensive and deterred the Argentinians from pursuing the SAS teams once the latter had begun their orderly retreat back to the LS.

TACTICS BEHIND ENEMY LINES

If an SAS team is larger than a four-man patrol and is not in a covert OP, then a base will be established from where operations can be launched. During World War II, for example, the SAS established many bases throughout France in the days and weeks following D-Day. Similarly, during the 1991 Gulf War SAS teams set up bases deep inside Iraq. During this campaign the Regiment was involved in various activities: aiding Allied aircraft by marking targets with laser designators, gathering intelligence on Iraqi Army and Republican Guard units, and operating in towns and cities disguised as Arabs to collect useful intelligence.

Winning over the local population is also a part of operating behind enemy lines. This is the 'hearts and minds' policy that was so successful in Malaya, Borneo and Oman. In Borneo in the 1960s, for example, some of the natives the SAS encountered along the border with Indonesia had never seen a white man. Nevertheless, through patience, medical aid, speaking their language and helping them, SAS soldiers were able to win over these people and enlist their help in the fight against Indonesian forces. Liaison with friendly partisans is also part of SAS procedures when operating behind enemy lines. During World War II, for example, SAS bases in France were frequently shared with *Maquis* units. However, the latter often displayed poor security, leading to the subsequent discovery of the bases by the Germans. SAS procedure now, therefore, is not to share bases with partisans.

Left: Like these Royal Marines collecting information, the main role of SAS soldiers behind enemy lines is intelligence gathering. The timely information that SAS teams can send back to headquarters is invaluable for the accurate planning of operations and assessing enemy strengths and dispositions.

Other operations undertaken behind enemy lines include ambushes. Like raids, they need to be planned thoroughly and the troops involved have to be highly trained in the necessary combat tactics. SAS ambushes fall into two categories: planned and unplanned. The former are elaborate affairs and are only mounted after the SAS receives specific intelligence on enemy activity, while the latter are improvised. When Intelligence reports that enemy forces are to be at a certain point, the scene is set for the SAS to mount a deliberate ambush. The first phase of the operation involves covertly moving into position – the ambush will fail if the enemy gets any inclination they are being tracked.

Ideally the ambush party will be landed behind enemy lines at night and then move under cover of darkness to the objective. Using SOPs, the team moves silently to the objective. The ambush commander will leave his troops in an FRV and go forward alone to conduct a close reconnaissance of the ground. He will select good fire positions for the main 'killer group' and positions for cut-offs. The latter have the task of giving early warning of the approach of the enemy and stopping anyone escaping from the ambush. Of crucial importance is the 'kill zone', where the SAS will trap the enemy in a hail of fire. It should preferably be devoid of cover to allow the SAS to kill everyone in it quickly.

SPRINGING AMBUSHES

After returning to his FRV, the ambush commander brings forward his troops and personally places them in position. He gives every man his arcs of fire, indicating the areas he needs to watch. Claymore mines or trip flares can also be placed in the 'kill zone' to make things even more difficult for the enemy. Once the ambush team are in position, the commander declares the ambush set. From now on no one is allowed to move in case they reveal their position to the enemy. Ambushes can be in place for a few minutes or hours. Keeping awake is vital. Tired and stressed soldiers, no matter how well trained, have great difficulty staying awake or alert while lying down in uncomfortable positions.

When the enemy appears, the commander always initiates the ambush, either by firing his weapon or detonating a Claymore mine. All hell breaks lose as the 'killer group' rakes the enemy with fire. If everything has gone according to plan no one should escape. In some cases the most effective thing for the enemy to do is charge straight towards the ambush party, in the hope that weight of numbers will overwhelm the ambushers (this is also a tactic used if SAS patrols are themselves ambushed). Claymore mines and

GPMGs are the best defences against these tactics. However, the SAS men are now in a very exposed position because they have revealed their presence.

It is now the job of the ambush commander to break contact. First he will call in his cut-offs and then move the 'killer group' back to the FRV. A small protection party at the FRV will count the members of the team as they return. After confirming that everyone is accounted for, the commander will then lead his patrol quickly out of the area – this drill takes no more than a few minutes at the most to complete.

Unplanned ambushes have much in common with the deliberate variety, though they are more ad hoc affairs. It is here that the intense SAS training shows its worth. If, for example, an SAS troop discovers it is being followed by an enemy force, the troop commander will decide to set up an ambush. Thinking on his feet, he will select cut-off positions and deploy his 'killer group'. For ease of command he could simply make two of his four-man patrols cut-offs and make the remaining two patrols his 'killer group'. There is little time for formal orders so the troop will have to stick to its ambush SOPs. As in the

planed ambush, it is up to the troop commander to initiate the firefight and make the crucial decision on when to break contact. With no time to set up FRVs and place rear protection parties, the latter is a risky business.

High standards of training ensure SAS ambush drills have an excellent chance of success. Operations behind enemy lines demand high levels of fieldcraft, discipline and fortitude. Above all, the SAS trains its men to stay hidden when behind the lines. Capture is to be avoided at all costs. Unnecessary contacts with the enemy are avoided as the SAS operates by stealth and cunning.

Above: An SAS patrol rests while searching for enemy guerrillas in Malaya. To operate for long periods behind enemy lines and in small, isolated teams requires great reserves of mental and physical fortitude. Each man must be on constant alert to guard against being surprised by the enemy.

Section V
COUNTER-TERRORIST TACTICS

'I heard someone shout "grenade", and I started to fire my [Heckler & Koch] MP5 at the terrorist, other soldiers opened fire. The terrorist fell to the floor and was lying on his back motionless', was how SAS soldier 'E' described what happened when he burst into a room filled with hostages during the Iranian Embassy siege. A pathologist later reported that the dead terrorist had received 39 firearm wounds. He had been shot in the trunk, both front and back, and in all four limbs.

Successful anti-terrorist operations are quick, violent and often bloody. The SAS has spent 20 years refining its tactics and is considered to be one of the world's foremost practitioners of this 'black' art. An SAS 'Sabre' Squadron is kept on 24-hour stand-by to respond to terrorist incidents anywhere in the world. With highly trained troops at their disposal, SAS commanders are able to deploy the Counter Revolutionary Warfare (CRW) squadron quickly, after only the briefest of orders. Highly practised drills mean all the specialist equipment and weapons the squadron may need are always packed and ready for use.

CONTAINMENT AND ASSESSMENT
When a terrorist incident occurs, the CRW squadron will be alerted and deployed to the scene as quickly as possible. Once at the incident, the squadron commander will make an immediate assessment. In the UK this is a straightforward matter: the SAS establishes a command cell in the police operations room. Senior SAS officers are also present in the emergency Government committee – the Cabinet Office Briefing Room – which handles the incident and has direct access to the Ministers who make the final decision as to whether to deploy the Regiment or not. Overseas, the situation is not so clear. The local government or security forces may have no experiences of dealing with terrorism, and local political considerations may also mean the chain of command at the site is confused.

For hostage incidents the SAS has developed a comprehensive checklist for different events to enable commanders to collect all the information they need to mount a successful rescue: for example, how many hostages are being held; what type of aircraft is involved; how much baggage is in the hold; how much fuel is in the aircraft's tanks. All this information is necessary to get an accurate assessment of the situation. The SAS has standard operating procedures (SOPs) for forcing entry into different types of aircraft, so once the type of aircraft is established the plan will be fairly straightforward. In most sieges the Government will begin negotiations with the terrorists to try to secure the hostages' release without recourse to violence.

ESTABLISHING AN ASSAULT PLAN
If the terrorists start killing the hostages immediately, the SAS commander will initiate his emergency rescue plan. This usually involves nothing more than a direct frontal assault. High casualties among the hostages and rescue team are likely if the emergency plan is used. Once the emergency plan is in place and the negotiators are working on the terrorists, the SAS will begin to plan its rescue in earnest. Detailed intelligence is needed on the locations of the terrorists and hostages inside the aircraft or building; on what they are wearing so they can be recognised instantly during the rescue; and, if possible, detailed psychological profiles on the terrorists and hostages to give the rescue force some idea how they will react if an assault is launched. Of great importance is what weapons the terrorists are carrying and if they have placed grenades or demolition charges near the hostages or in any other places. Observation of the target is one way to collect intelligence on the terrorists, and any released hostages will also be interviewed. This information will be collated by a special intelligence and surveillance detachment with the CRW squadron. The intelligence operatives will also try to get close to the target to make first-hand assessments of likely entry points and the terrorists' deployment.

Special eavesdropping equipment and photographic equipment, such as infrared and image intensifying, can also be used to try to get a clear picture of what is happening inside the hijacked aircraft or seized building. Any

Above right: As well as its hostage-rescue responsibilities, the SAS is also tasked with counter-terrorist duties in Northern Ireland. Laying in wait and springing ambushes on armed IRA terrorists is part of that work. It is a dangerous task. However, when it does go right, as at Loughall in May 1987, the results are spectacular. **Below right:** Black-clad members of 'Pagoda' Troop on the roof of the Iranian Embassy in May 1980, just prior to their assault. Hostage-rescue operations have necessitated the design of specialist clothing and equipment for such work.

Above: The front of the Iranian Embassy, 5 May 1980. Covered by police snipers, SAS soldiers lay their 'frame charge' against the window. Moments later the glass was blown in and the soldiers stormed inside – Operation 'Nimrod' was under way.

release document stating that the control of the incident has been passed to the SAS commander. The latter will then deploy his troops. Once they are in position he will give the order to attack. A cordon of snipers will be placed around the objective to prevent any of the terrorists escaping, and the SAS commander will also have a reserve force on hand in case anything unforeseen happens.

The assault falls into three distinct phases: the approach, the assault, and the hand over to the civil authorities after the operation. To succeed surprise is essential, so a covert approach and diversions are vital factors in any successful hostage-rescue operation.

Aircraft are probably the most difficult targets to assault. They are usually parked on airport runways or taxi-ways, so the rescue team may have to cross hundreds of metres of open ground to reach the objective. A night assault is one way to achieve surprise, another is to approach 'blind spots' under the wings or the tail of aircraft. Aircraft doors are also off the ground, so the assault teams have to carry special ladders to reach them. Foam rubber will be wrapped around the end of the ladders so the terrorist cannot hear them being placed against the aircraft. These were used by the GSG 9 team at Mogadishu in October 1977.

STORMING BUILDINGS

Covertly approaching buildings is slightly easier. SAS teams can abseil off roofs after being dropped onto them by helicopter, or cross over from neighbouring buildings. Blowing out dividing walls is a good way to surprise terrorists and gain entry at the same time. Garden hedges, trees and parked cars also provide good cover for assault teams. If possible, the SAS will stage a diversion to distract the terrorists' attention in the vital seconds before they make their entry. Civil aircraft routes can be changed, for example, to divert them low over the incident and drown out the noise of the assault team. In May 1977, Dutch Marines freed hostages being held on a train by South Moluccan terrorists after the latter had been distracted prior to the assault by Dutch Air Force jets flying low over the train and kicking in their afterburners. The negotiators can also play their part, lulling the terrorists into thinking the authorities are about to agree to their demands, which may result in them dropping their guard.

Entry techniques are numerous and depend on the particular location involved. Aircraft doors are best blown out by specially designed explosives called 'frame charges'. Standard demolition charges are obviously not recommended because of the injuries they would cause to any hostages nearby. Building windows or walls can also be blown out in a

negotiations with the terrorists will be closely monitored to ensure the SAS has up-to-date intelligence on the formers' state of mind (in any siege all telephone services to the building are severed, this is to ensure that all communications go through the negotiators and the terrorists have no access to the media). With accurate intelligence on the target, the SAS commander will formulate his plan and then stage detailed rehearsals at a secure location nearby. If possible, models of the objective will be built to test out assault tactics (one was built for the Iranian Embassy in 1980, for example). Contingency plans will also be developed to deal with any possible counter-moves by the terrorists.

When the SAS commander is happy with his plan he will tell the Government that he is ready to move against the terrorists. Any decision on launching an assault now lies with the police and politicians. Only when they decide that negotiations are fruitless, or any killing begins, will an assault be ordered. In the UK the local police commander will sign a

similarly controlled way. More covert entry methods are also possible, such as removing the putty or screws from windows and doors so all the assault team has to do is push them in. Pump-action shotguns are also used to blast hinges and locks off wooden doors.

Seconds before the assault force soldiers enter the objective, they will throw stun grenades, 'flash bangs', to disorientate everyone inside. These grenades make a loud bang and the magnesium inside then ignites, generating a 50,000 candlepower flash. Some versions of 'flash bangs' produce multiple bursts. To further confuse the terrorists, CS gas grenades can also be thrown into the objective – these were used at Princes Gate by the SAS in 1980. With the terrorists momentarily stunned, the assault force will move into the objective.

Dressed in black flame-resistant suits, balaclavas, body armour and wearing combined respirator/communications equipment, the rescue force is largely protected from the effects of its own stun and CS

grenades. The first objective is to reach the hostages to prevent the terrorists from killing any of them. Where positive intelligence has identified the hostages' location, the SAS will gain entry as close as possible to where they are being held. If their location is unknown, the SAS team will have to sweep through the objective to find them. Normal fighting in built-up areas (FIBUA) drills, involving throwing grenades into rooms before spraying them with submachine gun fire, are obviously not appropriate given the risk to the hostages; rather, the SAS relies on quick reflexes and accurate firepower – this is where the hours spent in the 'Killing House' pays off. SAS CRW training calls for soldiers to be able to differentiate between a terrorist and hostages, then pump the target full of bullets in under four seconds ('double taps', whereby the trooper fires two shots in quick succession, are often insufficient to deal with armed terrorists; accurate and sustained firing puts the target down and keeps him/her down, as well as keeping their hands away from any weapons).

Above: The Toyota van used by the IRA team at Loughall. Raked by hundreds of bullets fired by nearby SAS soldiers, the occupants didn't stand a chance. It was a black day for the IRA – eight of its East Tyrone Brigade was wiped out in the action.

HECKLER & KOCH MP5

The MP5 is the weapon most associated with the modern Special Air Service Regiment. The black-clad SAS troopers armed with MP5s who stormed the Iranian Embassy in 1980 gave the general public an image of the Regiment that will last for years to come.

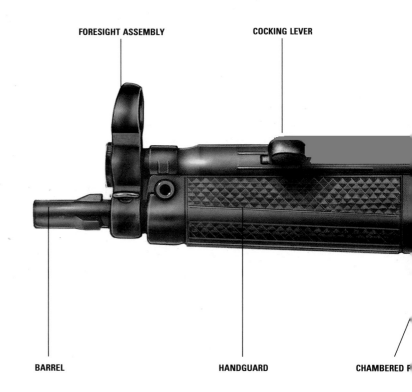

FORESIGHT ASSEMBLY

COCKING LEVER

BARREL

HANDGUARD

CHAMBERED F

HECKLER & KOCH MP5 SPECIFICATIONS

- **TYPE:** submachine gun
- **CALIBRE:** 9mm
- **WEIGHT:** 2.55kg (empty)
- **LENGTH:** 680mm (butt fixed)
- **EFFECTIVE RANGE:** 50m
- **RATE OF FIRE:** 800 rounds per minute (cyclic)
- **FEED:** 15- or 30-round box magazine
- **MUZZLE VELOCITY:** 400 metres per second

The MP5 submachine gun entered SAS service principally because two members of the Regiment saw it in action at close hand. In October 1977, a West German Lufthansa jet was hijacked by terrorists and ended up at Mogadishu airport, Somalia. After the pilot of the aircraft had been executed by the terrorists, the decision was taken to storm it using the GSG 9 anti-terrorist unit that was on the ground at the airport. The unit, led by Ulrich Wegener, was accompanied by two SAS soldiers, Major Alastair Morrison and Sergeant Barry Davies, who helped plan the assault. The aircraft's doors were blown in and the counter-terrorist

soldiers went in, armed with Smith & Wesson handguns and MP5s. Very soon three out of the four terrorists had been killed and the fourth had been severely wounded. All the hostages were freed, only three being wounded. Though the handguns used by GSG 9 were found to have insufficient stopping power during the rescue, the MP5 performed superbly, a fact noted by the two SAS men.

Three years later, the SAS was called upon to mount its own hostage-rescue operation in the centre of the British capital. The Regiment's principal weapon for such tasks had previously been the Ingram submachine gun.

Though it undoubtedly had a high rate of fire, its inaccuracy made it totally unsuited to this kind of work, especially for actions in confined spaces. Fortunately, however, by 1980 the SAS was armed with MP5s. Why is the later such a good weapon?

The most important aspect concerning the MP5 is that it fires from a closed bolt. Many other submachine guns operate with an open bolt – when the trigger is pulled the bolt flies forward to chamber a round – thereby causing a shift in the gun's balance which results in the shot often being off target. However, when the trigger is pulled on the MP5 all that happens is that the hammer is released to fire the cartridge (the MP5 starts with a closed bolt), thus making for much greater accuracy. In addition, because it is so finely engineered, the MP5 is a very reliable weapon. This is very important for hostage-rescue work. The action is invariably over in a matter of seconds and the first shot really does count.

Heckler & Koch produce a number of variants of the MP5, all of which are used by the SAS. There is the MP5A2 and A3 variants which were used at the Iranian Embassy, being identical but for the A3 having a single metal strut stock which is adjustable, whereas the A2 has a fixed butt stock. The MP5SD is the silenced version of the weapon and is designed so that the bullet leaves the

muzzle at subsonic velocity. The MP5K is a weapon specifically designed for counter-terrorist work, being shortened and so easier to wield in confined spaces, and it can also be concealed in clothing or the glove compartments of vehicles. All variants of the MP5 can be set to fire single-shot, full-automatic or, very useful for hostage-rescue work, three-round bursts.

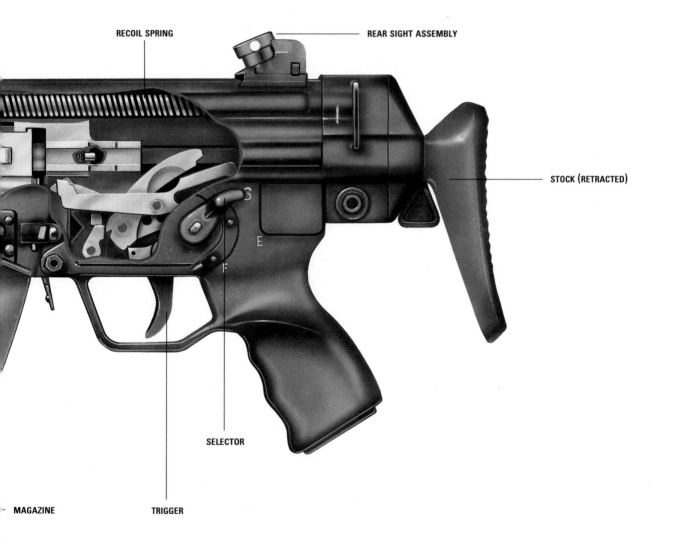

RECOIL SPRING

REAR SIGHT ASSEMBLY

STOCK (RETRACTED)

SELECTOR

MAGAZINE

TRIGGER

What weapons do CRW squadrons use? For hostage-rescue work Heckler & Koch MP5 submachine guns, Remington 870 pump-action shotguns and Browning High Power handguns are employed. The Heckler & Koch MP5 is extremely accurate and reliable. To allow unique high accuracy rounds to be used, a new curved magazine was developed for use with the MP5 to prevent stoppages. To fire baton rounds or CS gas grenades, the Arwen five-shot anti-riot weapon is also available. As a weapon of last resort, each SAS man carries the 9mm Browning which can be used with a silencer. The Browning, while not being the most modern handgun, is renowned for its accuracy at close quarters and stopping power – important considerations during anti-terrorist operations.

When clearing buildings SAS men work in pairs, and each pair is given specific areas to clear. As they enter a room each pair will identify any hostiles and, in around two seconds, neutralise them with sustained fire. When the terrorists are no longer a threat, the SAS men will radio that the room is clear. A sweep through a building is conducted methodically to ensure no terrorists are missed. In an aircraft fuselage killing the terrorists is more difficult. If they duck down between the rows of passenger seats they have to be individually searched for. This cat-and-mouse game takes time and gives the terrorists the opportunity to detonate explosives or shoot hostages. Aircraft fuselages are also very thin, and it is easy for high-velocity rounds to go straight through them and kill or injure people outside the aircraft (any firing will also probably result in injuries to the hostages because of the confined space).

BLOCKING OFF ANY ESCAPE ROUTES

During the rescue all terrorists are shot unless they unambiguously surrender. No chances are taken. If the terrorist is holding a gun or grenade he is presumed to be a threat and dealt with accordingly. Terrorists who fake surrender and then make moves towards concealed weapons are also shot dead. When the SAS commander thinks the besieged building or hijacked aircraft is clear of terrorists, the attention of the rescue force will then turn to quickly evacuating the hostages. They are in great danger as long as they remain at the scene of their ordeal. The terrorists may have placed delayed action charges, or the firefight could have set the building or aircraft on fire.

In the confusion it is common for terrorists to try to escape by hiding among the hostages – this happened at Princes Gate – in the hope that the rescue force will miss them. To guard against this the SAS bind all the hostages with

Far left: A posed shot of IRA terrorists on the streets of West Belfast. Despite having a rather amateur appearance here, the organisation's operatives are armed with sophisticated weaponry and are highly trained. For the SAS, the IRA is a deadly foe.

plastic wrist straps while they are being evacuated. Once in a safe area the released hostages will be closely searched to ensure they are not terrorists. Any terrorists discovered among the hostages are now arrested. Back at the scene of the incident, the rescue force will be administering first aid to any hostages or terrorists who may have been injured in the assault. The final act for the SAS commander is for him to declare all the hostages and terrorists accounted for. Once that is done he turns control of the scene back to the civil authorities.

Keeping one step ahead of terrorist tactics and threats is an uphill struggle. The CRW Wing has the job of making sure that the Regiment wins that struggle. In addition, the Operations Research Wing is responsible for the development and evaluation of different items of kit for hostage-rescue operations. This ensures that SAS troopers are armed and equipped with the best that is available. This can include assault ladders, abseiling harnesses and rope, specialised explosive charges and ammunition, as well as constantly refined assault clothing. Thus, for example, the S6 respirator has now been replaced by the more modern S10 version. The Ops Research Wing maintains the SAS's position as the world's premier anti-terrorist unit.

Section VI
HOSTILE ENVIRONMENTS

In 1952, 22 SAS was reformed to fight the guerrillas of the Malayan Races Liberation Army in Malaya's jungle interior. Over the following 40 years, the Regiment has had to fight its campaigns in some of the world's most hostile environments: jungles, deserts, mountains and arctic wastes. At times fighting the enemy has had to take second place to survival. Being able to operate in harsh terrain is imperative for units such as the SAS, which may be called upon to deploy to the world's most inhospitable environments at a moment's notice. For this reason all the Regiment's soldiers receive training in how to live in hostile regions.

MOUNTAIN AND ARCTIC REGIONS

On 22 April 1982, during the Falklands War, Mountain Troop of D Squadron, under the command of Captain John Hamilton, was tasked with landing on Fortuna Glacier, South Georgia, to establish observation posts (OPs) to gather intelligence on the strengths and dispositions of Argentinian forces. However, the massive glacier was a potential death trap. It had five arms which flowed down into the South Atlantic and was veined with hundreds of deep fissures and pressure ridges. At the top of the glacier, where the weight of the ice pressures downwards, it was comparatively level, but there were also hundreds of 1m-wide crevasses. These could swallow a man up to his waist, though if he was lucky the bulk of his bergen would break the fall. His colleagues would then have to drag him out. In good weather conditions this procedure does not cause too many problems. In sub-zero temperatures and gale force winds it is extremely hazardous.

Three Royal Navy Wessex helicopters flew the SAS men to the glacier just after midday on 21 April. The aircraft had to fly through a driving snowstorm to put the SAS men down on the glacier. As they were unloading their equipment and long, lightweight sleds (*pulks*) from the helicopters, the soldiers were sheltered from the worst of the weather. The helicopters' hot exhaust fumes gave the SAS a deceptive feeling of warmth. When the helicopters lifted off, the 16 SAS soldiers were

hit with the full force of biting 70km/hr winds. They soon realised what they were up against.

Temperatures were dropping rapidly and minutes after landing their weapons were frozen solid. During their short flight over the sea the warm metal of the SAS men's rifles and machine guns had attracted a thin film of water. On exposure to the wind it instantly froze, rending the weapons useless. It was imperative to get off the glacier before nightfall. Groups of men attached themselves to *pulks*, loaded with food and ammunition (some weighed up to 150kg), before moving off. As a basic safety precaution each group of three or four men was roped together. In a rising gale the men edged slowly forward. Within a few metres they came to a halt as the first man fell into a crevasse.

The ice surface of the glacier was covered with a light sprinkling of snow, which gathered in the crevasses. In some cases the SAS men could see the indentations in the snow, but others were only detected when the lead man plunged unexpectedly through the crust of snow. After a man fell through the ice, his colleagues would anchor him with ice axes before pulling him free. This was happening every 50m. Progress was at a snail's pace. By nightfall the SAS had travelled only one kilometre. The SAS found the 'least' exposed part of the glacier and dug snow holes for the night. Some soldiers tried to put up three-man tents, but they did not survive in the gale. Facing the threat of his men getting frostbite, Hamilton had no choice but to request immediate evacuation for the morning.

THE KILLER COLD

Mountain and arctic regions are characterised by cold weather and wind, the two together resulting in windchill which can freeze exposed flesh in minutes. To survive in such regions requires the correct clothing and the ability to get out of the wind when required. SAS soldiers are therefore equipped with windproof and waterproof clothing which covers the whole body. The key to keeping warm is the so-called 'layer system', whereby layers of clothing are added or taken away depending on the temperature and level of

Above right: A Long Range Desert Group (LRDG) patrol on the move in North Africa during World War II. During the early stages of its campaign in North Africa, the SAS used LRDG trucks to transport its men to targets. As well as the searing heat and the dangers of sand and dust storms, military forces are extremely exposed in the desert during daylight hours, particularly to enemy aircraft.

Below right: Sending a radio message during the Malayan campaign. The oppressive humidity of this environment results in men becoming tired very quickly. SAS soldiers required high levels of stamina to operate for long periods in the jungle.

Right: A Royal Marine moves up an ice wall in Norway. The cold, combined with strong winds, makes polar regions very hostile to military operations. Fingers and toes can be lost through frostbite and exposed flesh can become frozen in minutes. The correct clothing is essential for fighting in such conditions.

activity. Materials such as Gore-tex are worn which keep water out but allow moisture to escape (if trapped inside the garment, sweat cools very quickly in the arctic). Other items of kit worn include mittens, face masks, ski boots, snow shoes and skis. Keeping weapons in working order in these conditions means removing all unnecessary lubricants because in extremely cold conditions lubricants thicken, causing jams and sluggish actions. Therefore only the camming surfaces of the bolt are lubricated, the rest is left dry. Similarly, ammunition has to be cleaned of all oil, ice and condensation.

As the key to surviving in these environments is to get out of the wind and create a warm atmosphere, all SAS troopers receive training in how to construct shelters: snow holes, igloos and snow caves. In addition, they receive extensive instruction in ski techniques and navigation in arctic conditions.

SURVIVING IN THE DESERT

A different climatic situation was encountered by the SAS in the deserts of South Arabia during the 1960s and 1970s. During daylight the heat in these regions is unbearable. The heat and wind soon crack open the lips of Europeans. At night it is freezing cold. The people who have lived in these areas since biblical times are some of the poorest people in the Middle East. They exist off their goat herds and water is their most valuable commodity. The few streams or water holes therefore have great strategic value.

The region has little similarity to the deserts of the northern Arabian peninsula, with their shifting sands and featureless terrain. Fitness is the key to survival in the mountains, along with plentiful supplies of water. For soldiers manning well-supplied base camps water is not a problem; on a patrol deep into the mountains water becomes a matter of life and death.

In the desert SAS patrols have to balance their need for firepower and water (individuals often carry around 200 rounds of ammunition for the patrol's machine gun, in addition to over 500 rounds for their personal weapon). To survive in the heat soldiers need at least nine litres of water a day. Water replenishment in the field is usually impossible. The only sources of re-supply for patrols, therefore, are streams and water holes.

Proper clothing is imperative for desert warfare. During the day it must protect the wearer from the sun, at night it must keep him warm, and at all times it must be a barrier against bites and scratches (which can become infected very quickly). Headgear is essential to prevent sunburn and sunstroke, an Arab *shemagh* (headdress) is perfect for this because it can also protect the eyes, nose, mouth and

neck. Similarly, the correct footwear is also very important, the feet must be covered and protected from the sun. Weapons and ammunition must also be saved from the ravages of the sun which means regular cleaning and the removal of oil from the working parts (sand and oil do not mix!).

JUNGLE WARFARE

Jungle survival techniques are very different to those employed in the desert. Navigation in the thick jungles of Malaya and Borneo, for example, was a major problem for SAS teams. Aerial photographs or maps, if they existed, would be studied to find the landmarks such as rivers, streams or ridges. They would be matched to compass bearings by patrol commanders to allow them to be identified on the ground. To follow a compass bearing march through a jungle was a team effort. One of the patrol had to count paces to work out how far it had travelled. In thick jungle the lead man had to use his machete to clear a path which was often a painfully slow business. Each patrol member had to take turns because of the physical exertion involved. The high humidity made moving in the jungle exhausting, even without the added burden of having to cut a path through it. Water consumption was phenomenal, perhaps more than in the desert. Fortunately in the jungle their was plenty of water, even if it did contain very unhealthy organisms.

For SAS patrols on three-week patrols deep into the jungles of Borneo re-supply was difficult. They had to live on dehydrated rations yielding only 3500 calories per day. Weight loss was incredible. When some patrols returned to base they were almost skin and bone. It was estimated that even hardened SAS men could only endure three of these patrols before needing to be sent back to England for recuperation. In their weakened states SAS soldiers were very vulnerable to tropical diseases. Modern medicine has developed protection from many diseases, but in the unhygienic conditions encountered by troops in the jungle these are often of little use. Even the smallest cut would soon become infected in the jungle because it was almost impossible to keep it clean and dry (everything thrives in the jungle, including germs). Immediate evacuation by helicopter was essential if the victims of gunshot wounds, for example, were to survive.

Swamps proved a major hazard. The part of the body immersed in water was soon attacked by blood-sucking leeches which could consume up to a quarter litre of blood if not discovered quickly. A lighted cigarette had to be applied to the creature to get it to withdraw cleanly from the body. Malaria mosquitoes

would attack the part of the body above the water. Other animal threats include snakes, scorpions and insects.

Specialist clothing and equipment are essential for jungle warfare. The skin must be protected from bites and scratches which can become infected, this means rubber and canvas jungle boots, lightweight cotton shirts and trousers, and headgear. Because of the high humidity clothing can rot very quickly in the jungle. Therefore quick-drying cotton material is worn by troopers, though even this

will eventually rot because it is impossible to keep anything dry, including bodies, in the jungle (sweaty groins can result in fungal infections). All troopers are briefed on the need to maintain the highest levels of personal hygiene and to get immunisation against such things as malaria and dengue fever.

Troopers are also taught how to construct shelters from bamboo, rattan and palm fronds, though they will also carry ponchos with them which can be used to make 'bashas'. As in the desert and arctic, weapons need special

Left: With a Twin Pioneer aircraft in the background, SAS soldiers try to fix a Land Rover in Oman during the 1970s Dhofar campaign. Dust and sand get into everything in the desert, resulting in the frequent breakdown of machinery. Note the soldiers are all well covered. In the desert it is very important to protect flesh from the sun and thus prevent sunburn and sunstroke.

attention if they are to work properly, this means they have to be stripped and thoroughly cleaned every night.

SAS soldiers frequently train in the Middle East, the Far East and in the jungles of Brunei, as well as Norway and the arctic. These deployments ensure that the Regiment's squadrons have a high level of experience of fighting in hostile environments. There is also a great deal of cross-training with units such as the Royal Marines, the Gurkhas and US Green Berets.

Being able to fight and survive in some of the world's most hostile environments is a vital skill for the Regiment's soldiers, just as important as weapons expertise or physical stamina. The ability to live off the land when there is seemingly only a barren landscape, to construct shelters out of the most primitive materials, and navigate across the scorching, featureless desert and arctic wastes, are the skills that place the SAS above other units, when allied to the determination and physical fitness of its soldiers.

CHAPTER 4

WEAPONS AND EQUIPMENT

• SMALL ARMS

• SUPPORT WEAPONS

• LAND VEHICLES

• BOATS AND AIRCRAFT

'WITH ALL GUNS COCKED WE APPROACHED THE SILHOUETTED AIRCRAFT, AND AS WE CAME ALONGSIDE THE FIRST ONE, THE VICKERS "K's" OPENED UP WITH A MIXTURE OF TRACER, ARMOUR-PIERCING AND EXPLOSIVE BULLETS. I WAS MANNING THE FORWARD SINGLE VICKERS AND OUR REAR GUNNER HAD THE TWINS.'

JOHNNY COOPER, NORTH AFRICA, 1942

Section I
SMALL ARMS

The SAS has a surprising variety of personal weapons at its disposal, many more than the rest of the Army. This small, elite unit has a special dispensation to bypass the laborious trials and purchasing procedure that the Army normally undertakes. Many sources refer to the SAS trooper being allowed to choose any weapon he likes. This is not quite true. An SAS soldier has certainly more choice than the average infantryman, but there are still limits to what is available. What he can do though is select, within limits, the best weapon for his current mission. While personal preferences are considered important, the patrol or troop must have the correct mix of weapons to carry out its mission.

Any military weapon must have some, or all, of the characteristics listed below, but no one design can fulfil all wants. When selecting a weapon for a specific task, the SAS soldier has to analyse his mission then decide which of these requirements are vital and which can be compromised.

RELIABILITY FIRST AND FOREMOST

The most important prerequisite for an SAS weapon is reliability. In battle a regular infantryman will usually be surrounded by his comrades who will still be shooting if his own weapon jams. If an SAS man is in combat, he will be part of a small team or may even be on his own, thus a stoppage can be fatal. It is, therefore, better to have a weapon that will work every time rather than a superb precision instrument that is likely to jam at a vital moment.

Associated with reliability is ruggedness. SAS patrols must be prepared to operate anywhere in the world, perhaps for months at a time. They may also be hundreds of kilometres away from their own forces, with no chance of weapons being repaired or replaced. In these circumstances, their small arms must be tough enough to survive rough handling, and to remain functional in dry sand and dust, freezing snow and ice, or humid jungle. Ideally, cleaning and maintenance should also be simple, with the minimum of small fiddly components for a tired soldier to lose or break.

When Counter Revolutionary Warfare (CRW) operations are undertaken, this requirement is less important. The SAS team will normally be based in a well-equipped barracks or headquarters building, going into the field for short periods for specific operations. In these circumstances, weapons can be carefully maintained and cleaned in a comfortable environment (one reason why the precision-built Heckler & Koch MP5 is used for such work).

A soldier must be able to hit his target. Many factors influence accuracy including barrel length, ammunition size, ammunition power, rate of fire and the sighting system. A large, powerful round fired from a highly rifled barrel, for example, will fly straighter than a lightweight one. The interaction between firer and weapon is vital – if a gun is awkward or uncomfortable to shoot, the soldier is unlikely to use it well. For example, the 7.62mm rifles that most NATO forces used until recently are all superbly accurate weapons with ranges of many hundreds of metres. Their disadvantage is that they are heavy, with a noticeable recoil. Most countries are now changing to smaller 5.56mm weapons which are not as accurate beyond 400m. What armies have found, however, is that these weapons' light weight, low recoil and quieter report make them easier to use, enabling trainee soldiers to learn accurate shooting more quickly than before.

Accuracy may not be the prime requirement for many SAS operations. If a sabotage team is operating behind enemy lines, its weapons are largely for self-defence. In this case, reliability and rapid firepower are more important. A hostage-rescue operation, however, demands accurate fire to avoid hitting innocent people.

STOPPING POWER

A weapon must also be sufficiently powerful to kill or disable its target. Lighter weapons firing small calibre rounds, such as the 5.56mm M16, may need multiple hits to be sure of putting a enemy soldier out of action, especially if he is wearing body armour. Again, the individual mission should be considered. If weapons are carried for self-defence or if engagement ranges are likely to be short, a smaller calibre is fine. However, for long-range combat a larger round may be required, which means a heavier, larger weapon. Conventional ammunition (7.62mm and 9mm) can sometimes travel straight through the body without inflicting enough damage to instantly disable a determined adversary, i.e. to stop him. The SAS feels that it is essential to neutralise a hostage-holding terrorist with the first shot, so

Previous pages: The Heckler & Koch MP5 submachine gun. Used by the SAS primarily for hostage-rescue operations, it is a finely engineered weapon that is extremely reliable.
Above right: An example of SAS kit in Malaya. Note the weapons: M1 Carbine and Owen submachine gun.
Below right: The M16 is a weapon that is well-suited to close-range work, having a high muzzle velocity. However, for long-range work its 5.56mm round has been found to be wanting.

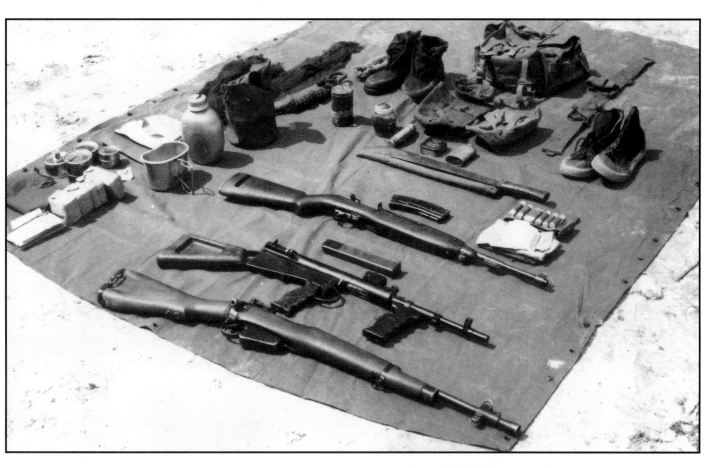

STEN GUN

Cheap, nasty and crude are all adjectives that can be applied to the Sten gun. Nevertheless, it performed well enough and the SAS used it widely throughout the war, especially in the weeks and months after the D-Day landings of June 1944.

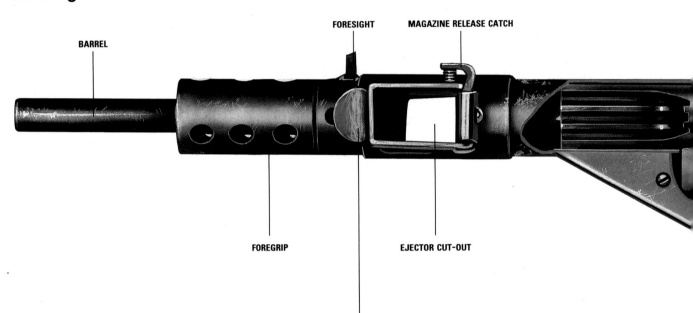

FORESIGHT   MAGAZINE RELEASE CATCH

BARREL

FOREGRIP   EJECTOR CUT-OUT

HOUSING ASSEMBLY CATCH

STEN GUN SPECIFICATIONS
- **TYPE: submachine gun**
- **CALIBRE: 9mm**
- **WEIGHT: 3.70kg**
- **LENGTH: 762mm**
- **EFFECTIVE RANGE: 40m**
- **RATE OF FIRE: 550 rounds per minute (cyclic)**
- **FEED: 32-round box magazine**
- **MUZZLE VELOCITY: 365 metres per second**

In World War II SAS soldiers, along with other special forces units on both sides, wanted weapons that had two main attributes: handiness and firepower. In most firefights SAS patrols, because of the nature of behind-the-lines, small-sized units, were invariably outnumbered. However, if they could lay down a barrage of fire that was heavier than the enemy then they could come out on top, or at least have the means to cover a hasty retreat. The standard bolt-action rifles of the infantry, though accurate and

firing a bullet with considerable range and stopping power which drilled a large hole in its target, did not have enough firepower. This is the reason SAS soldiers favoured machine guns and submachine guns, especially the latter. Their lethality at short ranges often tipped the scales.

After Dunkirk in 1940 the British Army found it had few weapons, as most had been left behind in France. It therefore needed to re-arm quickly to face the apparently impending German invasion. A request was therefore sent out for a

simple submachine gun which could be produced in great quantities very quickly. Within weeks two men named Shepherd and Turpin who worked at the Enfield Lock Small Arms Factory had come up with a design – the Sten gun was born. It certainly fulfilled all the criteria laid down by the Army.

The Sten had two main components: a pipe and a bedspring! In fact, it had been designed to be produced as cheaply as possible, with simple tools and a minimum of machining. The whole gun was held together by welds,

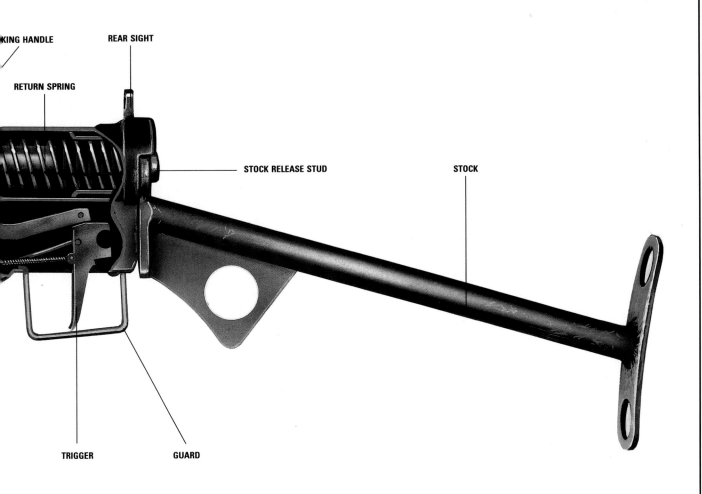

KING HANDLE

REAR SIGHT

RETURN SPRING

STOCK RELEASE STUD

STOCK

TRIGGER

GUARD

pins and bolts. Over 100,000 of the Mark I version were produced in a matter of months – testimony to the simplicity of the production process. The 'archetypal' Sten was the Mark II version which was all-metal, having a steel butt instead of a wooden one. It could also be quickly broken down into three parts (barrel, magazine and butt) which made it easy to conceal. This attribute made it an ideal weapon to be dropped to the French Resistance in large quantities, and very soon the Germans came to fear the Sten. Despite

its ungainly appearance, it was an effective killing device. After all, a bullet from a Sten was just as deadly as those fired from more elaborate weapons.

A silenced version, called the Sten Mk IIS, was produced in small numbers for Commando and raiding forces. However, SAS troops mostly used the standard versions of the weapon. They were also involved in training French Resistance (*Maquis*) fighters in the use of the Sten, a relatively easy task as the weapon was extremely simple. It was not particularly accurate and its

magazine often caused stoppages, and given the choice most SAS soldiers would have had a Thompson or German MP40. However, the Sten did have some good points: it was virtually indestructible; it required almost no lubrication; and it was easy to strip and maintain. Not surprisingly, the Sten was not used by SAS units after 1945. Despite its crude looks and bad points, the weapons filled a much-needed requirement and was invaluable for arming large numbers of Resistance fighters in the weeks after D-Day.

Above: Soldiers, including an SAS member, being trained in the use of foreign-made weapons. The Regiment puts great emphasis on its members being able to fire foreign weapons, particularly Soviet and Chinese models. This means patrols operating behind the lines can use the enemy's models if need be.

more advanced ammunition is used in such a situation. There are many types available, but in essence all variants work on similar principles. The idea is to transfer all the energy from the round into the target, causing massive shock and trauma to the body. Some rounds have unusual shapes to cause more damage to body tissue, others flatten or shatter on impact. The disadvantage of such rounds is that if a hostage is hit by accident they will almost certainly be killed instantly, an added incentive, therefore, for SAS teams to get their counter-terrorist drills right.

In some situations the quantity of rounds fired is important. If a patrol is ambushed, for example, it would want to lay down a short, heavy barrage to keep enemy heads down long enough to make an escape. Here, automatic weapons with large magazines and high rates of fire are desirable. If a team is acting in the fire support role, then it will need to put down heavy firepower at key points while their comrades are moving. In this situation, belt-fed machine guns are the best option. This is

where small calibre rounds have the advantage, as their light weight means that more ammunition can be carried, though this has to be balanced against the range and stopping power of a larger bullet.

A powerful, accurate, rugged and reliable weapon with great firepower inevitably means it will be heavy. It is here that the compromises and trade-offs in weapon design have most effect. If an SAS patrol is to operate in remote country or behind enemy lines, it will normally have to travel great distances on foot. Everything the soldiers need – food, clothing, radios, special equipment, weapons and ammunition – will thus have to be man-handled on their backs. A rifle that is a kilo or so heavier than it need be can turn into a nightmare load after a few hundred kilometres. A heavy rifle usually means that heavy, large calibre ammunition also has to be carried, and the weight of this limits the number of rounds which can be hauled. In such a situation, firepower and accuracy may have to compromised for lighter weight.

Another consideration especially important to special forces is the 'signature' or 'profile' of a weapon. In many situations, such as a night attack, a weapon with a loud report or large muzzle flash may not be desirable. The SAS has the option of using specially modified silenced weapons, such as the L34A1 Sterling submachine gun, where circumstances dictate. These weapons are also compromises, as the silencer usually absorbs much of the energy from the bullet, reducing the effective range of the weapon. Conversely, a patrol may want to make as much noise and cause as much confusion as possible, either as a diversionary tactic or in an ambush. Again, rapid automatic fire is useful in such a situation.

ASSAULT RIFLES

When on undercover or bodyguard duties, troopers need a weapon that is small, easy to conceal and can be brought to bear quickly, without a complicated loading or safety action. A handgun, such as the Browning High Power, fulfils this requirement.

A characteristic which is not often discussed is deniability. One reason for using the M16 in cross-border operations in Borneo was that it was not a standard British Army weapon. Spent cartridge cases or bullets found by the Indonesians could not be used to prove official British involvement. Leaving aside Irish Republican Army (IRA) accusations of SAS 'murder' squads, there is little concrete evidence that the SAS holds unusual weapons for such reasons today. There was an interesting report in the press in early 1992, however, that the British Government had been behind an attempt to buy a quantity of Czech-made Skorpion machine pistols which are tiny, easily concealable automatic weapons popular with terrorists and bodyguards.

Another aspect which must be considered is that of cost. While the SAS is able to procure weapons and equipment that is unavailable to the rest of the Army, it is not given carte blanche to purchase anything that takes its fancy. Every weapon must be justified operationally, and even then budgetary considerations may prohibit acquisition.

The basic infantryman's weapon is the rifle. Military rifles are nearly all self-loading: if a round is fired, the case is automatically ejected

Below: The Colt Commando, a carbine version of the M16 assault rifle. Compact weapons are a great asset to special forces as they can be brought to bear quickly and can be used in confined spaces.

L1A1 Self-Loading Rifle

The Belgian-designed SLR has been one of the most successful post-war rifle designs in the world. In service since the mid-1950s, the rifle has been widely used by the SAS in its campaigns.

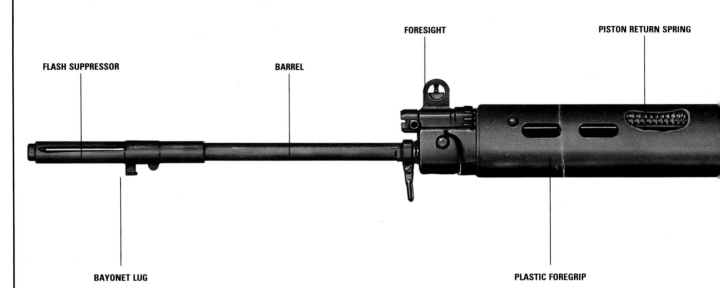

FORESIGHT

PISTON RETURN SPRING

FLASH SUPPRESSOR

BARREL

BAYONET LUG

PLASTIC FOREGRIP

L1A1 SELF-LOADING RIFLE SPECIFICATIONS
- **TYPE:** self-loading rifle
- **CALIBRE:** 7.62mm
- **WEIGHT:** 5kg (with full magazine)
- **LENGTH:** 1143mm
- **EFFECTIVE RANGE:** 600m
- **RATE OF FIRE:** single shot
- **FEED:** 20-round box magazine
- **MUZZLE VELOCITY:** 838 metres per second

Designed by the Belgian firm FN Nouvelle Herstal SA, this rifle was originally produced in 1948. It is a no-nonsense weapon that is made throughout from high-grade materials with much attention to fine tolerances and machining. It works on the gas system, whereby a gas regulation system taps off propellant gases from above the barrel to operate a piston that pushes back the bolt action for unlocking the breech. Automatic fire is possible on most models, though not those in service with the British Army, by use of a selector mechanism located near the trigger group.

The British version of the gun is designated L1A1 and was adopted for use by the UK only after extensive trials and modifications that saw the abandonment of the automatic fire feature. However, one important virtue the British Self-Loading Rifle (SLR) retained was the overall robustness of the weapon. This means the SLR is well able to withstand the rigours of the battlefield and general service life. It is, therefore, a weapon that endeared itself quickly to the SAS. The latter was not only attracted to its ruggedness but also to the range and stopping power of its 7.62mm round – when a man was hit by an SLR bullet he tended to stay down. The absence of the full-automatic facility did not trouble the SAS unduly, though individual troopers did try to get hold of M16s if they could, especially for jungle operations where firefights are often short and vicious.

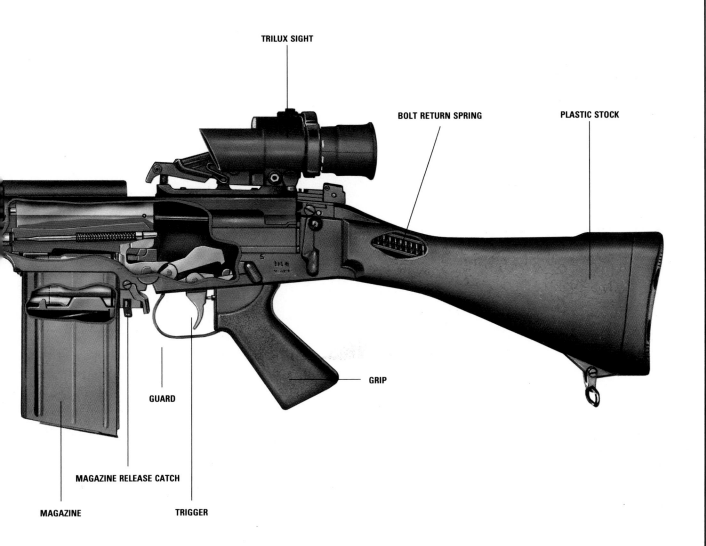

TRILUX SIGHT

BOLT RETURN SPRING

PLASTIC STOCK

GRIP

GUARD

MAGAZINE RELEASE CATCH

MAGAZINE

TRIGGER

The SLR appeared towards the end of the British campaign in Malaya (1948-60) and it was carried by SAS soldiers during that campaign. They also used it in Borneo when called upon to defend the area from Indonesian incursions. The use of the SLR in jungle conditions is interesting as the weapon, owing to its length, is not ideally suited to a jungle environment. In addition, the range of its 7.62mm round is really wasted in a terrain characterised by short-range visibility. Nevertheless,

SAS troopers liked the weapon enough to retain it for jungle use and found it performed almost as well as other, shorter models such as the M16. In Aden (1964-67) and Oman (1970-76) SAS soldiers found the SLR came into its own as its long-range accuracy allowed individuals to seek out targets of opportunity at great ranges. Another notable attribute of the SLR is its ability to work in any terrain, from the jungles of the Far East to the desert and the freezing conditions of the arctic. All in

all, the SLR is an excellent rifle and is not due to be phased out of British service until 1994.

In line with current military thinking regarding assault rifles, FN now produces a 5.56mm version of the weapon which is called the FNC. The latter was actually produced with SAS-type units in mind, being intended for use by troops who are operating without continuous logistical support. The FNC has allegedly been used by members of the Regiment.

and the next round pushed into place, ready to be fired. There are two main calibres in use. The traditional calibre is 7.62mm, used as standard by most NATO countries and others from the 1960s to the mid-1980s. 7.62mm rounds are powerful – they will put a man down at ranges of over 600m. The basic 7.62mm rifle in SAS service is the British Army L1A1 Self-Loading Rifle (SLR). Described in detail elsewhere, the SLR is a rugged and reliable weapon. It is somewhat heavy, however, and is cumbersome for urban or jungle conflict or for carrying in a vehicle. The SLR only fires single shots, but one hit is usually sufficient to disable or kill a man. The SLR is popular with the SAS, especially where long-range combat is anticipated. The rifle normally has a 20-round magazine, though it can accommodate the 30-round box used in the 7.62mm Light Machine Gun (LMG). Although being withdrawn from frontline service in the rest of the Army, the SLR will remain in SAS service for many years to come. The weapon underwent something of a renaissance in the Gulf War, where targets often needed to be engaged at long ranges.

The SLR was developed from the Belgian FN FAL rifle, the main difference being that the FN can fire fully-automatic. The Argentinians in the Falklands War were equipped with FNs, thereby allowing British soldiers to use captured ammunition. Some folding-stock FNs found their way into British use as war booty, and the SAS acquired its share of the spoils. The folding stock makes a handier weapon for vehicle crews or parachutists, and burst fire from a 30-round magazine can turn it into a makeshift LMG substitute.

SAS HECKLER & KOCHS

Another 7.62mm rifle sometimes seen in SAS hands, especially in Northern Ireland, is the Heckler & Koch G3. This is the standard rifle of the German Army and is in service with over 30 other nations worldwide. Similar in concept to the SLR, it uses an unusual bolt locking system derived from German World War II designs. The G3 is extremely accurate and reliable, though it demands a high level of maintenance and does not stand up to rough treatment as well as the SLR. The G3, which can fire single shots or bursts, uses the same ammunition as its British counterpart.

Most countries are replacing their 7.62mm weapons with smaller calibre 5.56mm equipment. Lower-powered rounds were introduced by the Germans towards the end of World War II after analysis of combat results indicated that most actions took place at ranges below 300m. They reasoned that powerful rifle rounds were largely wasted and so developed an intermediate cartridge and an automatic rifle to shoot it. This was dubbed the assault rifle, and was expected to replace the rifle, submachine gun and light machine gun with a single weapon. Many countries have since followed similar reasoning, to a greater or lesser degree. After the war, experiments were undertaken with smaller calibre rounds, again optimised for short and medium ranges. The first such weapon to enter service was the American M16, described in detail elsewhere. Its 5.56mm round is designed to 'tumble' once it hits, inflicting injury out of all proportion to its size. However, there are reported instances from Vietnam and the Falklands where enemy soldiers took multiple hits from M16s but still continued to fight on. Nevertheless, the M16 has been a popular weapon with the SAS, being light, accurate and effective at the ranges that count. The M16 requires careful cleaning and maintenance, as the American Army found out in Vietnam. Here, poor weapons maintenance and training caused the M16 to gain a reputation for being unreliable and prone to jamming. As the Americans eventually realised, the M16 needs to be looked after if it is to look after its user.

COLT COMMANDO AND SA-80

There is also a shorter variant known as the Model 733 Colt Commando. Combining the length of a submachine gun with the firepower of a rifle, the Commando is favoured by units such as the SAS. Its only disadvantages are relative inaccuracy and a large muzzle flash, though some special forces soldiers like the morale-boosting effect of this flash and its associated loud report.

The British Army is in the process of introducing a 5.56mm assault rifle of its own, the L85A1 Individual Weapon System. As detailed elsewhere, this light, accurate weapon, also called SA-80, is of an unusually advanced design. Its 'bullpup' design (where the magazine, chamber and mechanism are behind the trigger and grip) gives a much reduced overall length compared to conventional rifles. The SA-80 has suffered from persistent complaints about reliability problems and difficulties with maintenance and cleaning. Teething problems are inevitable with any new weapon, though the rifle has been through a long and detailed evaluation and development programme. The SA-80 uses the SS109 bullet, a heavier and more effective round than the original M193 fired by the M16. Later model M16s are also designed to use the SS109. The SAS does not seem to have taken to the new weapon. Reports from the Gulf War indicate that the M16 is still its 5.56mm weapon of choice, together with the tried and trusted SLR.

Far left: Two weapons that have seen extensive service with the Regiment: the SLR and Sterling submachine gun. The latter has been in British Army use for nearly 40 years. Despite this, there is no sign of it being phased out. The silenced version, the L34A1, is particularly favoured by the SAS for work in Northern Ireland.

ENFIELD L85A1 SA-80

The bullpup SA-80 is the new individual weapon of the British Army and the SAS. Following some initial problems, it has settled down to become a good replacement for the SLR.

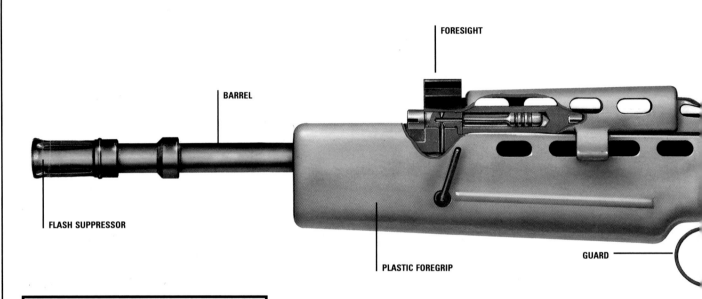

FORESIGHT

BARREL

FLASH SUPPRESSOR

PLASTIC FOREGRIP

GUARD

ENFIELD L85A1 SA-80 SPECIFICATIONS
- **TYPE:** assault rifle
- **CALIBRE:** 5.56mm
- **WEIGHT:** 4.98kg (with full magazine and sight)
- **LENGTH:** 785mm
- **EFFECTIVE RANGE:** 300m
- **RATE OF FIRE:** 650-800 rounds per minute (cyclic)
- **FEED:** 30-round box magazine
- **MUZZLE VELOCITY:** 940 metres per second

Initial deliveries of the SA-80 assault rifle, designated L85A1, were made in 1984 and, reportedly, the SAS was one of the first units of the British Army to receive them. This raises an interesting question: did the Regiment use them in the 1991 Gulf War against Iraq? At present there is no way of telling. However, it would seem reasonable to suggest that the SA-80 has been used operationally by the SAS, if not in the Middle East then in Northern Ireland.

The rifle has had what can be termed a 'bad press' since it entered service, and it has still not shaken off a number of criticisms. For example, the magazines fell off the early models when a soldier ran with it while slung across his chest because the magazine catch was positioned badly. These teething problems have, for the most part, apparently been ironed out and what is left is a weapon that is light, easy to handle, has a low recoil and

excellent sights, and one that is capable or semi- or full-automatic fire.

Its bullpup design makes it easy to handle in the confines of buildings, helicopters and armoured personnel carriers, the latter two important considerations for the infantry soldier of the twenty-first century. The design of the rifle is certainly markedly different when compared to the other standard-issue rifles of the British Army this century. It has a straight plastic foregrip

PLASTIC STOCK

BUTT PLATE

MAGAZINE
RELEASE CATCH

MAGAZINE

and pistol grip with the butt and backstop being integral with the trigger housing. It is also fitted with a 4x telescopic sight as standard, but retains fixed open sights as a backup. In addition, the muzzle is fitted with a flash suppressor which can also accept a bayonet and a variety of rifle grenades. It is a conventional gas-operated weapon that is fed by a 30-round magazine, being able to fire the M193 ball and the heavier SS109 steel-core round.

The Light Support Weapon (LSW) is a squad automatic variant of the SA-80. It does not have a quick-change barrel, though. As it is fed from a 30-round magazine, over-heating from sustained fire is not a problem.

The SA-80 is a weapon that is ideally suited to SAS operations, being light, easy to wield and having good accuracy up to a range of 300m. Though this is significantly less than the range of the rifle it is replacing, the SLR, this

cannot be helped as the 5.56mm round is generally less powerful than its 7.62mm counterpart. This may present problems for SAS teams conducting operations in the desert or terrain which allows long-range visibility; indeed, this drawback may have already been encountered in the Gulf. Nevertheless, on the plus side it is lighter than the SLR and considerations of weight are always a top priority for special forces units.

Other rifles have been seen in SAS use, though often only in small quantities for evaluation purposes. The Austrian Steyr AUG, for example, has accompanied some SAS patrols. This advanced technology weapon has a largely plastic frame, with an integral sight built into the carrying handle. Light, robust (it

accuracy well ahead of conventional assault rifles. If the technology can be made rugged and reliable enough for service use, a weapon based on the G11 may eventually see SAS service. However, as yet there are no takers for the G11. The German Army, for reasons of cost, has temporarily cancelled its order.

Above: When an M203 grenade launcher is fitted to an M16 assault rifle, as here, the result is a potent combination of firepower. For small-sized units grenade launchers can be significant force multipliers.

can survive being under the wheels of armoured vehicles) and effective, it is one of the most innovative of current assault rifles.

An interesting new development is the Heckler & Koch G11 rifle, a weapon that looks as if it should be on the set of science fiction movie. The G11 fires an unusual round which has no cartridge case – the bullet is sunk into propellant which is sufficiently rigid to require no container. As there is no need to extract an empty case, the rifle uses a patent rotary firing chamber which gives a very high rate of fire. The whole mechanism and barrel are spring mounted within a plastic casing. A three-round burst can be fired before this unit recoils against the casing, giving a level of

SUBMACHINE GUNS

Submachine guns (SMG) were originally designed for close-quarter trench combat and have been in use since the end of the World War I. Smaller and lighter than rifles, they normally use pistol rounds, the most common being the 9mm Parabellum. This has immense stopping power but is limited in range. Large numbers of bullets (normally around 30) are carried in detachable magazines, giving heavy short-range firepower. With the advent of the assault rifle, the SMG was expected to fade away into obsolescence. This it has failed to do. Short and light, these weapons are still retained for close-range work and self-defence. Units such as the SAS have found that SMGs, because of their high firepower and compact size, are particularly well-suited to counter-terrorist and hostage-rescue work.

The L2A3 Sterling is the standard British Army SMG which is used for self-defence by signallers and support troops. A well-made, reliable, if not especially accurate, weapon, it has been in service with the SAS for many years. The L34 variant has a built-in silencer arrangement, with a thick suppressor arranged around the barrel. Silencers absorb much of the energy of the expanding gases from a fired

it remains probably the finest weapon of its class. The MP5 is used by many of the world's top anti-terrorist teams and exists in a number of variants, some of which include integral silencers. The MP5 fires the normal 9mm Parabellum round, though special ammunition is often used for anti-terrorist missions.

During the 1970s the SAS used the Ingram Model 10 SMG to arm its hostage-rescue teams, but these have now been withdrawn. A tiny, easily concealed weapon, the Ingram is popular with bodyguards and is often used by

cartridge, reducing the report from the weapon. Most normal ammunition is supersonic and a silencer has no effect on the sharp crack thus caused. To be truly silent, a weapon needs to use special ammunition and the suppressor is normally an integral part of the design. The L34 is useful for night ambushes because, even if the enemy hears the report, the quiet popping sound is much harder to locate than the crack from an unsuppressed weapon.

Used by special forces around the world, and perhaps the symbol of SAS counter-terrorist operations, is the German-designed Heckler & Koch MP5 SMG. This superbly made weapon fires from a closed bolt, making it as accurate as a rifle up to a range of 100m. Ideal for precise shooting at close quarters, it requires careful maintenance and lacks the ruggedness for extended operations in harsh environments. When it is highly maintained, however,

organised criminal gangs and assassins. The short barrel and ferocious rate of fire made it insufficiently accurate for hostage-rescue work and it has now been replaced in SAS service by the MP5. However, the Regiment still uses the Ingram for counter-terrorist work in Ulster, attracted by its size and high rate of fire. A few Israeli Uzis have also been used by the SAS, though more for evaluation purposes than for actual operations.

HANDGUNS

Semi-automatic handguns are still favoured for close-range work and are carried as backup weapons by CRW teams. The SAS normally uses the standard-issue Browning 9mm High Power handgun, models of which have been in British service for over 40 years. The Browning carries up to 13 rounds in its magazine and weighs around .88kg. Its 9mm Parabellum ammunition may not give quite

Above: A soldier map reading on Dartmoor equipped with an SA-80 assault rifle. The latter is the new individual weapon of the British Army. Although, light and compact, it has been bedevilled by teething problems. Early reports suggest the SAS has not taken kindly to it.

FRANCHI SPAS 15

The shotguns produced by the Italian firm Luigi Franchi are ideal for law enforcement purposes. They can deliver a devastating amount of firepower and, importantly for the counter-terrorist unit, can fire a variety of munitions.

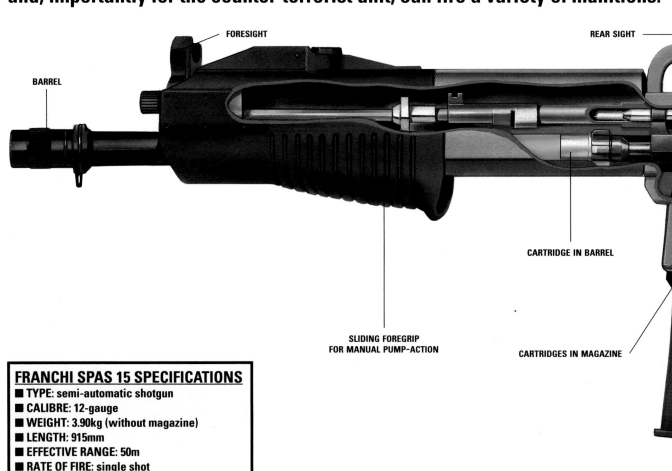

FORESIGHT

REAR SIGHT

BARREL

CARTRIDGE IN BARREL

SLIDING FOREGRIP
FOR MANUAL PUMP-ACTION

CARTRIDGES IN MAGAZINE

FRANCHI SPAS 15 SPECIFICATIONS
- **TYPE:** semi-automatic shotgun
- **CALIBRE:** 12-gauge
- **WEIGHT:** 3.90kg (without magazine)
- **LENGTH:** 915mm
- **EFFECTIVE RANGE:** 50m
- **RATE OF FIRE:** single shot
- **FEED:** 6-round box magazine
- **MUZZLE VELOCITY:** varies according to cartridge used

The lethality of modern 12-gauge shotguns cannot be doubted. A 12-bore slug, for example, can turn a small rock into powder at short ranges. This type of firepower is now used by many hostage-rescue units throughout the world, including the SAS. The range of Special Purpose Automatic Shotguns (SPAS) produced by Luigi Franchi of Italy is specifically designed with law enforcement in mind. The first of these weapons was the SPAS 12, a gun that

was something of a revolution in shotgun design. It is a short-barrelled semi-automatic shotgun with a skeleton butt which has a special device that allows the firer to carry and fire the gun one-handed if necessary (though a man requires great strength to do so). In addition, the gun is capable of full-automatic fire, unleashing four shots a second on this setting, which means that using standard buckshot rounds it is possible to put 48 pellets a second on

to a target one metre square at a range of 40m – ferocious firepower. The SPAS 12 even looks fierce, having a receiver made from light alloy and the whole weapon painted black.

The SPAS 12 was, and is, a great success. Following on from this, the company decided to change the 12 by replacing the internal tubular magazine with a box magazine. However, the development did not go smoothly and so the company decided to create a

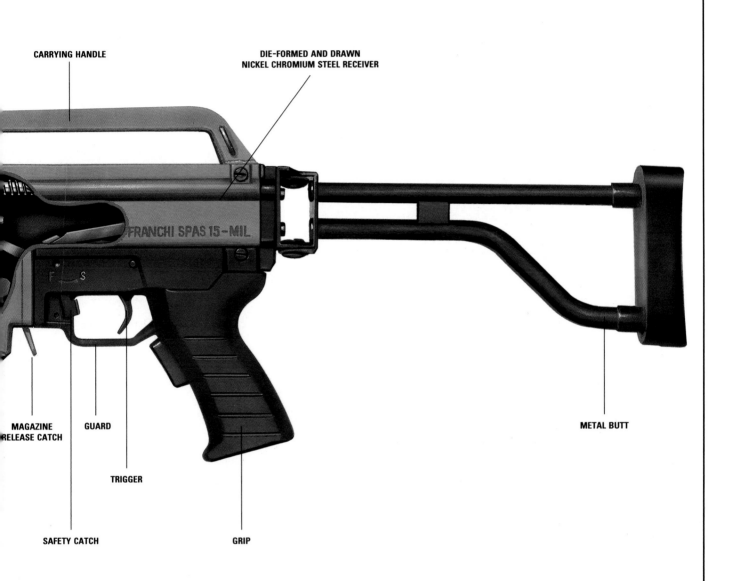

CARRYING HANDLE

DIE-FORMED AND DRAWN
NICKEL CHROMIUM STEEL RECEIVER

FRANCHI SPAS 15-MIL

F S

MAGAZINE
RELEASE CATCH

GUARD

METAL BUTT

TRIGGER

SAFETY CATCH

GRIP

new system. The result was the SPAS 15, a weapon capable of both pump-action and semi-automatic fire. Like the SPAS 12, the later shotgun can be fitted with a number of devices that allow a variety of cartridges to be used: buckshot, solid slug, small pellets and tear gas to name but a few. In addition, a grenade launcher can be fitted to the muzzle, allowing a grenade to be fired out to a range of 150m, and a special scattering device can be fitted which produces an instantaneous spread of pellets – very useful for indoor firing. The switch from a tubular magazine to the box variety is interesting. Though the latter are invariably bulky and protrude beneath the receiver, they greatly aid ease of loading, an important factor in counter-terrorist/hostage-rescue operations.

Undoubtedly the shotgun has added a whole new dimension to counter-terrorist warfare, though its use seems rather restricted in hostage-rescue work to the lesser, though still important, role of blowing door hinges and firing tear gas and smoke rounds into a building prior to an assault. As the spread of pellets from a round fired inside a room can be lethal to hostages as well as terrorists, it seems that assault shotguns will always be relegated to the secondary role during hostage-rescue operations, rather than being primary assault weapons.

the stopping power as the US Army's .45in round, but the SAS feels that it is perfectly adequate for the task. The Browning lacks some of the features seen on modern automatics, but has a long history of reliability under all conditions. The disadvantage with this vintage of weapon is that once a round is chambered the hammer is automatically cocked, making it unsafe to carry the handgun in this configuration in a holster. The hammer can be lowered by hand, but it has to be re-cocked in the same way before firing. A firer can thus lose a vital second after drawing his weapon from his holster. As the Browning tends to be carried as a backup weapon, however, reliability is the single most important characteristic, and with regard to the latter the High Power has served the SAS well.

Weapon design has moved on, and SAS soldiers have been seen with various new-generation pistols. The Austrian Glock 17 9mm pistol is a leading example, having a frame and receiver made from a light, though strong, polymer. The Glock has an internal hammer assembly and can be carried safely with a round chambered. There is no safety catch or cocking/uncocking levers, the safety locks are automatically removed as the trigger is pulled. A loaded and cocked pistol will not fire accidentally if dropped, but the advanced mechanism allows the user to discharge his first shot quickly, without pulling back the hammer or releasing any safety catch.

Other modern weapons include the German SIG-Sauer 9mm P226. All metal, it is a reliable and effective piece and has been adopted by many police and military forces. Again, the P266 has no safety catch, but has a lever to uncock the hammer. The first shot can be fired by the double-action trigger mechanism or, if time permits, the hammer can be raised manually for a more accurate first shot.

SHOTGUNS

Shotguns are deadly at short ranges, blasting a cone-shaped pattern of pellets which can inflict lethal wounds up to a range of 40m. The SAS was among the first to use the shotgun as a military weapon, finding its firepower devastating in the Malayan jungle. The most common shotgun in SAS service today is the Remington 870, probably the most popular police, military and sporting pump-action shotgun of the last 40 years. Special ammunition available includes buckshot, armoured-piercing projectiles, flechette rounds, rubber baton rounds and powdered CS. The Hatton round is specially designed to blow off the locks or hinges of locked doors, and it is in this role that SAS anti-terrorist teams employ the 'Remmy'. Interestingly, shotguns are never used by teams inside

Left: Israeli soldiers firing Uzi submachine guns. The Uzi has been around since 1949, and the SAS reportedly had a few in the 1970s as part of its hostage-rescue armoury. However, despite the Uzi's reliability, the Regiment adopted the MP5 for siege-busting operations. The German submachine gun is better made than its Israeli counterpart.

SSG 69 SNIPER RIFLE

Used by the SAS in the 1980s, this Austrian sniper rifle is a superb piece of engineering. In trained hands it can achieve a shot grouping of less than 40cm at a range of 800m.

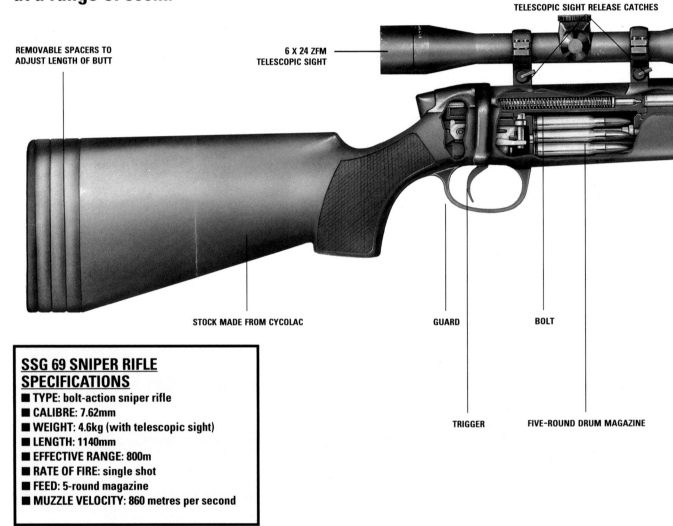

REMOVABLE SPACERS TO ADJUST LENGTH OF BUTT

TELESCOPIC SIGHT RELEASE CATCHES

6 X 24 ZFM TELESCOPIC SIGHT

STOCK MADE FROM CYCOLAC

GUARD

BOLT

TRIGGER

FIVE-ROUND DRUM MAGAZINE

SSG 69 SNIPER RIFLE SPECIFICATIONS
- **TYPE:** bolt-action sniper rifle
- **CALIBRE:** 7.62mm
- **WEIGHT:** 4.6kg (with telescopic sight)
- **LENGTH:** 1140mm
- **EFFECTIVE RANGE:** 800m
- **RATE OF FIRE:** single shot
- **FEED:** 5-round magazine
- **MUZZLE VELOCITY:** 860 metres per second

A cursory glance at the sniper rifles used by the SAS since World War II will reveal that they are all bolt-action models. This is not surprising with regard to the 1940s and 1950s because all sniper rifles at that time were bolt-action models. However, today there are many excellent rifles that are optimized for use by snipers but are also semi-automatic. Yet the Regiment has stuck to bolt-action guns. Why? There are two main reasons: bolt-action rifles are, as a general rule, more accurate than their gas-operated

counterparts; and there are less moving parts in a bolt-action rifle and so less chance of jamming. Though the most modern semi-autos are very accurate, there is always a nagging doubt about malfunctions. Therefore, the SAS has stuck with bolt-action models, and the Regiment's current sniping rifle, the Accuracy International PM, follows in that tradition.

The SSG 69 was in SAS service during the 1980s, between the time when the L42 was phased out and before the introduction into service of

the PM at the end of the decade. As well as its Counter Revolutionary Warfare (CRW) responsibilities, the Regiment also has its wartime role to fulfil if the need arises. Most of the hardware it selects, therefore, must be able to serve both roles. For such items as assault suits and stun grenades this does not arise because they have only one role. For items such as sniper rifles it is entirely different. The models used must be able to withstand the rigours of the battlefield, as well as fulfilling the criteria for counter-terrorist work. A

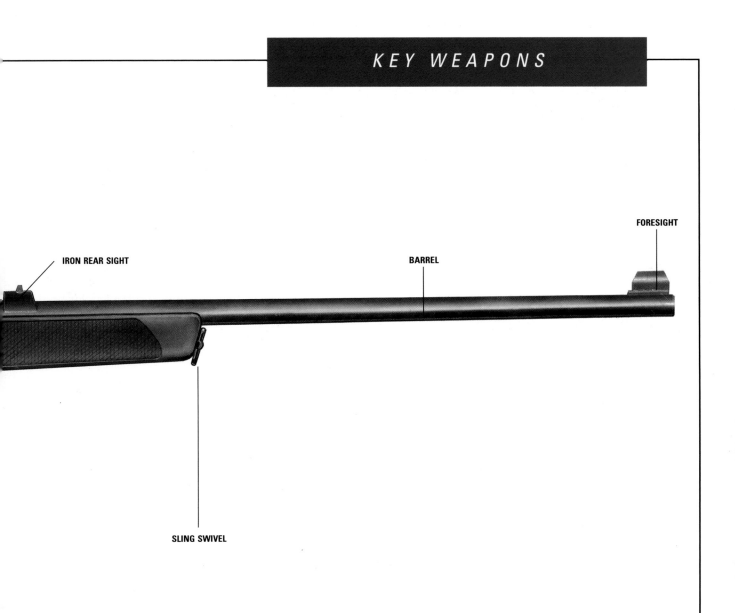

FORESIGHT

IRON REAR SIGHT

BARREL

SLING SWIVEL

bolt-action model such as the SSG 69 can fulfil both roles: it is robust enough for field use yet its accuracy compares favourably with the best sniper rifles currently available.

The rifle's barrel is made by the cold forging process which results in both the bore and the outside of the barrel being hardened. The trigger mechanism has a double pull, with the length and weight of the pull being both adjustable externally. The magazine holds five rounds, though a 10-round magazine is also available if required. The receiver is capable of taking a number of sights, though the standard one is the Kahles ZF69 which is graduated up to a range of 800m. The rifle is also fitted with iron sights. In keeping with the requirement for a rifle that can be lethal at long ranges, the SSG 69 is a 7.62mm-calibre weapon, though it can also fire the .243in round. Both rounds have good lethality over long ranges, something that the smaller 5.56mm round does not have (small calibre rifles are not suitable for long-range work).

What individual skills does an SAS soldier need to become an accomplished sniper? Good eyesight and ice-cool nerves are obvious requirements, but so too are high levels of camouflage and fieldcraft skills. In addition, the sniper must also be aware of his weapon: the sun glinting off bare metal will give his position away. Similarly, too much oil in the rifle will create a tell-tale puff of smoke when it is fired which will also compromise his location. However, excellent personal skills combined with a weapon such as the SSG 69 will result in a deadly sniper.

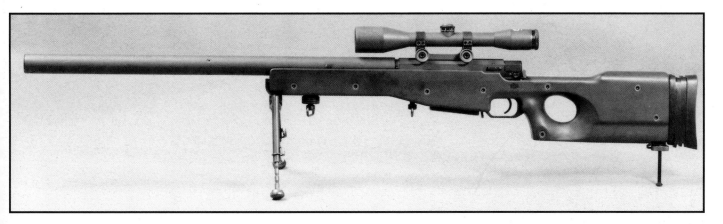

buildings or rooms, the wide spread of shot would inflict serious injuries on the hostages.

The Italian Franchi Special Purpose Automatic Shotgun (SPAS) 12 is a newer weapon, specially designed for military and police work. It is semi-automatic and can fire up to four rounds per second. The rounds need to be loaded into the tubular magazine one at a time, so the SPAS 15 has been developed which has an interchangeable box magazine. Both versions have a pump-action mechanism as a backup and for use when low-recoil special ammunition is being used. A new automatic shotgun which may see SAS service in the future is the American USAS-12. This looks rather like an oversized M16, with a similar carrying handle/sight unit and a box magazine. Some soldiers in the Regiment have doubts about the effectiveness of such automatic and semi-automatic shotguns, they feel they may be over complicated and less reliable than the pump-action Remington, and less able to cope with a wide range of specialist ammunition.

SNIPER RIFLES

Another type of weapons used by the SAS is the sniper rifle. The military sniper can have an effect out of all proportion to his actual firepower and the threat of a hidden rifleman, able to pick off with one shot the next man to move, can have a paralysing effect on the morale of a comparatively large unit. Modern technology is able to give the rifle an incredible level of long-range accuracy, and sports target shooters take full advantage of this. The military sniper has to balance accuracy against other factors: his rifle must be robust enough to withstand the rigours of operations; it should require the minimum of maintenance; it should be relatively easy to carry, especially when crawling through thick undergrowth; and it should be powerful enough to immobilise a target with one shot.

For over 30 years, the standard British Army sniper rifle was the L42, a 7.62mm bolt action weapon based on the venerable Lee-Enfield bolt-action rifle. Perhaps not the most accurate of weapons, it certainly met all the requirements for ruggedness and reliability, and was very popular with individual soldiers. For a few years in the 1980s, the Steyr SSG 69 was used by the Regiment. A more accurate weapon than the L42, the SSG 69 is a conventional bolt-action design made to finer tolerances and with a better finish.

THE ACCURACY INTERNATIONAL PM

The British Army's current sniper rifle is the Accuracy International PM, known as the L96A1. The L96A1 uses 7.62mm ammunition and is able to hit a target at ranges up to 1000m. The weapon uses a traditional bolt-action mechanism, which is surprising in that many other armies are moving to semi-automatic sniper rifles. A semi-automatic allows the sniper to fire a second shot extremely rapidly and gives him better chance of fighting his way out of trouble. The British argue that a bolt-action weapon still gives a more accurate shot and is more reliable. The L96 has a green plastic stock with adjustable butt and a built-in folding bipod. The construction is simple and the weapon is easy to maintain in the field. The L96 is a superb rifle and is rapidly gaining favour with the SAS and the rest of the Army.

An unusual recent addition to the armoury of the sniper is the extremely large calibre 12.7mm rifle. These weapons originally used the same round as the M2 heavy machine gun, but now have a range of specially designed ammunition including armour-piercing and incendiary types. These 12.7mm weapons can be used to attack vehicles, helicopters and parked aircraft, and the effects on humans are devastating. A US Special Forces sniper equipped with a Barret Model 82A1, for example, achieved a confirmed kill at over 1000m during the Gulf War. The disadvantages of these weapons are their massive size and weight. The Model 82 is over 1.5m long and weighs over 13kg when fully loaded. The signature on firing is large, with a loud

Above: The new SAS sniper rifle, the Accuracy International PM. Able to hit targets accurately at 1000m range and beyond, it gives the Regiment a state-of-the-art weapon for the next century.
Far left: Special optics and night sights have given units the ability to engage targets in low light and poor visibility.

Above: Snipers must have excellent fieldcraft techniques to move unseen on the battlefield and select their targets. However, equally important is having a good weapon. In the Accuracy International PM, shown here, the SAS has an excellent gun.

report and a cloud of dust kicked up around the firer when the trigger is squeezed. Large calibre rifles such as this may have applications in certain specialised situations, though their length and weight makes them unlikely to be carried on extended operations if vehicles are not available.

WEAPON SIGHTS

Many armies are now moving to optical sights for their infantry rifles which are sometimes built into a carrying handle. The British SA-80 rifle has the SUSAT (Sight Unit Small Arms Trilux) optical sight, a unit which gives 2x magnification and a remarkably clear sight picture. SUSAT contributes to the high levels of accuracy attainable with this weapon, though some soldiers feel that peering through an optical sight reduces the awareness of the surrounding environment, which is essential in fast-moving close-quarters combat. The L85 can be fitted with a conventional backup iron sight system if necessary. More powerful telescopic sights are largely used by snipers, and these systems normally magnify the scene by four or six times.

Infantry weapons can also be equipped with image intensifying sights for night combat. These amplify the tiny levels of ambient light

present and display a reasonably clear picture of the scene in the eyepiece. Early models were vulnerable to being swamped by light sources such as flares and vehicle lights, though later types have overcome this problem. SAS teams make extensive use of image intensifiers as they often move and fight at night. The two main disadvantages with image intensifiers are their expense and fragility, making then unsuitable for extended SAS-type operations.

Laser pointing systems are helpful in close-range combat, where they transmit a narrow point of laser light in the direction the weapon is pointing. The firer only has to place the laser dot on the target to know he is aiming correctly. Quick-reaction snap-shooting from the hip is possible using laser sights, a useful asset for hostage-rescue missions. The disadvantage is that these sights tend to be fairly large and delicate, and are reduced in effectiveness by rain, smoke or dust.

Some troopers prefer the singlepoint system. This unusual concept uses no light transmitted to the target; instead a coloured (usually red) dot is visible only inside the sight. The firer cannot actually see through the sight when he brings it to the aiming position because he has to keep his other eye open. If he is aiming correctly he will see the red dot superimposed on his target in a combined sight picture. Singlepoint gives an extremely fast, accurate snap-shooting capability and the firer keeps both eyes open and retains an awareness of what is going on around him. Singlepoint sights are also simpler and more reliable than laser systems.

COMBAT GRENADES

For close combat, grenades are a useful source of firepower to the infantry soldier. The traditional weapon is the hand-thrown, steel-cased fragmentation grenade, such as the British L2A2 model. Grenades have a tactical disadvantage in that the lethal radius of the projected fragments (10m) is about the same distance that the grenade can be thrown, which means the thrower must be in cover. Rifle-launched grenades are an attempt to overcome this. They can be fitted onto the barrel of a assault rifle, though a special blank propelling round needs to be loaded into the rifle. This complication, combined with a heavy recoil, caused the rifle grenade to fall from favour with the British, though modern versions are in service with other armies.

The current solution is to use the American 40mm cartridge-launched grenade. Developed in the 1960s, the 40mm grenade looks rather like a short, wide bullet. It was originally fired from the M79 launcher, a short-barrelled

weapon which could propel the explosive grenade to over 350m from the firer. Accuracy was limited: an individual foxhole could not be reliably hit at over 150m.

The M79 has now been replaced by the M203, a short, stubby launcher which clips under the barrel of an M16. The launcher barrel is slid forward to allow a grenade to be loaded, and the launcher unit comes complete with its own trigger and integral flip-up sights. The firepower of the rifle is unaffected, and the M203 gives an infantryman a lightweight method of supplementing the patrol's firepower.

There are also a range of hand-thrown grenades for delivering incendiary white phosphorus, thick screening smoke and coloured smoke. The most unusual grenade in SAS service was actually developed by the Regiment itself: the stun grenade or 'flash bang'. A bursting charge is surrounded by magnesium powder in a non-fragmentation casing. The 'flash bang' is used in hostage-rescue situations, where it can be thrown into aircraft or buildings where hostages are held. The charge ignites the magnesium causing a intensely bright flash and a loud bang (some models issue a succession of bangs) which can deafen and disorientate everyone for over 30 seconds. These few seconds are enough for the SAS team to enter the room, pick off the terrorists and free the hostages.

Below: Firing the Accuracy International PM. Traditionally snipers have employed large calibre weapons for their work. Though some police and counter-terrorist agencies use 5.56mm rifles for sniper work, the smaller round does not have the range or stopping power of larger calibre bullets.

Section II
SUPPORT WEAPONS

SAS soldiers normally fight in small groups, therefore they sometimes need to supplement the firepower of their individual weapons. A mission could also involve patrols taking part in larger pitched battles, and may even require fire support delivered from other arms. SAS units may be called upon to cause a noisy diversion, such as D Squadron's attack on Goose Green during the 1982 Falklands War. In such situations, support weapons – machine guns, mortars, anti-tank and air-defence weapons – are essential to reinforce the fire of individual weapons.

MACHINE GUNS

The latest section machine gun in the British inventory is the 5.56mm L86A1 Light Support Weapon (LSW). Based on the L85A1 rifle, the LSW has a heavier, longer barrel, an integral bipod and an extra grip beneath the butt. Most of the other components are identical to those found in the rifle, and it uses the same 30-round magazine. The LSW is light (6.88kg) and handy with a high level of accuracy up to 3-400m.

The LSW is not proving popular as a fire support weapon, however. Being magazine-fed, it cannot match the rate of fire of a belt-fed weapon. In addition, the 5.56mm rounds are too small and they have little chance of penetrating light cover such as thin walls or wood. Range is also insufficient. An enemy equipped with 7.62mm weapons, for example, could shoot at a British section at long ranges and the latter would be unable to return effective suppressive fire. When the weapon was introduced to infantry battalions, the standard eight-man section was split into four-man fireteams, each team having an LSW. In practice, the only way to achieve a reasonable amount of suppressive firepower is to group both LSWs together, defeating the purpose of the exercise. There are also lingering doubts about the reliability of the weapon, though these teething troubles have been largely overcome. The SAS is even less enamoured with the LSW, feeling that it cannot deliver heavy, reliable firepower.

The predecessor of the LSW is the L7A2 general purpose machine gun (GPMG). A much heavier, belt-fed weapon, the GPMG fires the same 7.62mm round as the L1A1 SLR. It is also based on a Belgian design, the FN MAG machine gun. Known to British servicemen as the 'gimpy', it has been the standard section machine gun for over 30 years and has a reputation for being tough and extremely reliable. It is relatively heavy for an infantry weapon: 10.9kg without ammunition. The weapon has a built-in bipod and its ammunition is loaded in 200-round belts which can be linked together in action to allow continuous fire. Mounted on its integral bipod, the GPMG is effective out to 800m. It can also be mounted on a tripod and fitted with a heavier barrel and dial sight for the Sustained Fire (SF) role. Properly mounted, a GPMG in the SF role can deliver accurate and devastating firepower out to 1400m.

The GPMG has been criticised for falling between two stools: lacking in true sustained fire capability, and being too heavy for the section machine gun role. But troops who have used the GPMG in combat find that this rugged, reliable weapon delivers the heavy, accurate firepower that they need, and that the extra weight is worth carrying. The SAS has made extensive use of the GPMG, and most four-man patrols will carry at least one. Sufficient ammunition has to be available, and so every member of the patrol will carry at least one 200-round belt. On many occasions, more GPMGs are used. When the 23 men from G Squadron were helicoptered in to relieve their hard-pressed comrades at Mirbat in July 1972, they carried nine GPMGs between them – a useful boost to their firepower. The weapon can also be mounted on SAS Land Rovers and will bolt on to most other vehicles if necessary.

THE BROWNING 0.5IN

There are occasions where even the firepower of the GPMG is insufficient, and here the SAS has relied on the veteran Browning M2 0.50in calibre heavy machine gun. A massive, heavy weapon, the M2 is not really man-portable, weighing in at over 38kg. The SAS used the M2 extensively during the 1950s and 1960s, mounting it on vehicles and in defensive emplacements. By the time the Argentinians had invaded the Falkland Islands in 1982, it had virtually disappeared from British infantry service. During this conflict many weapons were captured from the Argentinians, and the British soldiers who had come under fire from this powerful weapon were so impressed that the M2 has found its way back into limited

Above right: The Vickers heavy machine gun. This weapon was used extensively by the SAS in World War II, often mounted on vehicles, especially in North Africa.
Below right: An SAS three-inch mortar in action in Italy in World War II. Mortars were also employed as support weapons by SAS parties in northwest Europe after the D-Day landings.

MILAN

Used operationally by the SAS during the Falklands War, MILAN is not only an effective anti-tank weapon but can also be used to destroy enemy bunkers.

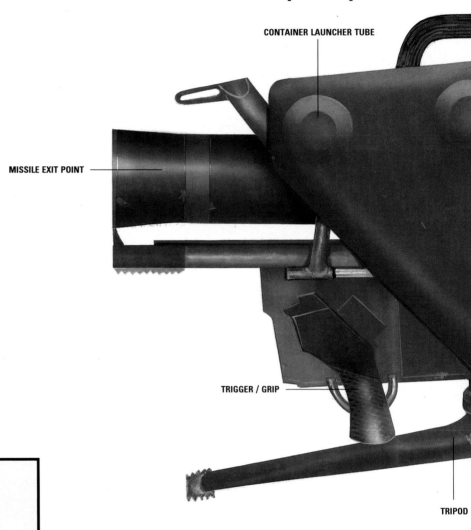

CONTAINER LAUNCHER TUBE

MISSILE EXIT POINT

TRIGGER / GRIP

TRIPOD

MILAN SPECIFICATIONS
- **TYPE: anti-tank guided missile**
- **WEIGHT: 27.68kg (launch weight)**
- **LENGTH: 765mm**
- **MAXIMUM RANGE: 2000m**
- **ARMOUR PENETRATION: 352mm**

During the 1982 Falklands War, two diversionary actions were mounted by the British to draw Argentinian attention away from the main landings that were to take place on East Falkland at San Carlos Water on 21 May 1982. One of these actions was a Special Boat Squadron attack on Fanning Head to the north of the bay. The other was conducted by a small force of SAS men from D Squadron commanded by Major Cedric Delves. Landed by Sea King

helicopters, the party marched south and engaged the enemy garrison at Darwin to prevent the latter moving up to San Carlos Water. The SAS men laid down such a ferocious barrage of fire with their machine guns, mortars and anti-tank weapons that the Argentinians reported they were under a battalion attack.

One of the weapons used by the SAS in the above action was the MILAN anti-tank weapon. It consists of a

launcher/guidance unit plus the missile, with the former having an optical sight, a tracking unit and a trigger. A MIRA thermal imaging sight can also be fitted for night-time use or for firing in smoke. The system has a Semi-Automatic Command to Line-of-Sight (SACLOS) guidance which means the firer must keep the target centred in his sight. The flight of the missile can be up to 14 seconds, though this would be at the missile's maximum range. Despite its

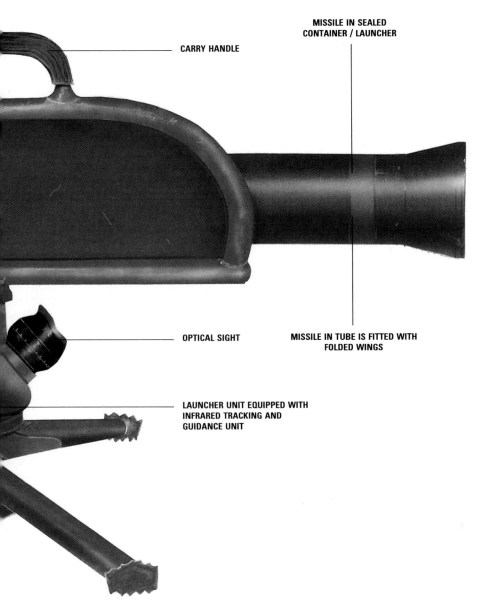

CARRY HANDLE

MISSILE IN SEALED
CONTAINER / LAUNCHER

OPTICAL SIGHT

MISSILE IN TUBE IS FITTED WITH
FOLDED WINGS

LAUNCHER UNIT EQUIPPED WITH
INFRARED TRACKING AND
GUIDANCE UNIT

excellent qualities, there are a number of drawbacks with MILAN, though they are common to all anti-tank guided missiles. First, the firer must remain immobile, and thus vulnerable, during the missile's flight (this is partly alleviated with MILAN because the sight is periscopic, allowing the firer to operate it from a prone position). Second, it has a significant backblast upon firing, again making the operator and the system vulnerable to discovery.

Third, its long-range tank-killing capability can be limited by terrain features. Tanks racing around from cover to cover would be able to take shelter before a missile could strike them. Fourth, and this is only pertinent to units such as the SAS, the weight of the system could prohibit its use. MILAN – the whole system – weighs 27.68kg (each missile weighs 6.66kg). Despite the fact that it is designed to be operated by two men, no SAS long-

range patrol could afford to take a MILAN along with each man already carrying over 60kg of personal equipment (the SAS soldiers at Darwin and Goose Green were dropped by helicopter and marched only a short distance carrying little personal kit).

Nevertheless, MILAN does have a place in the SAS armoury and, when it has been used, has proved itself to be a deadly anti-tank weapon that can also be used against enemy strong-points.

use. M2s were mounted on SAS Land Rovers during the 1991 Gulf War, where their long range was put to full use in the desert.

MORTARS

Simple, cheap, effective and reliable, the mortar can drop high-explosive or smoke bombs on enemy positions, or place illumination flares above them. Most mortars follow the same design principles: a smooth-bore tube is attached to a base plate on the ground, with the other open end pointing upwards and the whole supported by some form of bipod mechanism. The bombs have a propelling charge attached and are dropped tail first into the tube. A firing pin at the bottom detonates the propellant, throwing the bomb high into the air, where it arcs downwards, plunging onto the target. Range can be set by adjusting the angle of the tube and by changing the strength of the propelling charge. The stresses on the bomb as it is fired are much less than those on an artillery shell, so the bomb casing can be thinner, and more explosive carried. A mortar bomb is usually much more effective in the target area than a shell of similar weight.

The British 51mm mortar is a replacement for the wartime two-inch weapon, and is carried within the infantry section. The mortar weighs just over 6kg and is a simple tube with a fixed base plate. It has no sophisticated sight or firing mechanism, the operator simply wedges the base plate into the ground, holds the tube at the correct angle for the estimated range, and drops a bomb into the top of the tube. First-shot accuracy is difficult, though a skilled operator can quickly zero in on a target then fire up to eight rounds in a minute.

The mortar can be carried slung over the shoulder, and the ammunition distributed around the patrol. The 51mm can fire high explosive ammunition up to a range of 750m, though the SAS does not often use it in this way. It is more likely to be used as a quick method of creating smoke screens on the battlefield. The ability to drop a few smoke-producing bombs in front of an enemy position could save the lives of a patrol under fire. The other main use of the 51mm is to provide illumination at night. Even with the advent of night vision equipment and image intensifying sights, night combat is difficult without some form of artificial light. The mortar can launch flares which hang under a small parachute, each one lighting up an enemy position for a minute or so.

A much heavier weapon is the L16 ML 81mm mortar. Normally found in the mortar platoon of an infantry battalion, this is almost a miniature artillery piece. It weighs approximately 15kg with its steel baseplate, and is

around 1.3m long. An adjustable bipod supports the tube which holds the sighting mechanism. The 81mm has a maximum range of over five kilometres, so is usually fired indirectly, i.e. at a target identified by a forward observer. In this case, the mortarman uses a calibrated dial sight to aim the mortar on the compass bearing received over the radio. The bipod is adjusted to give the correct angle for the desired range, then the first bomb is fired. The distant observer watches where the shot falls then radios any necessary aiming corrections to the mortarman. The 81mm can also be fired at targets visible to the mortarman, though if this is necessary it usually means that the enemy is too close.

The 81mm fires high-explosive fragmentation bombs and also uses smoke and illuminating ammunition. Bombs can be fused to explode on impact, or a timer can be set to detonate them in the air above the target, showering blast and fragments into the bottom of trenches and emplacements. A new generation of electronic proximity fuses is also available, allowing air bursts to be detonated even more precisely. A good mortar team can fire up to 15 rounds a minute, creating a devastating barrage almost instantly.

Notable instances of mortars in SAS use include the Battle of Mirbat (July 1972) and during the Pebble Island raid (May 1982) in the Falklands War. The 81mm seems set to serve with the SAS and the Army for many years to come, as it is probably the most effective mortar of its calibre in the world. New types of ammunition are being developed, one of the most interesting of which is the British Aerospace Merlin round. This is a complex device with a millimetric wave radar seeker in the nose, a guidance electronics package and a shaped charge warhead. Merlin is fired like an ordinary bomb, but as it flies over the target area the seeker scans for metal objects (i.e. armoured vehicles) and guides the bomb towards the nearest, where it should achieve a direct hit. This will give mortar teams an effective long-range anti-tank capability, though precise coordination between observer, other anti-tank weapons and mortar would be necessary. Once the technology is fully developed, Merlin may see service with the SAS.

ANTI-TANK WEAPONS

The simplest anti-armour device carried by the SAS is the M72 LAW (Light Anti-tank Weapon). It is a light (2.4kg) single-shot rocket firing a 66mm shaped charge warhead capable of penetrating older tanks and all light armoured vehicles. A skilled operator can hit a moving target at a range of 150m, and a static one at 300m. The rocket is contained in an

Above: The MILAN anti-tank weapon is really too bulky and heavy to accompany long-range SAS patrols. However, for raids and diversions, such as the one mounted on 20 May by D Squadron during the Falklands War, it is excellent for destroying bunkers and trench systems.

extendable tube – 65cm long when retracted, 90cm when extended. To prepare for firing, protective caps are removed from each end of the launcher and the tube is extended, which causes the simple folding sights to pop up. The launcher is held on the shoulder and a trigger switch is pressed to fire. Once the rocket is launched, the tube is discarded.

The M72 has only marginal effectiveness against the new generation of tanks, but the SAS likes it for its light weight and general simplicity. In the Falklands, the LAW became popular as a 'bunker-buster', with infantrymen using it to blast enemy trenches and machine-gun positions. The SAS will still use it in this

role, and most patrols will sling a few of these handy weapons over their shoulders.

The British replacement for the L72 is the LAW 80, a much bigger and heavier weapon. LAW 80 works on similar principles to the M72, being a one-shot rocket fired from an extending tube. The warhead calibre is 94mm, and the 9.6kg weapon is 1m long (1.5m when extended). LAW 80 has an unusual aiming system. There is a 9mm spotting rifle built into the unit, with a fixed magazine of 5 tracer rounds with flash heads. When the launcher is extended, the firer puts it to his shoulder and takes aim through a simple optical sight. Once he thinks he is on target, he presses the trigger

which fires one of the spotting rounds. The tracer enables the flight of the round to be seen, and the flash head shows where it impacts. Once the spotting rounds are hitting the target, the firer moves a selector switch with his thumb and squeezes the trigger again. This time the main rocket fires and, as the spotting rounds are ballistically matched to the rocket, it should hit the same point.

The LAW 80 is a much more effective anti-tank weapon than the M72, though it too may have problems against new-generation vehicles equipped with explosive reactive armour. Weight and bulk are also a problem for SAS foot patrols, though LAW 80 was

carried on Land Rovers during the 1991 Gulf War against Iraq.

The most powerful anti-tank weapon available to the British infantryman is the European-designed MILAN missile. This guided weapon, fully described elsewhere, has an 80 per cent chance of killing a tank up to a range of 2000m (it can also destroy enemy bunkers and trenches). It can be fitted with a thermal imaging sight, allowing targets to be engaged at night, in fog or through smoke screens. However, the bulk and weight of this system is such that SAS patrols will only be able to carry it for long distances if man-handled by helicopters or vehicles.

Above: The 81mm mortar is one of the most useful support weapons currently available to the SAS. Accurate and able to fire a variety of munitions, the weapon was used to great effect by the Regiment during the Pebble Island raid during the Falklands War.

AIR-DEFENCE WEAPONS

The most basic defence against low-flying aircraft and helicopters is not to be spotted by them, and the camouflage skills of SAS patrols give them an excellent chance of avoiding detection. Failing this, the next line of defence are the machine guns and automatic weapons carried by patrol members, though the chances of them achieving an effective hit on a supersonic jet are poor. SAS Land Rovers carry GPMGs on trainable mounts, and these

Below: An IRA terrorist with an M60 machine gun. Though not an SAS weapon, the Regiment ensures that its soldiers are familiar with it and other foreign guns. It is always useful to be able to use an enemy's firearms.

target. Stinger, which is fully described elsewhere, has gained a reputation for being an effective and deadly weapon against low-flying targets. Earlier infrared guided missiles had to lock on to the hot engine exhaust of a target, usually after it had passed overhead (and made its attack). Stinger can engage targets from the front, though the infrared trace from the target is much fainter from this angle, making the missile more susceptible to countermeasures.

can give a good account of themselves at close ranges. Even if the machine guns obtain no hits, the sight of a stream of tracer bullets arcing towards his aircraft may disrupt the aim of an attacking pilot.

A more sophisticated system is the American-designed Stinger heat-seeking missile. This comes in a sealed container which also acts as the launch tube, and clips onto the sighting and electronic unit. The complete unit is held on the shoulder and, once switched on, the missile seeker looks for, then locks on to, the nearest strong infrared source, i.e. the signature of an aircraft or helicopter. Once locked on, the missile is launched and automatically homes onto its

A British equivalent to Stinger is the Blowpipe missile. Blowpipe is also a shoulder launched missile, but is slightly heavier than the American weapon, having a similar 5km range. Blowpipe uses a completely different guidance system: it does not track the target itself. The missile is guided by radio commands from the launcher unit, transmitted by the operator using a small joystick to steer it onto the target. The strengths of the missile are that it is an all-aspect weapon – most countermeasures do not work against it. The weakness is that it requires a highly skilled operator and is only really effective in the hands of specialist air-defence troops. It has not been a great success in SAS service.

Blowpipe has now largely been replaced by Javelin, a later development of the system. Javelin uses a more powerful rocket motor which greatly reduces the flight duration of the missile and gives the target less time to take evasive action. The big difference is that Javelin uses a Semi-Automatic Command to Line-of-Sight (SACLOS) guidance system. Here, all the operator has to do is keep his sight on the target. A TV camera on his sight unit tracks an infrared flare on the tail of the

can also be used in a hostage rescue. The British Arwen is good example. Arwen has a five-round rotating magazine, rather like a traditional revolver. It fires unique 37mm ammunition, normally plastic baton rounds which can temporarily incapacitate a target up to a range of 100m. Special rounds which can be used for anti-terrorist missions include variants that deliver CS gas, one which cuts through doors before spraying CS, and a baton round which, after it has struck the target and

Below: The Bren gun, seen here in the Malayan jungle, is probably the finest light machine gun ever built. Reliable, easy to fire and very accurate, it was used by the SAS throughout World War II and in the post-war era.

missile, and the electronics automatically send steering commands to the missile to place it where the operator is tracking. The skill level required to be effective with Javelin is greatly reduced compared to that needed for Blowpipe, though the operator needs to stand exposed to hostile fire while the missile is in flight. Even with these improvements, the SAS still prefers Stinger. It is simpler to use, and once it is fired the missile tracks automatically, allowing the operator to immediately take cover.

OTHER WEAPONS

Other support weapons that are in the SAS armoury include special anti-riot weapons that

knocked him down, sprays a cloud of CS gas at him. The single-shot version is Arwen ACE, and is sometimes more popular because of its smaller size and light weight.

Anti-personnel and anti-tank mines are also available to SAS teams, though the weight of these items prohibits their use by a patrol travelling on foot. The SAS is more likely to use the Claymore mine, a lethal area weapon effective in both ambush or defensive roles. A Claymore mine has a similar shape to a large book, but is slightly curved along its length. It is emplaced vertically on integral folding legs, with the long edge horizontal and the convex face towards the enemy. Inside is around 1kg of plastic explosive, with 800 or so ball

STINGER

Used by the SAS in the Falklands, the American Stinger system is an effective hand-held surface-to-air missile (SAM). It is ideal for protecting small, isolated units from enemy air attack.

STINGER SPECIFICATIONS
- **TYPE:** hand-held surface-to-air missile
- **WEIGHT:** 15.15kg (launch)
- **LENGTH:** 1.53m
- **RANGE:** 5000m
- **CEILING:** 4800m

On 21 May 1982, soldiers from D Squadron, 22 SAS, were returning from a highly successful action against Argentinian forces in the Darwin/Goose Green area. Their task, which they had performed admirably, was to act as a diversion for the British landings taking place to the north at San Carlos Water. Now, having accomplished their mission, the men were heading north in open order. An Argentinian Pucara ground-attack aircraft observed them and swooped down to strafe them with cannon fire. However, an SAS trooper carrying a Stinger spotted the aircarft, targeted it in his sights, and fired the missile. The latter streaked upwards and hit its target, causing it to burst into flames. This was the only time the Regiment has used Stinger in anger, and in fact the system had only been

TRAINING AID UNIT (OPTIONAL)

REAR OF CANISTER IS SET WELL BACK TO ENSURE FIRER IS NOT HARMED BY LAUNCH GASES

MISSILE INSIDE CANISTER IS ARMED WITH 3KG HIGH-EXPLOSIVE FRAGMENTATION WARHEAD

FIRER'S SHO RESTS H

purchased from the Americans by the SAS the month before.

The FIM-92A Stinger consists of a missile in a sealed launcher/storage canister, a gripstock/trigger assembly and an optical sight. The missile itself has a blunt nose containing an infrared seeker and a tapered tail which has four pop-out control canards and four folding tail fins. The warhead itself is a high-explosive fragmentation type fitted with contact and proximity fuses. The missile's infrared seeker is capable of all-aspect engagement and is resistant to flares and other simple infrared countermeasures. All-aspect engagement means the missile can engage targets head-on and laterally, and not just the rear quarters, i.e. the hot exhausts, of an aircraft. The sensors in the missile are sensitive enough to be able to track an aircraft by the less intense heat radiated (or reflected) by its airframe. Stinger is also fitted with an identification, friend or foe (IFF) interrogator which, in theory, sorts out the hostiles from the friendlies. When the seeker has achieved 'lock-on' the firer pulls the trigger. The missile then heads for the target, homing in autonomously.

Stinger is a capable anti-aircraft system that gives infantry forces the means of defeating enemy aircraft.

However, there are two tactical considerations to be addressed with regard to the SAS and its use of hand-held SAMs. First, can a deep-penetration SAS teams operating mostly on foot afford to carry Stinger missiles weighing 15kg each? Second, and much more important, SAS units have always relied on their high levels of fieldcraft and camouflage to stay hidden from enemy aircraft. This begs the question of whether the Regiment really needs weapons such as Stinger; after all, SAS patrols and observation posts in the Falklands were operating unseen in areas that were extensively patrolled by Argentinian aircraft and helicopters.

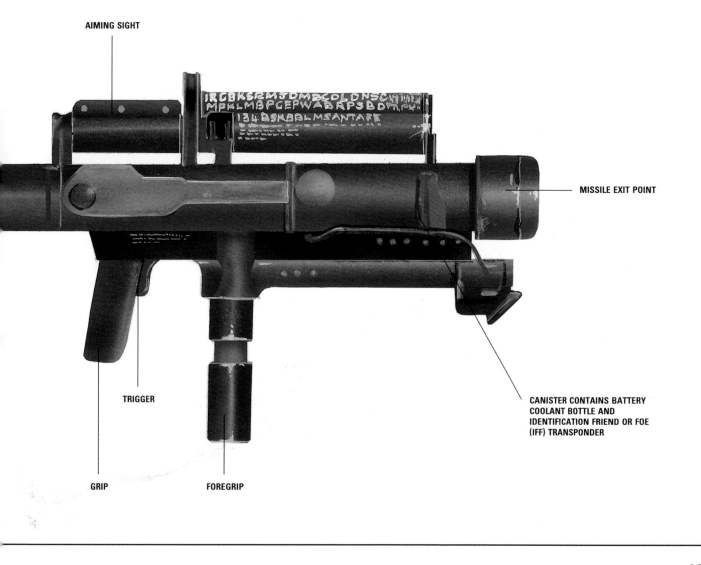

AIMING SIGHT

MISSILE EXIT POINT

CANISTER CONTAINS BATTERY COOLANT BOTTLE AND IDENTIFICATION FRIEND OR FOE (IFF) TRANSPONDER

TRIGGER

GRIP

FOREGRIP

Right: A Stinger surface-to-air missile (SAM) being fired. Despite the British Javelin system, the SAS prefers the American-built Stinger. This may be for one reason only: Stinger was fired in anger by an SAS unit during the Falklands War and was successful. The Regiment has traditionally stuck to using those things that have proved themselves in battle.

bearings embedded in it. The mine can be detonated by a trip-wire mechanism, or by an operator sending an electrical signal down a command wire. The ball bearings are blasted out in a triangular killing zone and are lethal up to 150m. Claymores are a spectacular way of springing an ambush, or they can be placed defensively to cover likely enemy approach routes. In addition, a blast from a Claymore may disrupt enemy troops long enough to allow an SAS team to break contact.

SAS patrols are also trained to call down fire from heavy artillery, helicopters and aircraft. The SAS observer radios the coordinates of a target back to the artillery fire-control centre, which passes the information direct to the guns (which can be 20km or more away). Aiming and ranging calculations are made by the gun-control posts and the first shells are fired. The observer spots where the shells land, then sends aiming corrections back until the shells impact on the target. A well-organised system with skilled operators can bring heavy artillery fire down on to a target within two minutes of the first sighting.

RANGEFINDERS AND IMAGERS

A simple laser rangefinder is sometimes carried which provides more accurate target range information to the observer. If artillery support is required at night, then some form of night vision is necessary. An observer can carry an image intensifier device, a larger version of the night sights that are attached to ordinary rifles. A more sophisticated system is the Thermal Imager (TI), which detects the heat radiated by objects in its field of view. Men and vehicles are clearly visible through a TI, and it can see for thousands of metres in darkness and through smoke, fog and dust. TIs are complex devices which require careful maintenance and need a supply of filtered cooling air and batteries, so they tend only to be carried when a vehicle is available. The Observer's Thermal Imaging System (OTIS) is specifically designed for artillery spotting. It comprises a heavy, long-range TI, a tripod and a co-sighted laser rangefinder. The SAS is more likely to use the Hand Held Thermal Imager (HHTI), a much smaller, lighter device easily carried by a soldier.

SAS patrols can also call in strikes from tactical aircraft which can attack with guns, bombs, rockets and missiles. For the ultimate in infantry fire support, a laser target marker can be pointed at a target, enabling a laser-guided bomb to steer accurately at the designated spot. The Regiment demonstrated the power of such a land/air combination when hunting Iraqi Scud missile launchers during the 1991 Gulf War.

Section III
LAND VEHICLES

An observer in certain parts of the Iraqi desert during January 1991 would have come across a sight similar to that seen in an earlier desert war some 50 years ago. He would have seen a Land Rover vehicle, laden like a Christmas tree with stores, equipment and ammunition and bristling with machine guns. This strange apparition would have been crewed by scruffy, bearded men wearing a mixture of western military clothing and Arab headdress. At first glance the method by which SAS soldiers ride to war does not appear to have changed much in five decades.

SAS LAND ROVERS

The modern SAS Land Rover can be regarded as the direct descendant of the armed jeeps of World War II, and today's vehicles are also flexible, well-armed and effective transport, reconnaissance and raiding machines. Land Rovers have been in British Army service since the late 1950s, though current models are more advanced than the earlier versions. They come equipped with either petrol or diesel engines, and are used in both short and long wheelbase variants. Most military Land Rovers have a four-cylinder petrol engine with a four-speed gearbox. Under normal road conditions, the Land Rover uses conventional two-wheel drive, but when travelling cross-country four-wheel drive can be selected by pushing an auxiliary gear lever. In extreme conditions, or when towing a heavy load, another lower set of gear ratios can be selected by moving yet another gear lever. Later models make use of a larger 3.5 litre V-8 petrol engine and a more sophisticated five-speed gearbox in permanent four-wheel drive.

While there are many combinations of fittings, all SAS Land Rovers are based on the long wheelbase chassis, with recent vehicles using the V8 engine and a new gearbox. SAS vehicles have to carry heavy loads over some of the roughest terrain in the world, so the suspension is stronger than on a standard machine. The cabin is stripped down to the level of the hull and the windscreen usually removed. A simple roll bar can be fitted, though this is not normally used on operations.

SAS vehicles have fittings to attach armour plates around key areas, giving a measure of protection to the crew. Thick armoured glass screens can also be attached in front of the driver and on any weapons mounts to give

some protection to the gunner. However, armour carries a weight penalty which adversely affects the vehicle's performance and range, and so most SAS patrols prefer to do without. The only armour that is normally fitted is a steel plate under the chassis to give some protection from land mines.

The SAS Land Rover normally has a crew of three: a driver, a commander and a gunner. The commander sits alongside the driver and sometimes his seat is slightly raised for better visibility. The gunner sits in the rear compartment. More people can be carried, though the space devoted to equipment and supplies must be reduced accordingly. At first sight the pink paint scheme (hence the nickname 'Pink Panther') seems a strange choice for a military vehicle, but it blends exceptionally well into a sandy desert background.

'PINK PANTHER' EQUIPMENT

A vehicle patrol is expected to operate independently of support and re-supply, so everything needed for an extended mission is carried on board. There are extra stowage racks for fuel and water cans, spare parts, camouflage nets, personal equipment, weapons, ammunition, radios, food and anything else likely to be needed. Smoke dischargers are fitted to the front and rear, and detachable searchlights are positioned on each side on trainable brackets. A camouflage net is usually rolled up across the bonnet and can be quickly extended to cover the vehicle. Metal sand channels are strapped to the outside of the hull and, when needed, are placed under the wheels to help the vehicle free itself from soft sand. Standard procedure is for the crew to pack their personal equipment and weapons in such a way that they can be quickly removed if the patrol has to continue on foot. As on other SAS operations, troopers carry their personal survival belt at all times, in case they have to hastily abandon the vehicle.

SAS Land Rovers are armed with a variety of weapons. The commander usually has a single GPMG mounted in front of him, allowing him to cover the complete frontal arc and one side arc of the vehicle. The main weapons installation is to the rear, usually a rotary mount with a 360-degrees traverse. This can hold one or two GPMGs, or even the much heavier Browning 0.5in calibre machine

Above right: The Longline Light Strike Vehicle. Allegedly used by the Regiment in the 1991 Gulf War, the dune buggy-type vehicle seems to have found favour with special forces units, especially the Americans.

Below right: The SAS 'Pink Panther' Land Rover. The Regiment continues to use Land Rover vehicles as the primary means of transporting its soldiers through desert terrain.

Above: Festooned with petrol and water containers and armed with Vickers 'K' machine guns, a World War II SAS jeep photographed during the North African campaign. The SAS first acquired jeeps in mid-1942, but from then on they became an integral part of operations, taking part in many raids against airfields behind enemy lines.
Right: SAS Mobility Troops experiment with all forms of land transport. In recent years trail bikes have been used as a method of tranporting men over inhospitable terrain.

gun. When weapons such as these are vehicle mounted, their ammunition belt is folded into a metal box which is clipped to the side of the gun. A canvas bag is usually tied on to catch the hot cartridge cases as they are ejected from the weapon, together with the metal links from the ammunition belt.

There are also mounts available for the much heavier 20mm cannon, electrically powered 7.62mm chain guns and the three-barrelled 7.62mm minigun. One British manufacturer also offers a power-assisted mount with a raised seat for the gunner, but there is a heavy weight and space penalty associated with such a system. It is also possible to mount the MILAN missile launcher on the vehicle, turning the Land Rover into a makeshift tank destroyer. None of these heavy and complex options seems to have been used operationally by the SAS because of weight considerations.

During the 1991 Gulf War, SAS vehicles also carried weapons on board which could be quickly removed for use on the ground. These included the LAW 80 anti-tank rocket launcher and the shoulder-launched Stinger

surface-to-air missile. In this way the SAS teams had a reasonable chance of protecting themselves from light armoured vehicles, helicopters and low-flying aircraft.

Navigating in relatively featureless terrain is a difficult art, though essential for long-range special forces operations. Technology has now made this easier than before, with the advent of satellite navigation (SATNAV) systems. The most widespread SATNAV system for military and civilian users is the American Global Positioning System (GPS). A GPS receiver can be mounted on a vehicle or carried in the hand. The receiver compares the signals from four or more of the constellation of 18 satellites in fixed orbits around the earth. By comparing the differences between these precisely coded signals, the receiver can calculate its position to within a few hundred metres. Military users have access to an encrypted set of signals which enable their position to be calculated to within 15m.

SAS vehicles in the Gulf War carried SATNAV systems which gave a simple read-out of their position. GPS coverage of the

region was not constant over 24 hours, however, and complex electronics can fail or suffer damage, so the SAS retained more traditional methods such as sun compasses and star sightings. A sun compass is simply a small disc mounted horizontally on the front of the vehicle, with a central vertical spike rather like a sundial. If the disc is rotated to the correct angle for the time of day, a reading of the current compass bearing can be made from the shadow of the spike. Conventional magnetic compasses are time-consuming, as the user needs to move far enough away from the vehicle for its metal bulk not to affect the reading on the compass.

Other hi-tech equipment carried in the Gulf included sophisticated satellite communications (SATCOM) systems which enabled SAS teams far behind the lines to talk directly to their operating base or to airborne command posts. They also carried the PRC 319 special forces radio, a lightweight man-portable device which uses burst transmission techniques to avoid detection by enemy radio-location units. Laser rangefinders and thermal imagers were also included in the equipment pile.

Fully loaded SAS Land Rovers have a range of over 650km with full tanks which can be greatly increased by carrying extra petrol on the vehicle. Maximum road speed is around 120km/h, though cross-country travel tends to be much slower. The Land Rover is not the last word in off-road vehicle technology, but it has developed a reputation for being tough and reliable. Should something go wrong, simple design and construction make the vehicle easy to repair. The SAS feels that its 'Pink Panthers' are worthy successors to David Stirling's World War II jeeps.

THE LIGHT STRIKE VEHICLE
A type of vehicle which has seen recent SAS use is the Light Strike Vehicle (LSV). They are based on the 'dune-buggies' that American youths used to race around the beaches of California. A simple tubular steel frame and roll cage holds a powerful petrol engine to the rear, with two seats in the middle and four fat, low pressure tyres at each corner. There is little else – no roof or body panels and no windscreen. Military LSVs have a steel belly plate to give some protection from mines, but they have no other armour protection or even weather cover.

The ultimate military hot-rod, these small, extremely powerful vehicles can travel across terrain impassable to jeeps or Land Rovers. Their low profile, relatively quiet engine and reduced radar and infrared signature makes them hard to detect and even more difficult to hit. They are also light enough to be man-handled out of trouble should they bog down.

The British company Longline designed and built the LSV. Payload is more limited than on the Land Rovers, though the LSV has likewise sprouted external brackets and boxes to hold fuel, water and equipment. Maximum range with one fuel tank is around 200km. It has been claimed that an LSV can carry up to 12 people in an emergency, though unless they sit on each other's shoulders it is hard to see where they would fit on the vehicle.

GPMGs and heavier machine guns can be fitted behind the crew, normally above the level of the roll cage. SAS LSVs can also carry LAW 80 anti-tank rockets and some have been seen carrying the man-portable MILAN guided missile. A detachment of LSVs carrying MILAN firing posts would make an ideal anti-armour raiding group or even a delaying force in suitable terrain. MILAN posts could be set up in suitable cover, a missile fired at a target, the launchers loaded back on to the LSVs and rapidly driven away from retribution, all within a few minutes. LSVs have also been seen with permanent on-board mountings for MILAN and the US TOW missile, though such modifications reduce the inherent flexibility of the vehicle.

THE LSV IN THE GULF WAR
US Special Forces used their 'dune buggies' extensively during the 1991 Gulf War, roaming the desert ahead of the advancing Allied armies. They also played a major role in 'The Great Scud Hunt', being equipped with thermal imagers and laser designators to target Scud launchers for Allied aircraft. The SAS was not so happy with their LSVs, however, feeling that their comparatively short range was a major hindrance to desert operations, and the lack of carrying capability prevented long-distance missions in the expanses of Iraq. There were also doubts expressed about the robustness and general reliability of the LSV. SAS teams deployed to the Gulf quickly decided that their faithful Land Rovers were much more reliable. Airlifted into their operating areas by RAF Chinooks, these elderly vehicles operated with distinction throughout the war.

SAS Mobility Troops also use light motor bikes for cross-country reconnaissance and transport. Motor bikes are easily carried behind enemy lines by helicopter and can be dropped by parachute. If the troop or squadron is to be inserted behind the lines in four-man patrols, a few motorbikes are useful if the SAS force subsequently needs to be concentrated for a major attack. The noise from such machines means that movement must be planned with care. They also have little load carrying capability, though they can be driven and manhandled across much rougher terrain

Right: Light Strike Vehicles. Though the LSV is undoubtedly fast, agile and highly manoeuvrable, its lack of range and limited payload capacity mean it requires some form of 'mother' vehicle in support. There have also been some questions raised concerning its ability to stand up to heavy punishment in the field.

than almost any other vehicle. Motorbikes in SAS use are usually lightweight civilian trials and 'dirt' bikes, normally Japanese designs such as Honda. The only concession to military service is usually a coat of green paint.

Apart from logistics and administration vehicles such as trucks and liaison cars, there are few other vehicles permanently assigned to the SAS. One which may see use in certain circumstances is the Fairey 'Supacat', now in service with 5 Airborne Brigade as a cross-country load carrier and supply vehicle.

Supacat looks rather like a six-wheeled bathtub, with the driver at the front with a motorbike-style handlebar control. It is very much an off-road vehicle, but it can carry loads of up to 1000kg over terrain that would otherwise require a helicopter. Supacat is of a simple construction and uses a civilian Volkswagen engine. While it is in no way a combat machine and lacks the range for operations behind enemy lines, it would be useful for re-supplying SAS teams in larger operations such as those carried out in Oman.

For operations in arctic conditions, the Swedish Bv 202 is in service with the Royal Marines and the Army. A fully tracked load carrier with an enclosed cabin and an articulated, powered trailer, the Bv 202 is optimised for crossing thick snow and ice. Not really designed as a personnel carrier, it can be useful as a re-supply vehicle for SAS bases. An unusual method of moving ski-equipped troops is to tow them behind the vehicle, this is known as as 'ski-joring'. The Regiment has also used ski bikes for fast arctic travel.

The SAS does not possess a vast fleet of vehicles, though there are trucks, Land Rovers and staff cars based at Hereford. Unmarked vehicles such as Range Rovers have been used to move Counter Revolutionary Warfare (CRW) teams without attracting attention, such as the during the deployment for the Princes Gate rescue in 1980. The Regiment's soldiers remain very much foot-powered, though where necessary patrols will utilise any form of transport necessary to carry out their mission.

Section IV
BOATS AND AIRCRAFT

The very first SAS mission (November 1941) used a parachute drop as a means of arriving behind enemy lines, and the SAS has used air transport ever since. Helicopters are the main aircraft used today, though fixed-wing transports remain an important facet in many of the Regiment's operations.

Helicopters are used to insert SAS teams into an operational area, withdraw them at the end of the mission, and, where possible, deliver supplies and evacuate casualties. The Regiment generally calls upon the Army Air Corps (AAC) to provide the machines and their crews, though transports from the RAF and Royal Navy are also available. A detachment of the AAC is permanently at Hereford (until the 1980s this was from 658 Squadron, but it is now known as 'S' Detachment). Having their 'own' helicopters allows SAS soldiers to plan and execute missions independently of other agencies, ensuring security and the guaranteed availability of transport. If they have to request the use of other AAC, RAF or RN machines, they are then competing with all the other units clamouring for helicopter support.

SCOUT AND AGUSTA HELICOPTERS

For many years the Westland Scout was associated with 658 Squadron, and up to three of these aircraft were permanently based at Hereford. The Scout first entered Army service in the early 1960s as a general purpose helicopter, occasionally being armed with machine guns and SS 11 wire-guided anti-tank missiles. Small and light, it has room for four (cramped) passengers and the pilot, and has a tactical radius of around 250km. The Scout uses no advanced technology and requires more maintenance than later machines, but it is tough and reliable. The Scout has been used by the Regiment many times over the years, the 1982 Falklands War being a case in point. Some Scouts remain in Army service, mainly in Northern Ireland, and they are still seen on SAS duty in the UK mainland.

The other helicopters regarded as 'belonging' to the SAS are a small fleet of Italian-designed Agusta A-109As. Two Agustas were captured from the Argentinians during the Falklands War and were quickly spirited back to the UK. The A-109 is a sleek, modern machine with a sprightly performance. It can carry up to six passengers and a two-

man crew and is fitted with a full set of sophisticated navigation and communications equipment. Two more A-109s have since joined the fleet. Officially assigned to HQ 7 Regiment AAC (coincidentally based at Hereford), the A-109s are seldom seen in public, but when they are they are usually wearing civilian-style colour schemes: blue/white and yellow/white, though all four carry military serials. It seems the A-109s fulfil a liaison and transport role, though they have been seen overflying Counter Revolutionary Warfare (CRW) exercises in the UK. It is not known if any special equipment has been fitted to these machines.

The AAC uses two other types of tactical helicopter, the Gazelle and the Lynx. A French design licence-built by Westland, the Gazelle is a small liaison and reconnaissance aircraft which has largely replaced the Scout in Army service. Of advanced design, it includes glass fibre main rotor blades and an unusual tail rotor which is fully enclosed by the tail fin. British Army Gazelle AH.1s are not normally armed, though machine guns, rockets and anti-tank missiles are carried by foreign users.

The Gazelle has room for two crew members at the front with a three-man bench seat behind. The Gazelle is handy for moving two or three SAS men around the battlefield, though they cannot carry much in the way of bulky or heavy equipment. It is quite a noisy machine with a distinctive turbine whine, but can deliver its passengers out to a radius of around 350km. Gazelles proved to be rather fragile during the Falklands War, and in some situations the SAS still prefers to use the older, more rugged and quieter Scout.

LYNX – FAST ATTACK HELICOPTER

The British-designed Westland Lynx is a larger machine than the Gazelle and is used by the Army as a general purpose transport and anti-tank helicopter. The Royal Navy also has a version for the ship-borne anti-submarine role. The Army's Lynx AH.1 is one of the fastest and most manoeuvrable helicopters in the world, and carries two crew plus up to a maximum of 10 passengers. TOW anti-tank missiles are often attached to pylons alongside the fuselage, with the co-pilot having a stabilised, roof-mounted sight. The Lynx AH.1 can insert a fully equipped SAS patrol up to a radius of 300km from its take-off point,

Above right: A Chinook helicopter in night camouflage. Chinooks were used to insert SAS teams into Kuwait and Iraq during the 1991 Gulf War against Iraq. In one incident a CH-47 landed in the middle of a minefield, damaging its undercarriage. However, with great difficulty it managed to take off and limp back to base.
Below right: Subskimmers, which can be 'parked' on the sea floor, give clandestine infiltration missions a greater chance of success.

though this is reduced if tactical 'nap-of-the-earth' (NOE) flying is necessary. The Lynx is also a noisy machine, but the later AH.7 version has an improved tail rotor which makes it much quieter. For low-level night operations, the crew must wear night vision goggles (NVG) as the helicopter has no infra-red or radar systems for navigation. The newer AH.9 Lynx is a bigger machine with a wheeled undercarriage and is used as a transport by 24 Airborne Brigade.

Larger helicopters are under the control of the RAF, but the SAS and other Army units are able to request transport missions to be flown on its behalf. The Puma HC.1, another French design built in Britain, can carry 16 troops in relative comfort or 20 in high-density configuration. The Puma has an operational radius of 280km and is unarmed in British service. RAF machines have normal radio navigation aids, but no special night vision equipment, for low-level flying in darkness.

CHINOOKS IN THE GULF WAR

The Chinook HC.1 is even bigger, able to carry up to 44 fully equipped troops or up to 12,000kg slung beneath the fuselage. An American design, known in US military service as the CH-47, the Chinook is a tough work horse, able to carry heavy or outsize loads in all conditions. During the Falklands War, for example, an overloaded RAF Chinook carried over 75 troops squeezed into the fuselage. Chinooks were used during the 1991 Gulf War to carry SAS Land Rovers deep into the Iraqi desert, the vehicles being slung below the helicopters. A few RAF Chinooks were modified to carry an inflight refuelling probe, a terrain avoidance radar and cockpit lighting compatible with NVGs. Painted in an unusual desert pink and green disruptive camouflage, these were often associated with special forces operations. A disadvantage with the Chinook is that the noise from the large twin rotors carries some distance, though it is very difficult for a listener to tell from which direction the low frequency beats are coming.

An older machine still in RAF service is the Westland Wessex, able to carry up to 16 troops. The RAF Wessex unit is 72 Squadron, based in Northern Ireland, and is often used to insert SAS patrols at night or remove them after an anti-terrorist ambush.

The Royal Navy also has transport helicopters, normally used for the airborne assault role with the Royal Marines. The main Commando helicopter is the Sea King HC.4, a troop carrying version of the anti-submarine Sea King. Some of these are also compatible with NVGs, and all are able to carry up to 28 troops or a 3600kg underslung load. It was a Sea King HC.4 of 846 Squadron that crashed while flying between ships during the Falklands War, killing 18 members of D Squadron. It was another 846 Squadron machine that was found burnt out in Chile, an event still not satisfactorily explained by the British Government. Other naval helicopters are flown by the Commando Brigade Air Squadron (CBAS) which has Gazelles and Lynxes identical to those in Army service, and these too may be used by the SAS. The Navy still has a few Wessex helicopters, and it was these aircraft that operated with the SAS on Fortuna Glacier, South Georgia, in 1982.

FIXED-WING AIRCRAFT

Fixed-wing mobility for the SAS is almost exclusively provided by the RAF's C-130 Hercules. A four-engined tactical transport, the big, tough Hercules is an American design in service with over 50 countries. The RAF Hercules C.1 can carry 92 troops or 64 fully equipped paratroops, or up to 19,000kg of cargo. Light vehicles can also fit into the capacious hold, including up to three short wheelbase Land Rovers. A 'stretched' version, the C.3, has space for 128 troops, 92 paratroops, or bulkier cargo. The Hercules is able to land on unprepared strips or sections of road and the large rear loading ramp enables cargo to be driven straight out of the aircraft. Paratroops are dropped from the side doors or they can run off the open rear ramp. Heavy loads and vehicles can also be fitted with large parachutes and pushed out the back.

The SAS usually operates with crews from the Special Forces Flight of 47 Squadron, RAF Lyneham, for parachute insertion missions. Troopers can be dropped from low altitude, with the aircraft below the detection range of many air-defence radars. Alternatively, extremely high altitude drops can be made, with the SAS patrol using High Altitude, Low Opening (HALO) parachute techniques, or the alternative High Altitude, High Opening (HAHO) method. Using these techniques a parachutist is able to travel some distance after leaving the aircraft, making enemy detection of the drop zone difficult.

The Controlled Air Delivery System (CADS) is a steerable ramair parachute which is radio-controlled from a distant transmitter. Using CADS, heavy equipment can be dropped from high altitudes alongside the troops, one of whom has the radio control device. As he steers his own parachute in the long descent, he can also ensure the CADS systems stays nearby, thus allowing the cargo to be easily found after landing – a great asset to clandestine missions. The radio control transmitter can also be stationed on the ground, with the parachute programmed to automatically steer towards it.

Far left: Because the Scout helicopter is a very stable platform, it is ideal for special forces troops to deploy from. With a top speed of 211km/hr, the Scout is also ideal for rapid movement over the battlefield.

Above: The C-130 Hercules is the principal long-range transport aircraft used by the SAS. The addition of inflight refuelling probes means a greatly extended range, thus making the airborne insertion of teams deep behind enemy lines much easier.

Right: Canoes are traditionally associated with units such as the SBS. However, SAS Boat Troops also employ them as a means of silently inserting men onto a shoreline or along a river.

The SAS has also experimented with slightly more esoteric aircraft such as the simple one-man microlights popular with sports fliers. These could be an effective way of moving small groups across enemy territory because they could be modified to have virtually no radar signature. The engine noise would have to be suppressed, but the great advantage would be that they could be easily hidden when on the ground.

BOATS AND SUBMARINES

SAS Boat Troops specialise in all forms of water transport and are able to use any kind of small boat. They train closely with the Royal Marines' Special Boat Squadron (SBS) and give the Regiment the ability to operate autonomously in rivers, lakes and coastal regions.

The smallest boat in use is the canoe, useful for covert approaches along rivers, across lakes or in coastal areas. The Klepper, in service since the 1950s, is made from a wooden frame covered by rubberised canvas and polyester, with inflatable air bags to give extra buoyancy. It can be stored on a vehicle or submarine and can be manhandled (with difficulty) for short distances over land. There is also a similar Klepper Mk 13 collapsible boat.

Slightly larger Gemini inflatable boats can carry three men and their equipment. Made from rubber and canvas, these boats have very little radar or infrared signature, though their

40hp outboard motor needs a muffler over the exhaust to give a silent approach. Geminis are easily portable by ship, vehicle or aircraft, and they can be packed inside a submarine. D Squadron's Boat Troop used five Geminis to land on South Georgia during the Falklands War, though engine failures meant that only three made the objective. The other two boats drifted away in high winds but their crews were eventually rescued.

The Rigid Raider is bigger and more powerful then the Gemini and is also used by the Royal Marines and the SBS. The Rigid Raider has a flat 'Dory' hull shape and can carry up to 10 men and their equipment. It uses a double-skinned fibreglass method of construction with polyurethane foam between the skins. British Rigid Raiders are powered by a 140hp engine, and this power, combined with the Dory shape, makes the boat 'plane' on the water surface, giving a fast, if sometimes bumpy, ride. Rigid Raiders usually demand a skilled coxswain who stands or sits at a steering console towards the rear of the boat. The only disadvantage with the Rigid Raider is its weight. Solid construction makes for a heavy boat, and the engine alone needs at least three men to lift it. The SAS used Rigid Raiders on their diversionary attack on Port Stanley harbour at the end of the Falklands

Right: The British nuclear-powered submarine *Triumph*. Like most submarines, this 'Trafalgar' class vessel is capable of transporting special forces teams, such as the SAS, to their targets. On such missions the final leg of the journey to the shore is usually undertaken in inflatable rubber boats.

War. On this occasion the sturdy construction proved its worth when the boats were repeatedly hit by gunfire but kept afloat.

An unusual form of water transport that seems likely to enter SAS service is the subskimmer. A futuristic combination of inflatable boat and submersible, this unusual vehicle can carry a crew of four divers. The vessel is powered by a 90hp outboard motor which gives a speed of around 25 knots when operating on the surface. The subskimmer has a large air-filled buoyancy tank in the centre of the hull. When this is vented and filled with water, and the hull sides are deflated, the boat runs just below the surface. The outboard motor will continue to run as it is water-sealed and protected by a snorkel air inlet system. If the buoyancy tank is filled with more water,

the vessel becomes totally submerged. Two steerable battery-driven electric motors then propel the craft and give an underwater range of around 5km. To regain the surface, stored compressed air is used to purge the buoyancy tank of water and inflate the hull sides.

Together with the SBS, SAS divers use Royal Navy submarines to get close to their targets, exiting the vessels underwater via the escape chambers. The Royal Navy's new 'Upholder' class would seem an ideal vessel for special forces missions, and no doubt the SAS will be training with them before long.

Whatever mode of transport is chosen, the needs of the mission remain paramount. The SAS remains true to David Stirling's original philosophy of using whatever means are necessary to get to the target.

SAS WARRIORS

This chapter lists only a small number of the hundreds of men who have made their mark on the SAS. This is partly due to lack of space and partly because of the secrecy with which the Regiment cloaks its actions. Many of the heroic deeds of the SAS have never achieved public knowledge, and never will. All the men listed here (in approximate chronological order) have in some way helped shape the history of the Regiment, and will have to stand as representatives for the thousands of others who have worn the Winged Dagger since 1941.

On the SAS memorial at Hereford is inscribed the following quotation from James Elroy Flecker's poem *Hassan*:

'We are the Pilgrims, master; we shall go
Always a little further: it may be
Beyond that last blue mountain barred
with snow
Across that angry or that glimmering sea...'

Here then are the stories of some of the pilgrims who went that little bit further.

LIEUTENANT-COLONEL DAVID STIRLING

The man who founded the SAS was born in 1915 and spent his childhood in Scotland. He was keen on outdoor activities such as hunting, shooting and mountaineering. When World War II broke out he joined the Scots Guards as a second lieutenant. After a frustrating few months without seeing action he volunteered for No 8 Commando, a unit largely formed from the Guards Regiments. 8 Commando was sent to the Middle East at the end of 1940, as part of the composite Layforce.

The story of Layforce and its problems has been related earlier, as has Stirling's frustration with its lack of success. On his own initiative he attempted to develop an airborne capability for 8 Commando and was injured during his first, untutored, parachute jump. It was during the two months he spent in a British military hospital that Stirling crystallised his ideas for the creation of a new raiding force. In a series of handwritten memoranda, he cogently analysed the progress of the war and explained how a suitably trained force could hinder the enemy by operating in small groups behind the lines. He also set out guidelines for the selection, training, employment and tactical principles of this force. With hindsight, it is amazing how many of these principles are still followed by the modern SAS.

Rather than send his proposals through normal channels, Stirling bluffed his way in to see General Neil Ritchie, the Deputy Chief of Staff at Middle East Headquarters. His bare-faced cheek paid off, and at 24 years old the young subaltern was given the chance to select, train and lead his own unit.

As well as formulating the guiding principles of his new force, Stirling was determined to lead his men from the front. He commanded one of the patrols on the first disastrous raid in November 1941 and took part in virtually every mission after that. While the young commander could have usefully spent more time on the administration and training of his new unit, he felt that the kind of men selected for the SAS would only respect a leader who ran the same level of risks as they. His slightly reckless temperament also naturally inclined him to this course.

He was constantly open to new ideas, and the methods of the SAS were continually adapted to changing conditions. The use of Long Range Desert Group (LRDG) transport after the failure of the first parachute drop is an example of this, as was the change in tactics to driving armed jeeps across the target airfield. Stirling also had the ability to select and recruit the right kind of officers and men for his unit. A surprisingly soft-spoken, polite man, the tall officer inspired loyalty and confidence in all who served under him.

By early 1943, the constant operations had taken their toll and Stirling was suffering from strain and fatigue. Just as the North African war was coming to an end he was captured while trying to cross Tunisia to meet up with the Allied armies coming from the west. Following four escape attempts he was sent to the maximum security camp at Colditz Castle, finally being released as the war ended. Stirling never again commanded the SAS, he spent the years after the war setting up a security consultancy company which employed many ex-members of the Regiment.

He was knighted in 1990, and died later that year. Stirling possessed an unusual blend of foresight, strategic grasp and aggressive leadership. If he had any faults it was in his willingness to expose himself to risks that some thought unneccessary, and in his tendency to keep his future plans for the Regiment largely to himself, which presented problems after he was captured. He was, however, one of the few original military thinkers who was given the opportunity to put his ideas into practice – and this he did with stunning success.

LIEUTENANT-COLONEL 'PADDY' MAYNE

There are probably more stories and legends surrounding 'Paddy' Mayne than any other figure in the history of the SAS. A large well-built man, he had been an Irish rugby international and an accomplished boxer before the war. At the time of his recruitment by Stirling he was a member of No 11

Left: David Stirling, the founder of the Special Air Service. The principles and aims that Stirling established for the SAS have survived through to the present day. He is also reported to have invented the Regimental motto: *Who Dares Wins*.

Above: 'Paddy' Mayne photographed in North Africa during World War II. Mayne was a born leader of men and fearless in battle. Off the battlefield his conduct was less exemplary: he was prone to bouts of heavy drinking which often landed him in trouble. One of these involved knocking out the Provost-Marshal in Cairo whilst on leave, an event which landed him in jail. Nevertheless, he was awarded no less than four DSOs during the war, testimony in itself to his military capabilities.

Commando, though at the time he was under arrest for punching his commanding officer. Mayne was normally quiet and courteous, an officer who took a keen interest in the welfare of his men. There was a darker side to his character, however. A ferocious temper and a low boredom threshold meant that he was liable to get himself into various drunken scrapes when not in action.

Nevertheless, Mayne was probably one of the finest fighting soldiers in the Army and was an ideal officer for the SAS. Quick thinking, aggressive and courageous, he led the first SAS patrol to achieve success: the raid against Tamet airfield. After this dramatic start, he was to see continuous action until 1945.

Mayne was no administrator; when left in charge of the SAS base camp in January 1942, for example, he achieved little and was thoroughly unhappy until he returned to operations. By late 1943 he was promoted to lieutenant-colonel and given command of 1

SAS following Stirling's capture. He succesfully led the unit under its various guises for the rest of the war. There are many acts of heroism in the 'Paddy' Mayne story; indeed, he ended the war with four DSOs. He inspired those serving under him and many feel that he should have been awarded the VC for his feats. His weakness was his temper and thirst for action, and even when a comparatively senior officer he was arrested for brawling with six Military Policemen in Cairo.

It was Mayne who ensured the survival of the SAS when Stirling was captured at the end of the desert war, and it was his fighting spirit that created many of the legends of the wartime SAS. 'Paddy' Mayne survived the war to form a solicitor's practice in Northern Ireland, but was killed in a car crash in 1955.

LIEUTENANT 'JOCK' LEWES

'Jock' Lewes was among the first officers recruited by Stirling and was responsible for devising the training programme for the new unit. Orignally from the Welsh Guards, he too had volunteered for No 8 Commando out of frustration. It was Lewes who scrounged the parachutes for Stirling's famous descent in 1941. A quiet, thoughtful man, Lewes also had strong practical abilities, demonstrated when he developed an explosive/incendiary charge specifically designed to destroy parked aircraft – the Lewes bomb. This was after a Royal Engineers explosives 'expert' had told him such a weapon was impossible.

He was a determined and skilled fighting soldier, taking part in the early SAS desert raids. Lewes was killed in December 1941 when his truck was strafed by an Italian aircraft. He was only with the Regiment for a few months, but in that short time had helped lay the groundwork for its future successes.

LIEUTENANT-COLONEL JOHN COOPER

Johnny Cooper was a private soldier in the Scots Guards, who along with David Stirling and others volunteered for 8 Commando. One of the original recruits to L Detachment, he took part in many of the SAS desert missions, usually in Stirling's party. He was one of the first SAS troopers to become fully trained as a desert navigator. In January 1943, Cooper was commissioned by Stirling in the field, though this highly irregular action was not recognised by the Army. The young 'lieutenant' therefore had to be sent to an officer training school on his return to Britain in the summer of 1943. He stayed with 1 SAS as a troop commander during the invasion of France (June 1944) and the final operations in Europe.

After the war and demobilisation, he joined the Territorial Army, though by 1952 he was a regular again with 22 SAS. In Malaya he reached the rank of major and fulfilled both squadron commander and administrative posts. He was largely responsible for developing the technique of 'tree-jumping', being injured in such a jump.

Cooper commanded A Squadron in Oman, taking part in the assault on the Jebel Akhdar (January 1959). He retired from the British Army in early 1960, taking a commission in the Sultan of Oman's armed forces. He later worked with Royalist guerrillas in the Yemen and Aden and was recruited by David Stirling into his private security company.

LIEUTENANT-COLONEL WILLIAM STIRLING

A quiet figure who was a much better administrator than his illustrious brother David, he too joined the Scots Guards on the outbreak of war. By September 1942 he was a lieutenant-colonel in command of 62 Commando in Algeria. This unit was disbanded by the end of the year, but in the meantime he was asked to form 2 SAS by David. He did not have the help of characters such as 'Paddy' Mayne or 'Jock' Lewes, but he did have the opportunity to learn from their early efforts. The training and selection regime he created followed the same principles and standards as those laid down in 1 SAS, and their effectiveness was proven by his unit's showing in Italy in 1943.

Like his brother, Bill Stirling had very clear ideas about the correct employment for the SAS, and was continually arguing against those senior officers who saw the Regiment as a special airborne assault unit or as a tactical recconnaissance force. Matters came to a head during the early planning for 'Overlord', when it was intended to use the SAS as jeep-mounted reconnaissance patrols against German armour. Stirling resigned in protest, an action which almost caused the dissolution of his regiment. Lieutenant-Colonel Brian Franks was appointed its commanding officer and managed to put the unit back on an even keel. However, William Stirling's ideas were vindicated. The plans were changed, and 2 SAS was to operate sucessfully behind the lines in France.

BRIGADIER 'MAD MIKE' CALVERT

Mike Calvert was one of the leading experts in irregular warfare in the British Army, and was responsible for the recreation of the regular SAS after the war. He originally joined the Royal Engineers in the 1933, though after a few years was posted to Military Intelligence Research where he helped organise stay-behind guerrilla units in Britain for activation if the country was invaded. For most of the war, he fought with the 'Chindits', the long-range penetration group which operated behind Japanese lines in Burma. For a few months in 1945 he was given command of the SAS Brigade until its disbandment in October.

By 1950 he was in a staff post in Hong Kong, but was asked by the Commander-in-Chief Far East, General Harding, to make a study of the deteriorating situation in Malaya and come up with suggestions as to how victory could be achieved. Calvert's plan (made after extensive personal research), with its twin elements of 'hearts and minds' and aggressive long-range jungle patrols, was soon implemented and has since become a classic blueprint for anti-guerrilla operations.

To fulfil part of his plan he raised the Malayan Scouts which eventually became 22 SAS. His original concept was for a unit to be recruited from soldiers already in the region, then disbanded once the 'Emergency' was over. Similar units would be formed in other parts of the world as necessary. Experience with the Malayan Scouts soon showed that the

Below: 'Mad Mike' Calvert. He was instrumental in the creation of the Malayan Scouts and the 'hearts and minds' concept that is still part of SAS procedure.

Above: Johnny Cooper (right) fought with the SAS in World War II, in Malaya and Oman. In the early 1960s he was involved in clandestine missions in North Yemen. Cooper was actually commissioned in the field by David Stirling, though the military authorities insisted he attend training school before his rank was acknowledged.

rigours of the long-range jungle operations demanded a special breed of soldier and an extensive selection and training programme. Such requirements could not be met by the temporary unit, thus 22 SAS was formed as a regular formation. In 1952, illness and over-work forced Calvert to be invalided home, but his legacy was a set of principles that were to form the cornerstone of future SAS operations.

LIEUTENANT-COLONEL JOHN WOODHOUSE

John Woodhouse has been acknowledged by David Stirling as being the father of the modern SAS, having done more than anyone else to restore the foundations of pro-fessionalism and dedication which form the core principles of the Regiment. He was one of the original members of the Malayan Scouts, being recruited by Mike Calvert to be the Intelligence Officer. With Major Dare Newell he became involved in reorganisation and training after the problems identified during the first jungle operations. By mid-1952 he was sent to the UK to organise the selection and training of future members of the Regiment. The principles and systems he devised still form the basis for today's Selection and Continuation Training. Wood-house returned to Malaya in 1954 as a squadron commander and became the Commanding Officer of the Regiment in 1962.

He was responsible for creating the scattered network of patrols and their native 'eyes and ears' in the Borneo campaign, and it was his firm advocacy of offensive action that persuaded the Government to authorise the cross-border 'Claret' patrols into Indonesia. Woodhouse left the Army in 1965.

LIEUTENANT-COLONEL JOHN WATTS

Johnny Watts was the commander of D Squadron when it was ordered to Oman in 1958, where he took part in the Jebel Akhdar campaign. He then led B Squadron in Borneo, eventually rising to command the Regiment in 1970. He devised the 'hearts and minds' strategy that was used to win the campaign in the Dhofar, during which he personally led Operation 'Jaguar', the 1971 assault on the Jebel Dhofar. He retired from the Regiment at the end of 1971, being regarded as the architect of victory in the Oman campaign.

MAJOR MICHAEL KEALY

Originally an officer in the Queen's Regiment, Mike Kealy joined 22 SAS in 1971. He had been a full member of the Regiment for only a few months when, in July 1972, his nine-man team fought the Battle of Mirbat. His exemplary leadership during the desperate action, when around 250 *adoo* guerrillas tried to take the town, was enough for the Army to award him the DSO. Kealy drove himself hard, and in 1979 attempted again the SAS Selection march as a 'refresher' before being posted to Ireland. The cold and the mist conspired against him and he died in the hills from hypothermia. Kealy's death stands as a reminder that weather and terrain can overcome even the most experienced soldier.

LIEUTENANT-COLONEL MIKE ROSE

Mike Rose was the commander of 22 SAS during the 1982 Falklands War, and it was his lobbying of Brigadier Julian Thompson, 3 Commando Brigade, that resulted in the Regiment being included in the landing force. Rose was responsible for planning the deployment of SAS reconnaissance patrols operating on the islands, and continually put forward other suggestions for missions. He was very conscious of the effects of psychological warfare on the Argentine conscripts, and continually broadcast 'doom and gloom' over their radio nets, in cooperation with Captain Rod Bell, a Spanish-speaking Royal Marines' officer. When the Argentinian commanders asked for a ceasefire, Rose and Bell flew into Stanley by helicopter to undertake the negotiations that led to the surrender.

GENERAL SIR PETER DE LA BILLIÈRE

Perhaps the best known SAS figure of modern times, Peter de la Billière joined the Regiment from the Durham Light Infantry in 1955. He fought in Malaya, and was in comand of the troop that hunted the notorious terrorist Ah Hoi in the Telok Anson swamp (1958). He also took part in the assault on the Jebel Akhdar in Oman (1959). On one occasion he led his troop on a daring attack on some caves in which some guerrillas were hiding. Standing in the middle of a natural depression, over-looked by guerrilla positions, his men fired anti-tank rockets into the mouths of the caves, then had to withdraw while under heavy fire, an action which won him the Military Cross.

In 1964 he commanded A Squadron in the Radfan, and created the first SAS Close Quarter Battle course for the undercover 'Keeni Meeni' squads. In Borneo he was responsible for reorganising certain facets of the Regiment, especially the logistic support of patrols in the field. His A Squadron launched a series of cross-border 'Claret' raids and he himself undertook a number of solo reconnaissance missions in the jungle. By the end of the Borneo campaign he had been awarded a second Military Medal.

In 1972, de la Billière was promoted to command 22 SAS, during which time he was instrumental in creating the Counter Revolutionary Warfare (CRW) Wing and developing the SAS anti-terrorist role. By the time of the Princes Gate rescue in 1980 he was

in overall charge of the SAS Group, a command which at that time included all supporting elements and the TA Regiments. He came into the limelight in 1990 when, as a lieutenant-general, he was appointed to lead the British land forces sent to the Gulf. His previous experience of the region and his fluent Arabic were vital assets to the overall commander, General Schwarzkopf. The two men quickly established a cordial working relationship, and it was de la Billière who persuaded Schwarzkopf of the usefulness of special forces operations. As a reward for his part in the success of the land offensive, de la Billière was made a full general at the end of 1991. A charismatic figure, his blend of strategic thinking and aggressive fighting skills is typical of the officers that are attracted to the Special Air Service.

Above: General Sir Peter de la Billière, the commander of British forces in the 1991 Gulf War and an SAS veteran. During his illustrious career with the Regiment, de la Billière saw service in Malaya, Oman, Borneo and Aden.

GLOSSARY

Armalite US-made assault rifle. SAS troops are often referred to as carrying Armalite and/or M16 rifles. To all intents and purposes, they are the same weapon. The Armalite, designated AR-15, was developed by Eugene Stoner while working at the Armalite Division of the Fairchild Airplane Company. Production was eventually licensed to Colt and the rifle became known as the XM-16. It was formerly adopted by the American armed forces in 1967 as the M16.

'badged' Word used to describe those recruits who have successfully passed the selection and continuation courses for entry into the SAS. On being 'badged' the new SAS recruit is assigned to one of the SAS's 'Sabre' Squadrons and to one of the four troops within each squadron.

'Bandit Country' A general British Army term, also used by the SAS, to describe South Armagh, Northern Ireland. The area is noted for high levels of IRA activity and attacks on members of the security forces. Between 1976 and 1978, the SAS was concentrated in South Armagh in an effort, which was successful, to reduce terrorist activity.

'beasting' A term used to describe a practice, now abandoned, carried out by SAS instructors during the Selection course whereby they would attempt to de-motivate recruits undertaking endurance marches by suggesting they take a short break or give up altogether. This formed part of the sifting process whereby the instructors would weed out those men who lacked the necessary physical and mental stamina for the Regiment.

'beating the clock' SAS slang for staying alive. Traditionally, those SAS soldiers killed in action had their names inscribed on plaques which were attached to the Regimental Clock Tower at Hereford. When the new barracks, Stirling Lines, was completed the plaques were mounted outside the Regimental Chapel.

'bin' SAS slang for anything that is rejected. It is also applied to those men who fail Selection Training and are 'binned'.

'bingo book' Journal carried by SAS soldiers on active service in Northern Ireland. Continually updated, it contains the names of wanted terrorists, suspected terrorist 'safe houses', and details of hijacked vehicles.

'boss' Term used by individual SAS troopers and NCOs when addressing their officers, as opposed to 'Sir'. This is symptomatic of the informal, no-nonsense attitude to soldiering that characterises the Special Air Service.

Bradbury Lines The former name of the SAS barracks block and headquarters of 22 SAS at Hereford. After it was rebuilt the block was renamed Stirling Lines in honour of the Regiment's founder, David Stirling.

'bullshit' In SAS phraseology 'bullshit' has two meanings: talking a load of rubbish, and any action which serves no useful purpose, such as spending hours cleaning a pair of boots until they shine.

'bug out' SAS term for immediate evacuation. Usually applied when a patrol is surprised and individual team members have to run for their lives.

'bumped' SAS term used when a patrol is observed or, more usually, attacked by the enemy. Often means a serious and bloody encounter with the enemy.

'Chinese Parliament' Informal meeting held by the commanding officer of an SAS team prior to an operation to discuss the plan of action. Each man, regardless of rank, is free to suggest ideas or offer criticism. The 'Chinese Parliament' indicates that the Regiment tolerates no sense of class, and that troopers (who are often NCOs before they join the SAS) can have considerable military experience.

Continuation Training The course held after Selection in which recruits are instructed in SAS patrol skills.

'contact' A phrase used to describe when an SAS team engages an enemy force.

cross-training System whereby the SAS ensures every one of its soldiers has at least one patrol skill and one, probably more, troop skill. This ensures SAS soldiers are multi-skilled individuals.

CRW Counter Revolutionary Warfare. As applied to the SAS, it means all aspects of counter-insurgency warfare plus hostage-rescue and bodyguarding.

'double tap' Two shots fired in quick

succession from a pistol. A tactic no longer used by SAS soldiers.

'Fan Dance' Name given by the SAS to the 60km timed, solo navigation march over the Brecon Beacons that is the culmination of SAS Selection Training. The route, over some of the most difficult terrain in the British Isles, must be completed in under 20 hours for the volunteer to pass.

'flash bang' SAS term for a stun grenade. The name derives form the action of the grenade when detonated: a blinding flash and deafening bang.

four-man patrol The smallest operational SAS unit.

'full battle order' SAS term meaning fully armed.

'gimpy' SAS nickname for the 7.62mm General Purpose Machine Gun (GPMG).

'green slime' SAS nickname for the Intelligence Corps. The name derives from the green berets worn by the latter's personnel.

'head shed' SAS slang for senior officers.

'hearts and minds' SAS tactic whereby individual troopers and patrols endeavour to gain the confidence and trust of the indigenous population by learning their customs and language. In this way the locals provide intelligence to the SAS soldiers and support the British cause.

'hide' SAS term for a covert observation post or lying-up position.

'hot-bedding' The sharing of one or two sleeping bags by a four-man patrol inside an observation post. Only two bags are required at any one time because two men are always on duty.

'Keeni Meeni' A Swahili phrase used to describe the movement of a snake in long grass. It was also applied to SAS undercover operations in Aden in the mid-1960s.

'Killing House' Name of the SAS Close Quarter Battle building at Stirling Lines, Hereford.

'Kremlin' Nickname for the SAS Operations Planning and Intelligence cell at Stirling Lines.

'Long Drag' Another name for 'Fan Dance'.

LSV Light Strike Vehicle. Light attack vehicle currently in service with the SAS.

Mars and Minerva Regimental journal of the Special Air Service.

MP5 Heckler & Koch submachine gun favoured by the SAS for hostage-rescue operations.

'9-milly' Nickname for the Browning High Power handgun used by the SAS.

O Group Orders group. Name of meeting which is always held by SAS teams before any action.

OGs Olive-greens. SAS and general British Army term for military clothing.

OP Observation post. OPs form an essential part of SAS intelligence gathering.

'Phantom Major' Nickname given by the Germans to David Stirling during the North African campaign in World War II. The name derives from the behind-the-lines activities of the SAS and the Germans' inability to track down the hit-and-run troops.

'Pink Panther' Nickname for SAS desert Land Rovers. The name derives from the colour the vehicles are painted for camouflage.

'Rupert' SAS term, often used disparagingly, for officers.

RV SAS term for rendezvous.

'Sabre' The name given to the four SAS squadrons of 22 SAS Regiment. Each 'Sabre, or fighting, Squadron is divided into four troops of 16 men.

Selection Training The four-week course run by SAS at Hereford that all prospective recruits to the Regiment must pass.

'shake out' SAS term for preparing for combat.

SLR Self-Loading Rifle. 7.62mm semi-automatic rifle used by the SAS since the late 1950s. Has now been replaced by the SA-80.

Stirling Lines Regimental Headquarters of 22 SAS. Named in honour of the Regiment's founder, David Stirling.

'Tailend Charlie' Name given to the soldier bringing up the rear when a four-man patrol is in line of march.

PICTURE CREDITS

Aviation Photographs International/Flack: 79 (bottom), 131 (top and bottom), 210 **Aviation Photographs International/Shakespeare:** 219 **Gordon Beckett:** 42, 55 **Graham Bingham:** 79 (top), 90-91, 186-187, 194-195 **Brown Packaging:** 12, 28-29, 37 (top), 41, 53 (bottom), 63 (bottom), 64-65, 66, 84-85, 88, 89, 92, 96, 100 (top and bottom), 113 (bottom), 118 (bottom), 125, 129, 140-141, 143 (bottom), 150, 150-151, 176-177, 181, 216, 217 **Peter Bull:** 10, 19, 26, 27, 34 **Robert Burns:** 46, 55 **Johnny Cooper:** 121 (bottom), 218 **Terry Hadler:** 22-23, 38-39, 50-51, 58-59, 70-71, 102-103, 122-123, 146-147, 162-163, 166-167, 170-171, 174-175, 178-179 **Keith Harmer:** 62 **Imperial War Museum:** 9 (top and bottom), 17 (top), 20, 21, 24, 32-33, 45 (top), 49 (top and bottom), 52, 53 (top), 93, 105, 113 (top), 121 (top), 124, 132-133, 137 (top), 153 (top and bottom), 156-157, 161 (top), 185 (top and bottom), 193, 200 **Malcolm McGregor:** 11, 13, 18, 35, 43, 47, 54, 63 (top), 75 (bottom) **Bob Morrison:** 77 (bottom) **Military Picture Library:** 2, 87 (bottom), 95 (bottom), 110-111, 114, 143 (top) **Military Picture Library/Robin Adshead:** 31 (top), 80, 83, 87 (top), 98, 138-139, 155, 158-159 **Military Picture Library/Patrick Allen:** 119 **Military Picture Library/Tim Fisher:** 95 (top), 115 **Military Picture Library/Peter Russell:** 107, 118 (top), 126, 135, 190-191, 191, 203, 207 (top and bottom) **Henry Nolan:** 74 **Pacemaker Press:** 57 (bottom), 61, 67 (top and bottom) 145, 148-149, 192 **Photo Press:** 6-7, 161 (bottom), 180, 199 (top), 201, 204-205, 208, 210-211, 212-213 **Popperfoto:** 69 (top) **Press Association:** 57 (top), 144 **Tony Rogers:** 127 (top and bottom), 173, 182, 183, 199 (bottom) **SAS Regimental Association:** 37 (bottom) **Steve Seymour:** 78 **Soldier Magazine:** 164, 168 **Telegraph Colour Library:** 14-15, 46, 99 (top and bottom) **TRH Pictures:** 17 (bottom), 31 (bottom) 40, 45 (bottom), 69 (bottom), 72, 75 (top), 77 (top), 82-83, 106 (top and bottom), 108-109, 116-117, 137 (bottom), 189, 196-197, 214